MANUAL OF GRAPHIC TECHNIQUES 1

FOR ARCHITECTS, GRAPHIC DESIGNERS, & ARTISTS

TOM PORTER AND BOB GREENSTREET

ILLUSTRATIONS BY SUE GOODMAN

Charles Scribner's Sons · New York

Acknowledgments

The authors would like to thank the following architecture students at Oxford Polytechnic, who contributed project works:

John Alwell, Neil Armitage, David Clennett, Paul Cook, Robert Finch, Rob Green, Paul Hodgkinson, Paul Johnson, Max Neal, Peter Risbey, John Stewart, and Giuliano Zampi.

Special thanks are due to Iradj Parvaneh for all monochrome photography, and to Richard Tymons, Ray Norton, and Jim Dunford for their help and advice.

Library of Congress Cataloging in Publication Data

Porter, Tom.
Manual of graphic techniques for architects, graphic designers, & artists.

Includes index.
1. Graphic arts—Techniques. I. Greenstreet, Bob, joint author. II. Title.
NC1000.P67 741.6'028 79-26599
ISBN 0-684-16504-X

This book published simultaneously in the United States of America and in Canada.

9 11 13 15 17 19 Q/P 20 18 16 14 12 10 8

Pages 33-48 printed in Japan by Dai Nippon Printing Co. Ltd.
Printed in the United States of America.

TABLE OF CONTENTS

Introduction

MANUAL OF GRAPHIC TECHNIQUES has developed from its authors' desire to provide a comprehensive support handbook for students of design that illustrates in graphic, self-contained page layouts the full range of design tools useful in the development and communication of ideas.

Its contents are arranged in an easy-to-follow format, reflecting as closely as possible an evolving sequence of design. The mark-making ability of mediums, such as pencils and brushes, and techniques of application, plus their interaction both with surface and ideas, are shown—many illustrated by actual student projects.

A variety of drawing systems and their potential in describing space are also explained, together with step-by-step information on analytical drawing techniques and basic methods of graphic transformation, reproduction, and simulation.

Finally, as the design cycle moves from its idea and experimentation stages (the private phase) to its final presentation (the public phase), concluding sections contain hints on what presentation graphics will best convey design proposals to others.

1 SURFACE, LINE, AND TONE

Opaque Papers and Boards

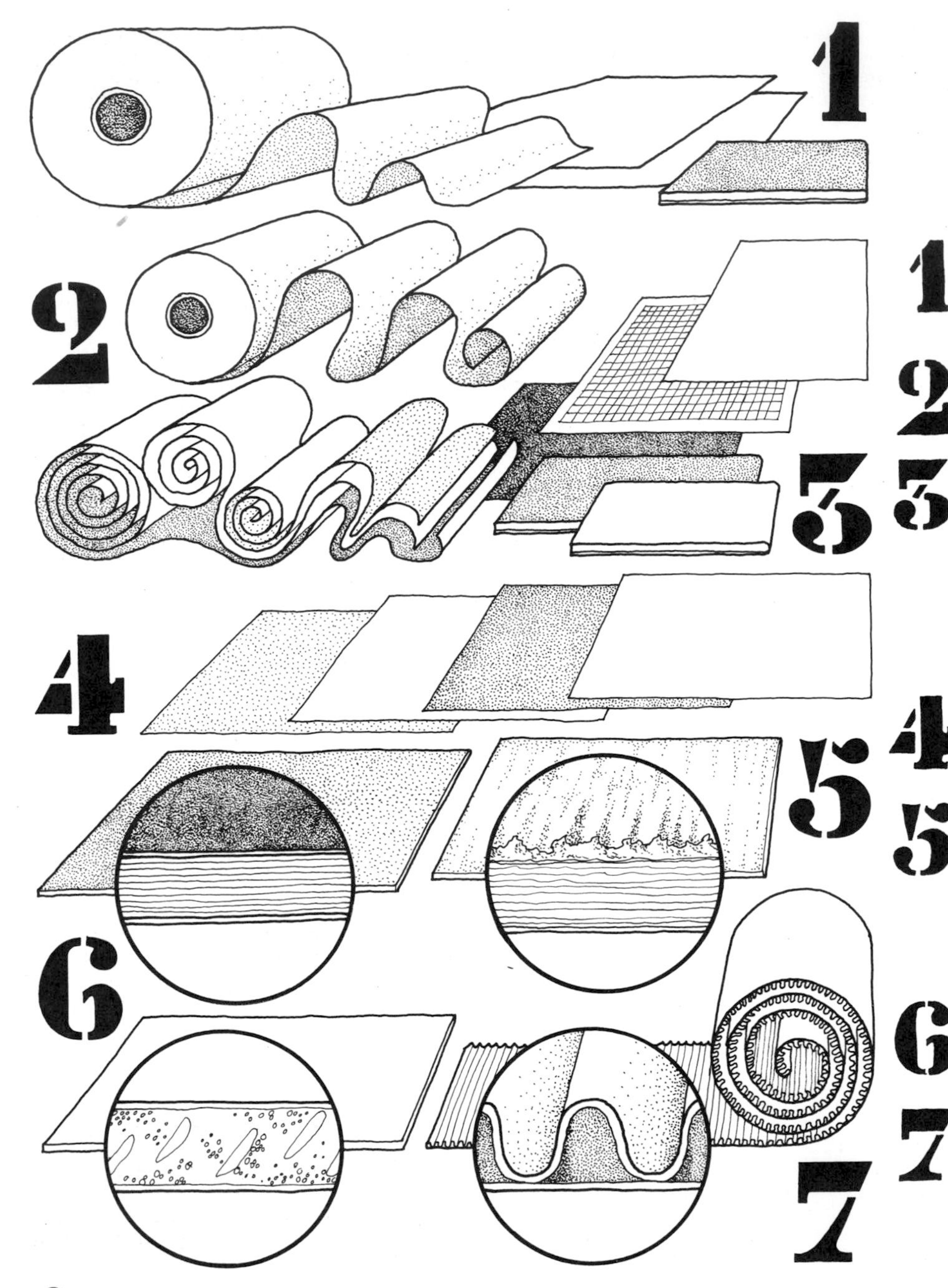

There is a multitudinous range of drawing paper, which is graded according to its weight (thickness) and tooth (degree of surface texture). When selecting a drawing surface it is important to establish several points: whether the artwork is a rough draft or a presentation drawing; whether the image requires reproduction; which medium is to be used; and the desired graphic effect. Apart from these factors, the final decision is one of personal taste developed from experiment and experience.

1 Newsprint is an inexpensive but fragile wood pulp paper. Manufactured for the newspaper industry, it is white, smooth, and absorbent. It is suitable for artwork of a rapid, temporary nature such as large design sketches and throwaway drawings worked in charcoal or crayon. Newsprint is available in pads, sheets, and from 5-foot-wide rolls.

2 Butcher paper is a more robust white paper produced in 36-inch-wide rolls. It is excellent for larger artwork using soft pencils, crayons, markers, inks, and gouache.

3 Drawing paper is obtainable in an extremely wide range of qualities, thicknesses, tooths, and in coordinated colors being supplied in various sized sheets, pads, and rolls. Graphed drawing paper is also obtainable with various squares to the inch lined in blue, green, orange, or black. As a general guide, pens and markers respond to heavier, smoother grades; pencil and paint to more textured, medium-weight surfaces; crayons and pastels respond to surfaces with a more pronounced "drag." Before using pen or pencil on drawing paper, carefully check each side, as many sheets offer a smooth (clay-coated) drawing surface and a rough (uncoated) obverse.

4 Speciality papers include custom surfaces prepared for charcoal, pastel, watercolor wash, ink line, and oil paint. Paper colors are infinite and offer matte or glossy finishes--some being sticky-backed for collage work.

5 Illustration board has a high-quality white rag surface affixed to a cardboard backing. It is produced in a range of sheet sizes which include smooth cold pressed (CP), faint grain hot pressed (HP), and a rough uneven texture (R). It is used for finished presentations worked in watercolor, crayon, airbrush, or pen and ink--the smoother surfaces being ideal for fine line work. Bristol board offers a white drawing surface in two finishes (smooth and slightly textured) and is produced in thicknesses ranging from 1 to 5 ply.

6 Mat board (mounting card) is of lighter weight and lesser quality. It is available in assorted colors and mainly used for matting, model-making, surface or window mounting artwork--but it can be used as a drawing or painting surface.

7 There is a great variety of cardboards in many thicknesses, surface textures, and colors. White clay-coated, smooth paper facings which sandwich a laminate of polystyrene foam (foam-core board) are best for all-around studio work. They are useful for display work, model-making, and for charcoal drawing or painting in watercolor or oilcolor. A plasticated card sheet is also manufactured which is extremely useful in prestigious modelmaking.

Translucent Paper and Transparent Film

1 Detail paper is a form of smooth greaseproof paper sufficiently translucent for copying, tracing, and--depending upon its light transmission--for diazo reproduction. Available in sheets, pads, and rolls, it is extremely popular with designers for developing design ideas and layout work in pencil and pen.

2 Layout paper is a brilliant white translucent paper mainly used for composing layouts or visualizing new ideas. It is marketed in roll or pad form and in a variety of surface qualities ranging from one especially made to accept markers, to others receptive to pencil, charcoal, pastel, pen, ink, and brush.

3 Yellow tracing paper is an inexpensive tissue paper with good transparency. It is useful for sketching and layout drawing, being obtainable in various roll widths.

4 White tracing papers range from clear, translucent, to opaque and offer various degrees of tooth and thickness both in plain and graphed sheets, pads and rolls. Thinner papers are widely used for design orientation and sketching, while the medium-grade, smooth surfaces are good with pen and ink. The more abrasive, matte surfaces tend to abrade pencil leads and are susceptible to smudging. There are two kinds of tracing paper--natural and vellum. Vellum is treated with oil to achieve translucency and is more expensive, whiter, and more durable, but is less transparent than the natural variety. Tracing papers are usually employed in overlay work, tracing, and for drafting requiring reproduction, but they are dimensionally unstable, as they distort in humid conditions.

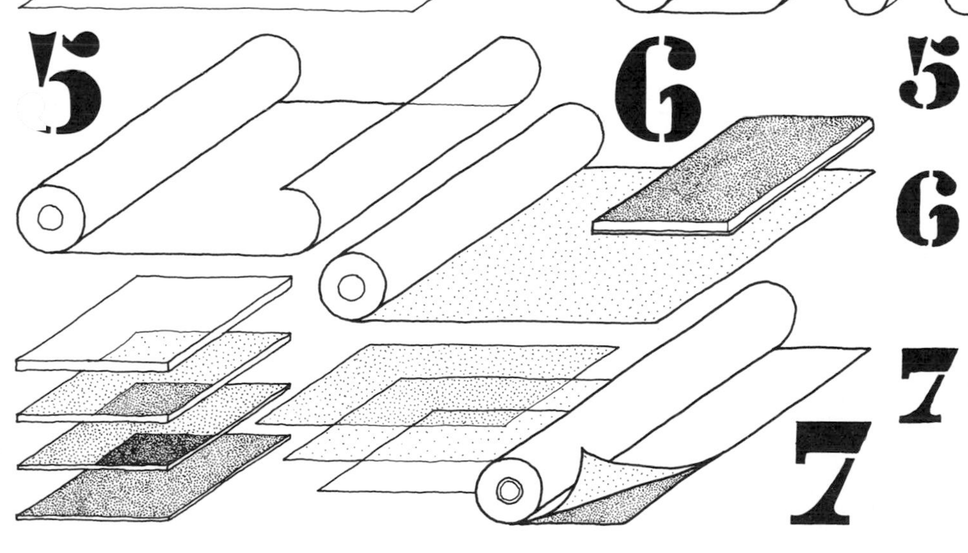

5 Clear plastic tracing film is a non-absorbent, stable drafting medium for pencil and technical penwork. It is formulated from polyester or acetate and has largely replaced other surfaces for high contrast reproductive drafting. Usually one side is gelatin-coated for a glossy finish.

6 Matte frosted acetate film has one or both sides roughened by chemical or mechanical abrasion--a surface upon which special plastic leads, pen tips, inks, and erasers should be used. If the acetate has a smooth side, it permits the use of nylon-tipped markers. There is also a specially prepared acetate which accepts paint and ink like paper, mistakes simply being corrected with water. Films are manufactured in sheets, pads, and rolls.

7 Colored acetate sheets and rolls are produced in vivid transparent hues. These are useful in overlay work, as pages in reports, in the preparation of slides for overhead projection, and in collage and artwork requiring a transparent colored background. Clear and colored acrylic sheets are manufactured in 1/8" (3 mm), 1/4" (6 mm), and 1/2" (12 mm) thicknesses. They are very expensive and suitable only for prestigious display work, framing, and modelmaking using the special cement adhesive.

Translucent Paper and Film in the Design Process

1

Tracing paper is used for extracting, transforming, or transferring drawn information from one surface to another. The overlay process in design is excellent for planning and analyzing basic spatial and component relationships.

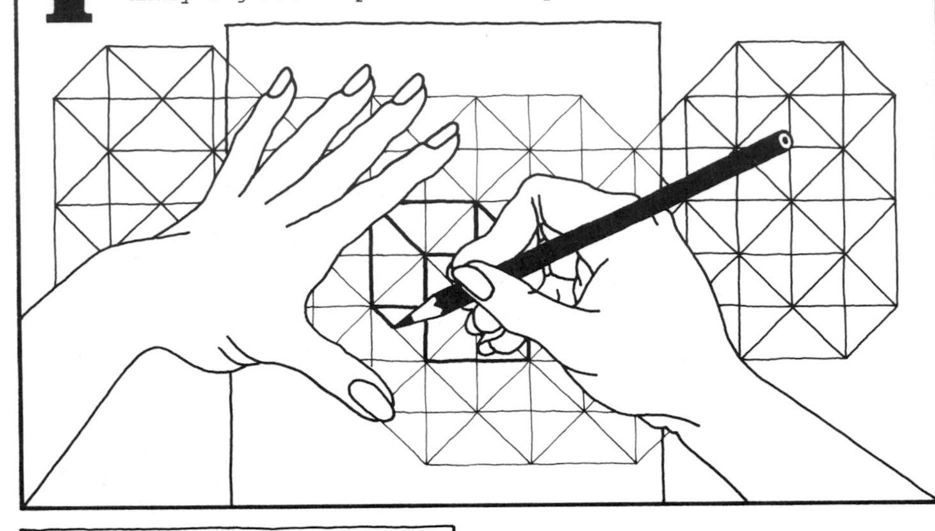

2

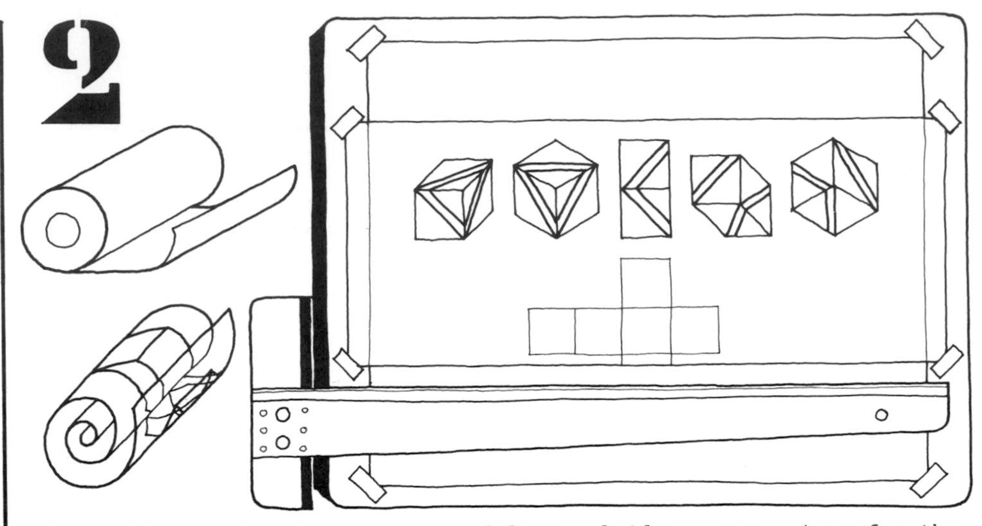

By working on tracing paper or film overlaid over a series of orthographic views drawn on a white paper backing sheet, developing concepts can be visualized three-dimensionally. This visual testing process aids a design attitude sensitive to movement around objects in space (see page 70).

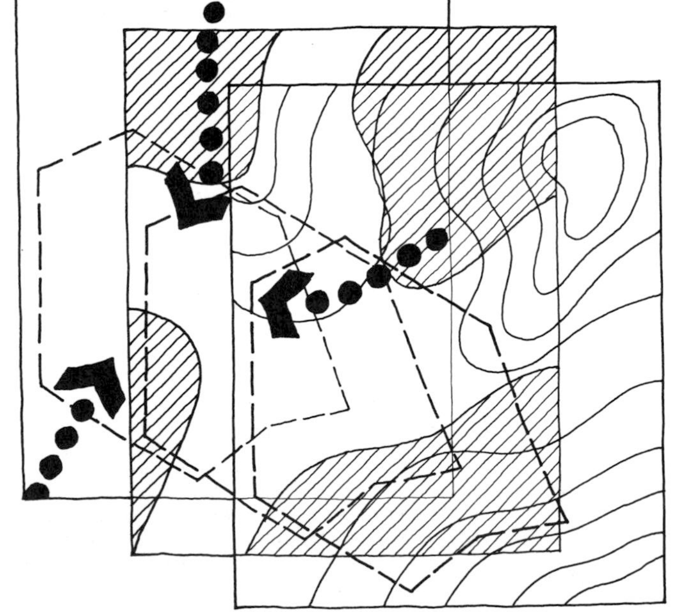

Various facets of a developing idea can be synthesized using successive clear film overlays worked in nylon markers or ink. Physical and non-physical considerations can be fused and graphically realized, as this procedure allows the designer to "see through" more complex relationships.

4

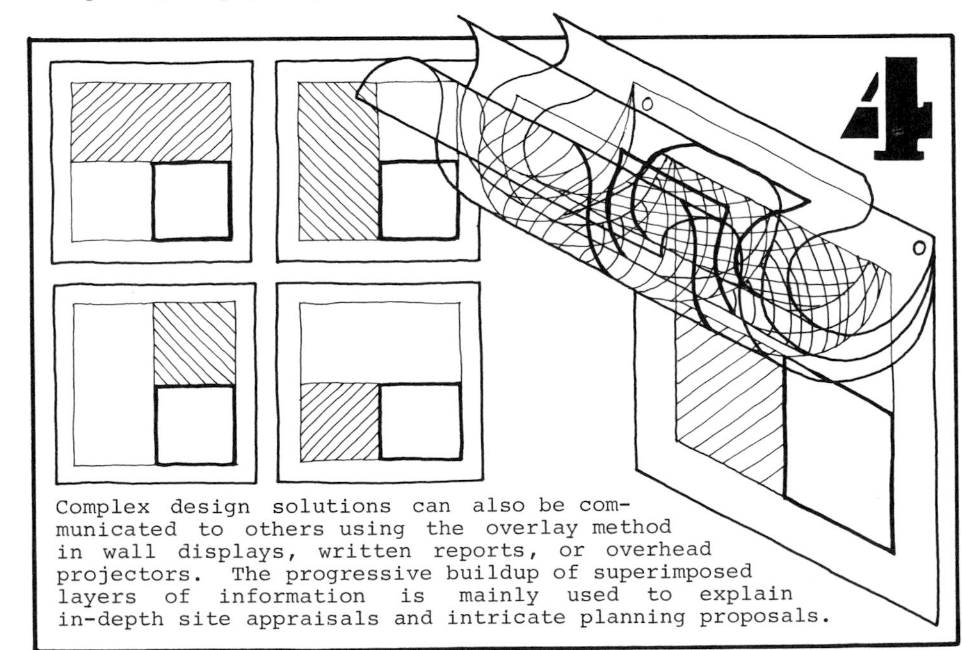

Complex design solutions can also be communicated to others using the overlay method in wall displays, written reports, or overhead projectors. The progressive buildup of superimposed layers of information is mainly used to explain in-depth site appraisals and intricate planning proposals.

Paper in the Design Process

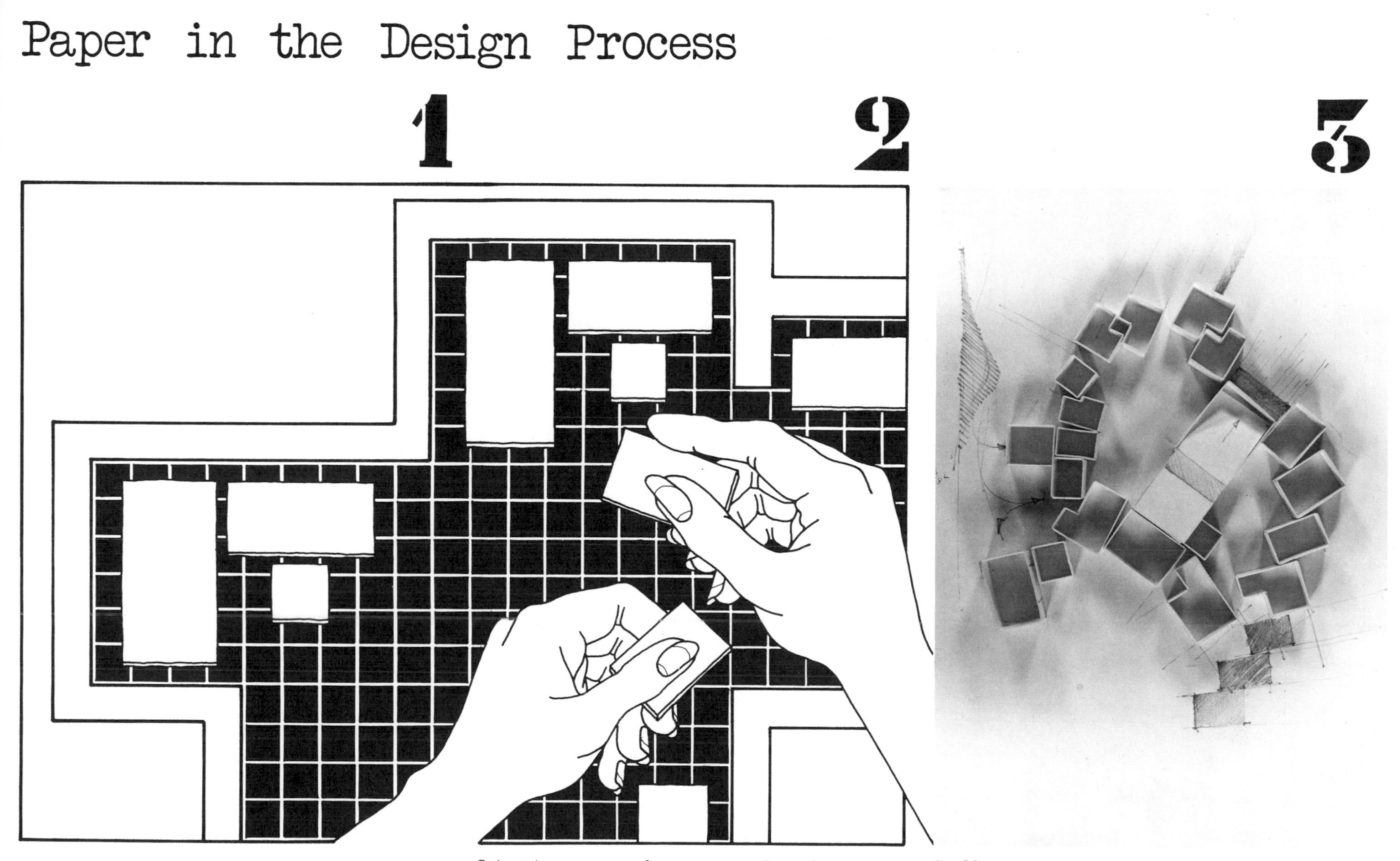

Paper is an essential component of a graphic design process. Always collect waste scraps of paper, for they are very useful in a variety of design functions such as sketching and trial drawing, collage work, spraywork masking, modelmaking, and mounting small photographs and artwork.

Cut-out paper shapes can--depending upon their implied scale--represent objects within an interior plan or elements in a site plan. These can be maneuvered until satisfactory planning arrangements are achieved, before moving ahead in the design sequence. This process is more rapid and flexible than working exclusively in line--especially in conceptual design stages.

Small paper constructions can quickly project an embryonic idea directly from the drawing board into three dimensions. An actual space can then be experienced, modified, and transferred back into graphics. This moving of concepts back and forth between drawings and simple paper models encourages an awareness of the implications of physical space in design.

Pencil Leads

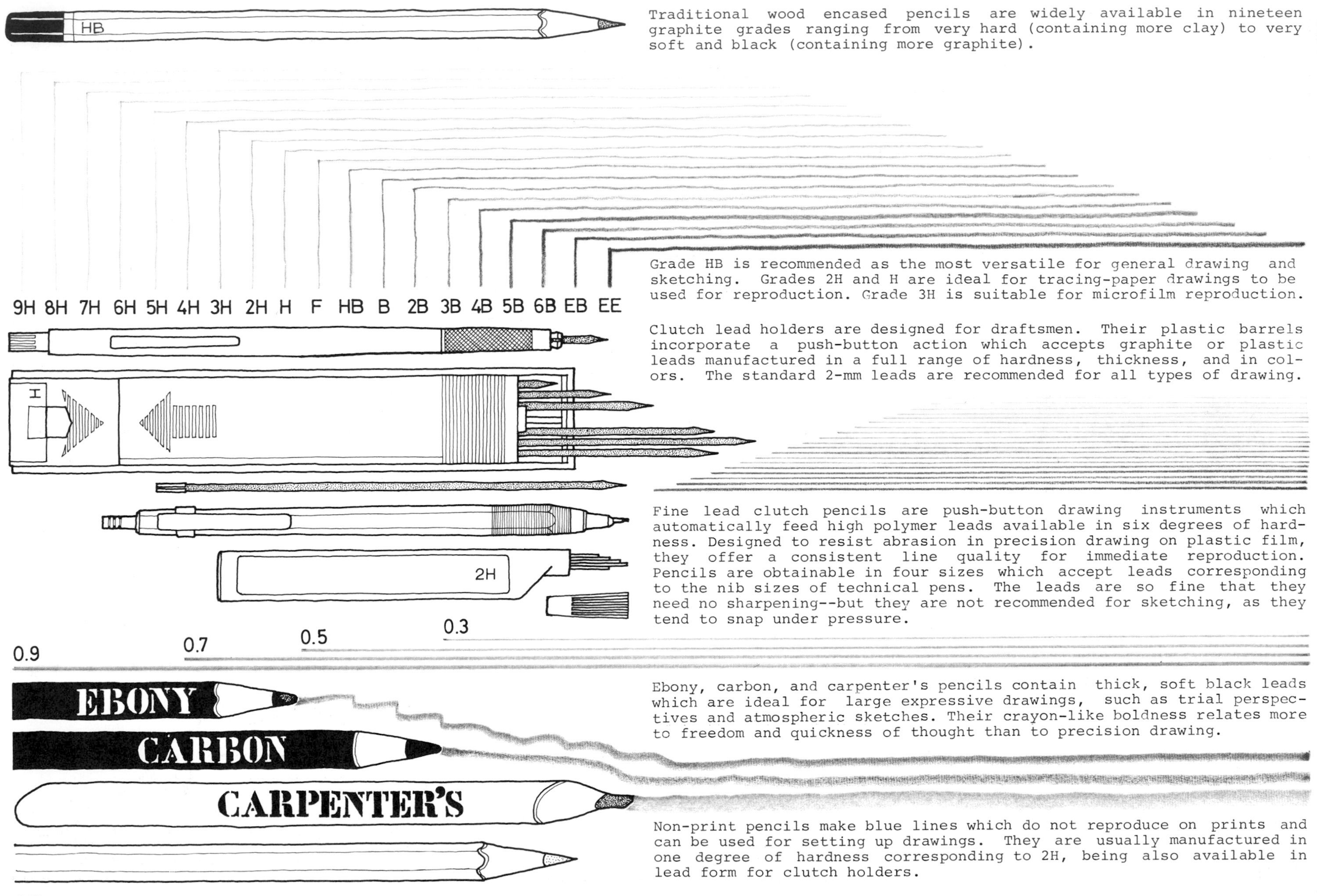

Traditional wood encased pencils are widely available in nineteen graphite grades ranging from very hard (containing more clay) to very soft and black (containing more graphite).

Grade HB is recommended as the most versatile for general drawing and sketching. Grades 2H and H are ideal for tracing-paper drawings to be used for reproduction. Grade 3H is suitable for microfilm reproduction.

Clutch lead holders are designed for draftsmen. Their plastic barrels incorporate a push-button action which accepts graphite or plastic leads manufactured in a full range of hardness, thickness, and in colors. The standard 2-mm leads are recommended for all types of drawing.

Fine lead clutch pencils are push-button drawing instruments which automatically feed high polymer leads available in six degrees of hardness. Designed to resist abrasion in precision drawing on plastic film, they offer a consistent line quality for immediate reproduction. Pencils are obtainable in four sizes which accept leads corresponding to the nib sizes of technical pens. The leads are so fine that they need no sharpening--but they are not recommended for sketching, as they tend to snap under pressure.

Ebony, carbon, and carpenter's pencils contain thick, soft black leads which are ideal for large expressive drawings, such as trial perspectives and atmospheric sketches. Their crayon-like boldness relates more to freedom and quickness of thought than to precision drawing.

Non-print pencils make blue lines which do not reproduce on prints and can be used for setting up drawings. They are usually manufactured in one degree of hardness corresponding to 2H, being also available in lead form for clutch holders.

How to Sharpen Pencils

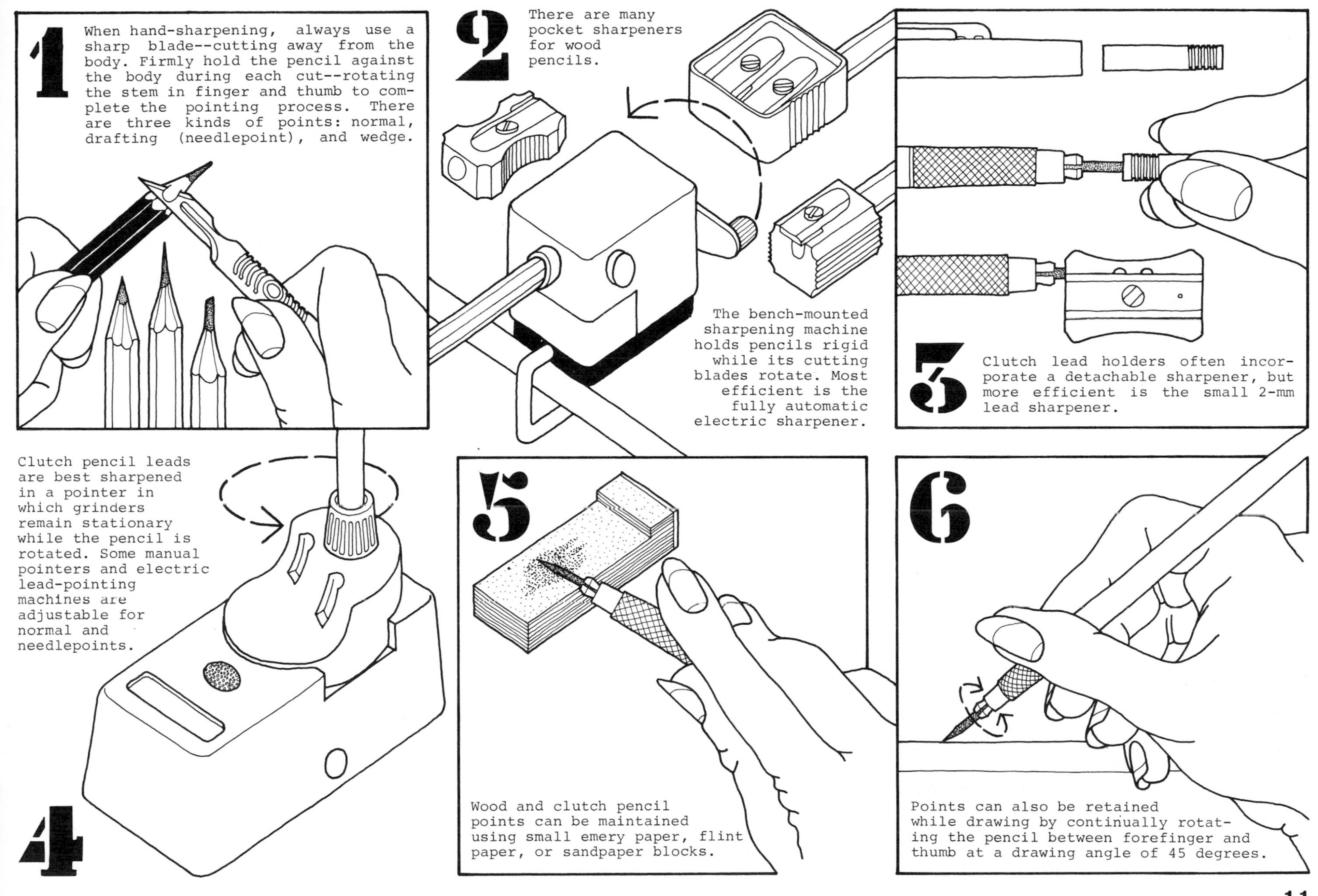

Pencil Shading Techniques

Pencil leads offer a wide range of line weight and quality dependent upon graphite grade, paper texture, and degree of pressure on pencil.

4H
3H
2H
H
F
HB
B
2B
3B
4B
5B
6B
EE

A wide range of shading effects can be achieved within one graphite grade, e.g., HB. Shading can be hatched in freehand or ruled, dotted, worked solid, or scribbled into tonal structures to simulate an endless variety of textures.

For sharp edge definition, mechanical shading can be worked against a ruler. More subtle, atmospheric shades can be produced by finger-smudging soft graphite or applying graphite dust from a pointer with tissue paper or cotton wool; sharp edges and highlights can later be "cut" using a soft eraser.

Widen your graphic experience by experimenting with combinations of shading techniques in one drawing.

Objective Freehand Pencil Drawing

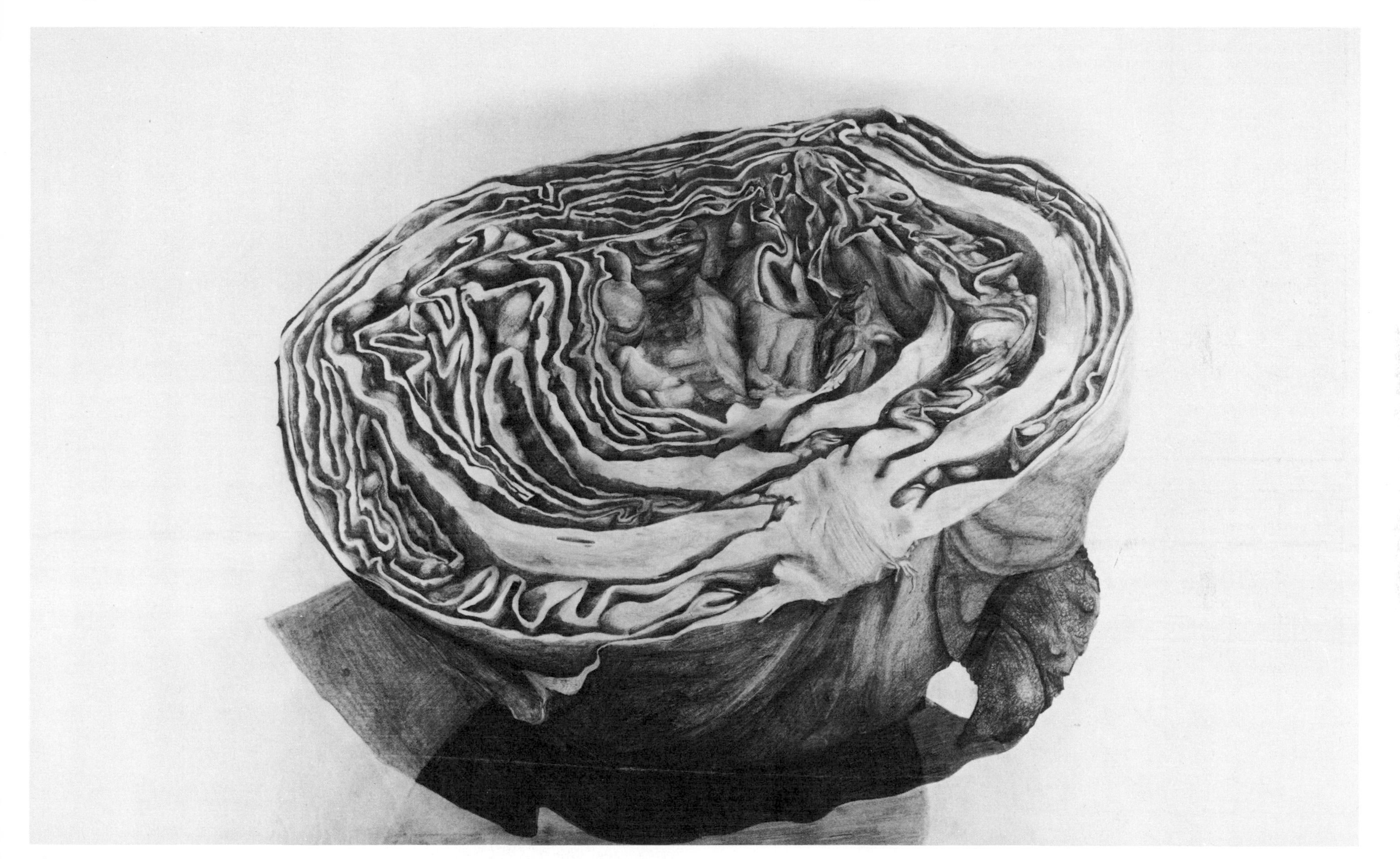

The tonal structure of a sliced cabbage tonally "sculpted" by a first-year architecture student in HB pencil on layout paper. In this drawing, the student aimed to record meticulously both the shape and value of tones within his perception of the object.

Pencil in the Design Process

1 Graphite is the most responsive and versatile of all the drawing mediums. At the outset of design, pencils are commonly employed to respond to the sensitive externalization of new concepts--ideas which hitherto were experienced purely in the mind's eye.

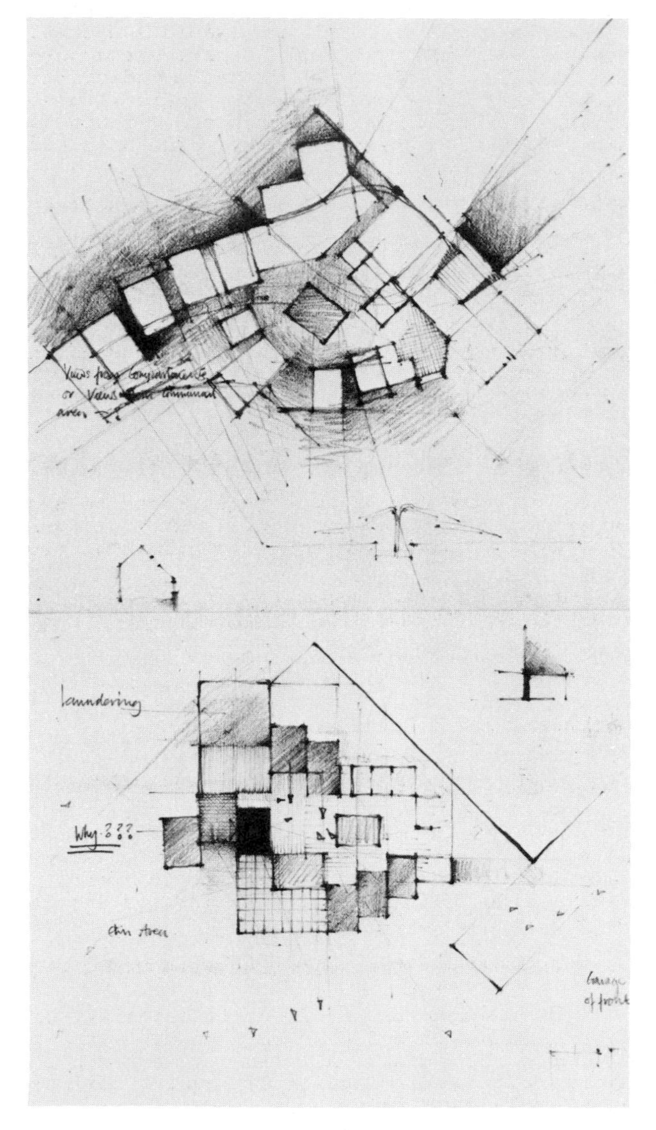

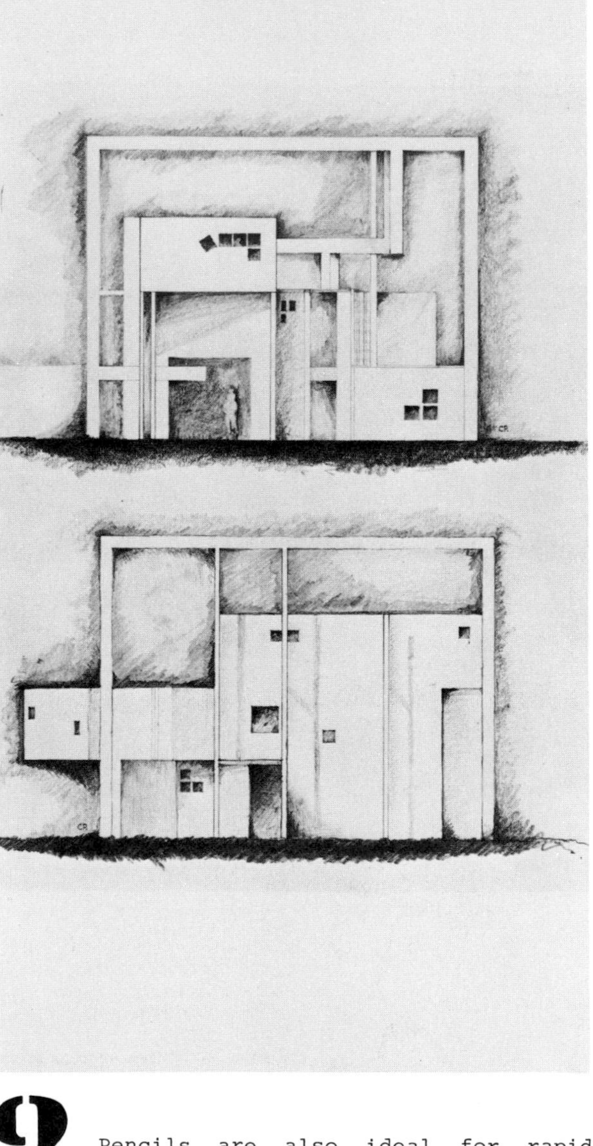

2 Pencils are also ideal for rapid freehand sketching and the final presentation of design ideas.

3

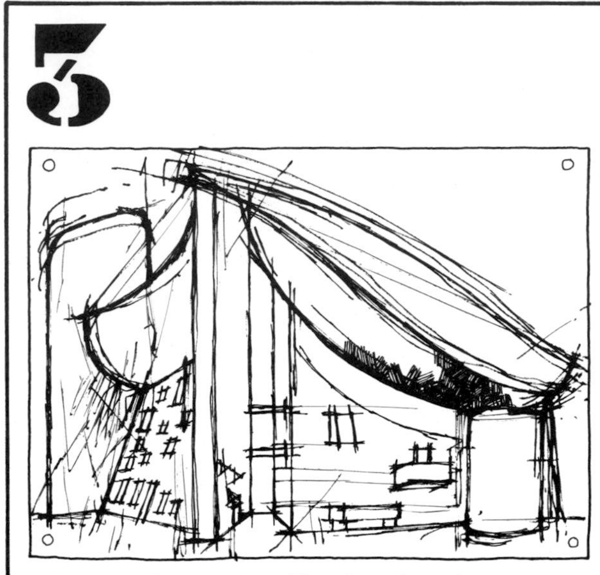

A layout for a pencil sketch using a non-print pencil on tracing paper can be corrected and revised many times without affecting the surface or the later application of a final medium.

When the layout is redrawn with a graphite pencil or a pen, the blue recedes to an unobtrusive undertone which completely disappears in subsequent photocopies or diazo prints.

Chalks and Crayons

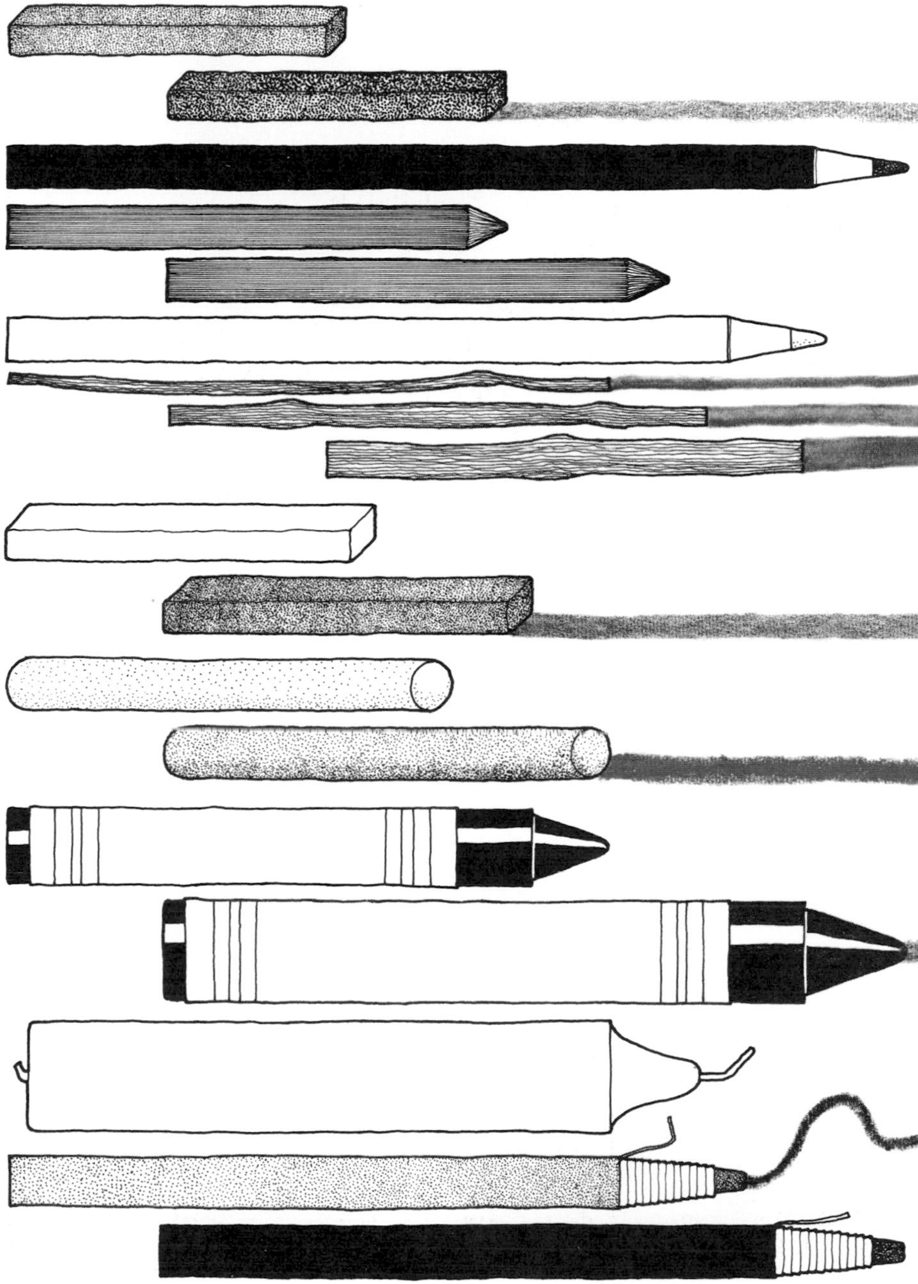

Graphite sticks are available in soft, medium, and hard grades. Like all drawing sticks, both the end and the side can be used for drawing lines or rendering tones.

Charcoal is made from charred willow and is supplied in natural twig, compressed stick, and wood-encased pencil form--each available in soft, medium, and hard grades. Black charcoal is ideal for rapid sketching and large exploratory drawings worked on most paper surfaces--especially those offering a textural drag. Being an unstable medium, it is easily rubbed away--either for effect or by accident. There is also a white charcoal pencil which is used for chiaroscuro drawings, sketching on toned paper, and providing highlights in graphite or black charcoal renderings.

Conté crayon is a form of refined charcoal stick, as it is harder, finer, and therefore less dusty. It is made in France and imported in three degrees of hardness, and in black, white, sanguine, and several colors. It is obtainable in both stick and pencil form--both ideal for freehand renderings.

Blackboard chalk is brittle and gritty. It is made in assorted colors and can be mixed with charcoal, graphite, or Conté for highlight effects. Le Corbusier used chalk on his massive studio blackboard to quickly explore design ideas on a large scale.

Black wax crayons produce dense, glossy lines applicable to almost all kinds of surface, including wood and metal. Being water-repellent, they can be used as a resist (white candle wax providing a clear resist) under watercolor and ink washes. Wax crayons can be sharpened with a blade for producing finer lines in drawings.

China marking pencils or "grease" pencils work on all smooth and glossy surfaces including glass, plastic, film, and slides. They can also be used in wax-resist work or for fine detail rubbings. Many china pencils are obtainable in the self-sharpening form, i.e., by pulling the little cord to unwrap a new length of wax core.

Experience with chalk and crayon complements the finer line quality of pencil leads. They respond to extremes of boldness and sensitivity in drawing, textured surfaces, and quick ideas. All (except wax) can be worked into with soft erasers, cloth, or fingertips; require fixing; and are useful as a preparatory medium for painting.

Crayon and Charcoal Drawing

Conté crayon is ideal for rapid, on-the-spot sketching. This sketch was made in seconds using both the end and the side of the stick by a student who, during a brief site appraisal, produced several such lightning images to explain the edges of his site.

The mark-making potential of both charcoal and Conté crayon.

Erasing and Fixing Graphite and Chalk

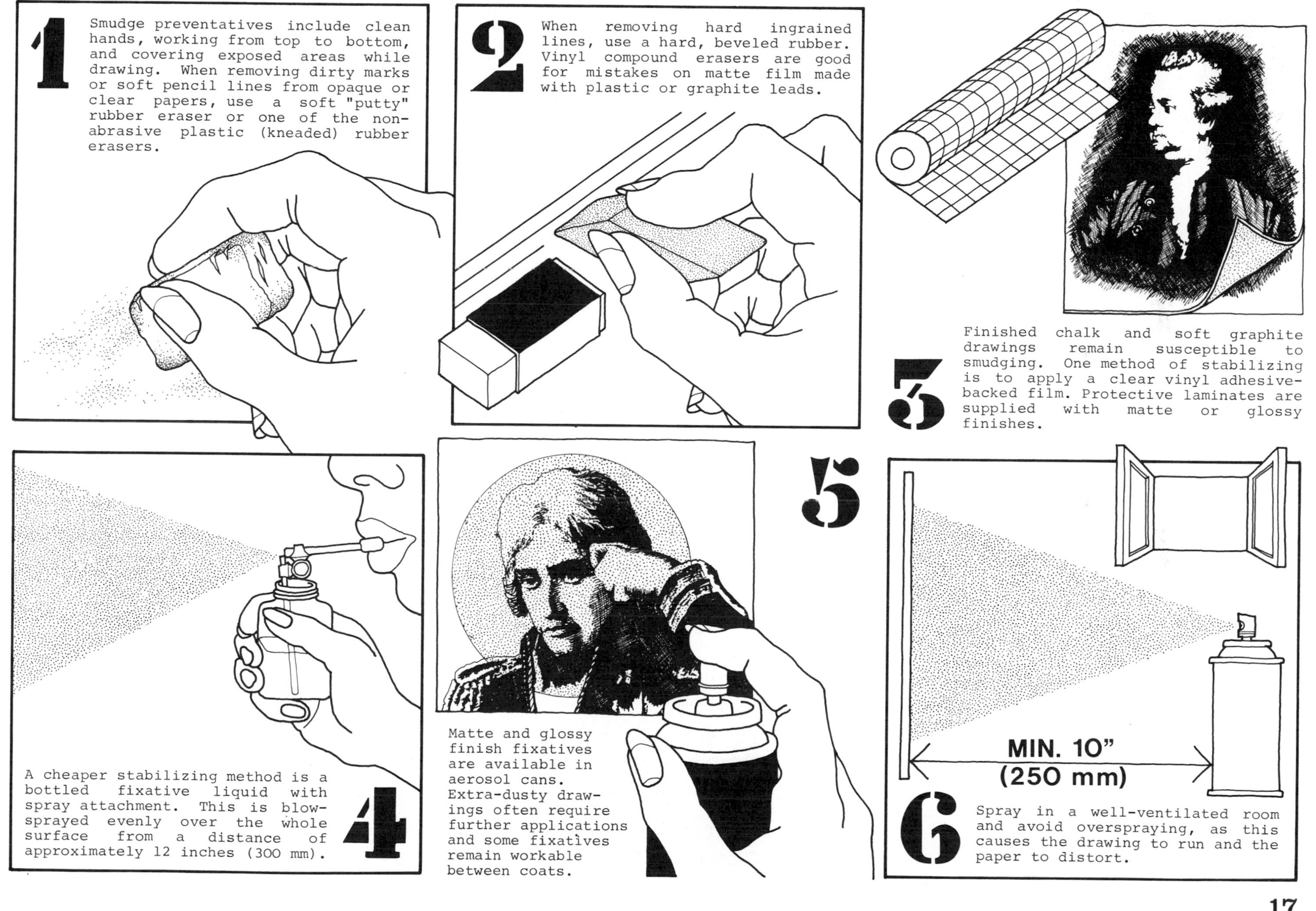

1 Smudge preventatives include clean hands, working from top to bottom, and covering exposed areas while drawing. When removing dirty marks or soft pencil lines from opaque or clear papers, use a soft "putty" rubber eraser or one of the non-abrasive plastic (kneaded) rubber erasers.

2 When removing hard ingrained lines, use a hard, beveled rubber. Vinyl compound erasers are good for mistakes on matte film made with plastic or graphite leads.

3 Finished chalk and soft graphite drawings remain susceptible to smudging. One method of stabilizing is to apply a clear vinyl adhesive-backed film. Protective laminates are supplied with matte or glossy finishes.

4 A cheaper stabilizing method is a bottled fixative liquid with spray attachment. This is blow-sprayed evenly over the whole surface from a distance of approximately 12 inches (300 mm).

5 Matte and glossy finish fixatives are available in aerosol cans. Extra-dusty drawings often require further applications and some fixatives remain workable between coats.

6 Spray in a well-ventilated room and avoid overspraying, as this causes the drawing to run and the paper to distort.

Pens

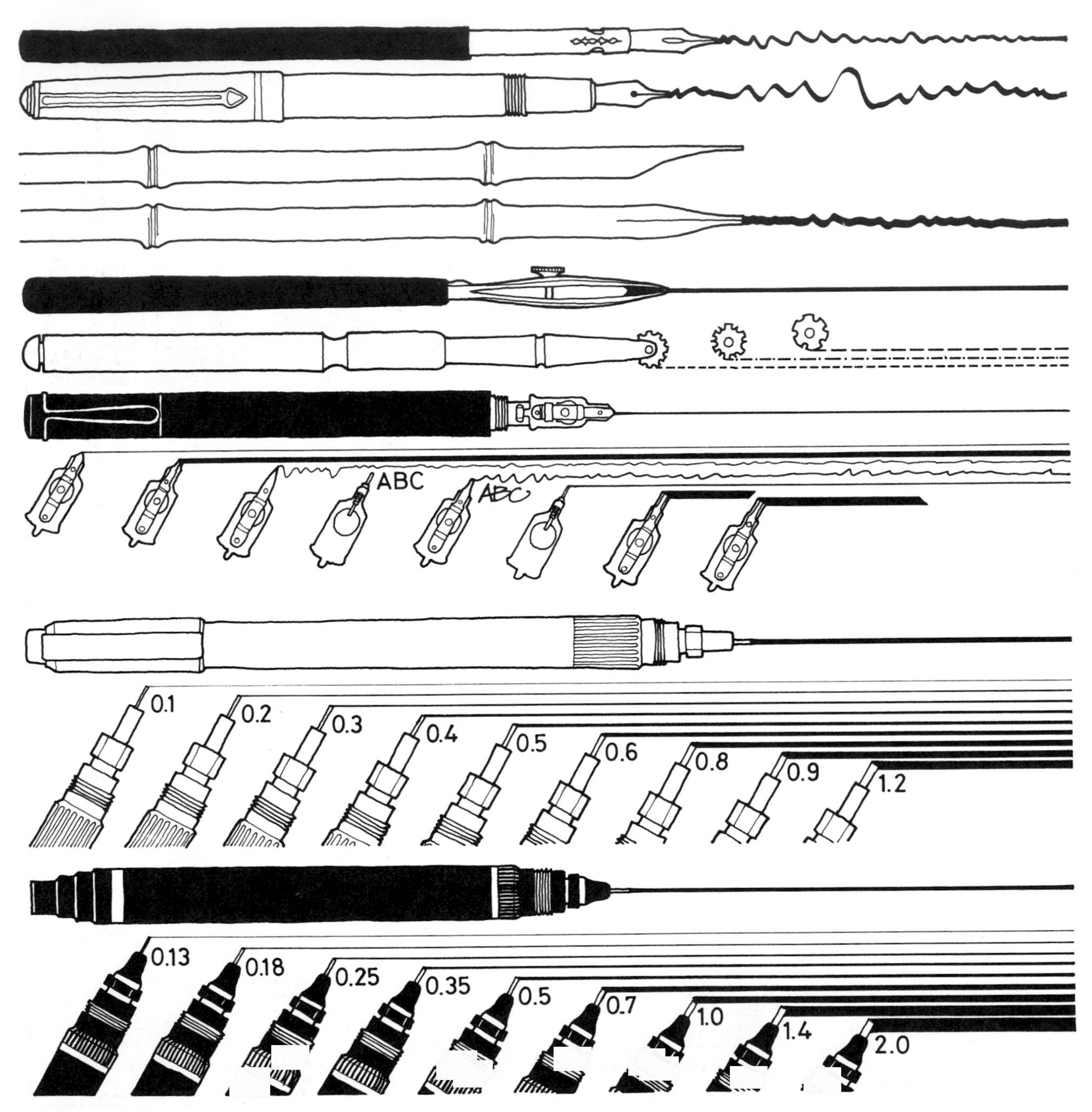

Traditional dip pens and fountain pens (with sac or cartridge ink reservoir) have flexible nibs which produce fluctuating line widths in response to finger pressure while writing or drawing.

Bamboo pens are do-it-yourself drawing instruments cut from a length of cane. The nib can be whittled with a sharp knife to produce the required line width. They are remarkably sensitive to objective drawing--as used by Van Gogh.

Ruling pens are drafting instruments for precision ink drawing on opaque and transparent surfaces. Variation of line width is controlled by the screw adjustment.

Dotted line pens are specialized instruments for technical and working drawings. Interchangeable wheels offer a variety of dotted, broken, and chain dotted lines.

Graphos drawing pens operate in conjunction with over sixty easily interchangeable nibs. There are eight basic types--each designed for specific artwork functions: fine line ruling, broad line ruling, freehand drawing, stenciling, freehand lettering, quick sketching, technical drawing, and oblique line. These pens are normally available with an integral or cartridge reservoir--and can be fitted with one of three feeds which control ink-flow speeds.

Technical pens operate with tubular nibs. Unlike the Graphos, each nib has its own cartridge ink-reservoir assembly. Although associated with precision drawing requiring diazo copying or microfilming, they are widely used by designers for general artwork.

A typical traditional range of nibs comprises nine line widths. Three nibs recommended for the beginner: 0.2 mm, 0.4 mm, and 0.6 mm.

The modern range of technical pen nibs are produced in nine internationally recognized line widths or isometric sizes which are specifically designed for the requirements of reduction techniques. Three nibs recommended for the beginner: 0.35 mm, 0.5 mm, and 0.7 mm.

Technical pens are available specifically for stenciling. Especially toughened sapphire and tungsten carbide nibs are marketed for use on abrasive film surfaces.

Drawing Inks

Permanent writing ink for ordinary fountain pens is water soluble and suitable for general drawing and sketching. As part of a basic color range, blue-black changes color when diluted.

Shellac-free India ink can be used in ordinary fountain pens. It is almost waterproof when dry, and suitable for drawing, lettering, and ruling on paper, cloth, and film.

Encre de Chine drawing inks for use on drawing papers and art boards are available in a wide range of opaque and transparent colors--the opaques being suitable for diazo reproduction. They should not be used in tubular pointed pens.

Chinese stick ink is diluted in water to make a color wash. This is usually brush-applied to add tonal gradations to pen or pencil line drawings (see page 44).

All drawing inks can be diluted with water--preferably boiled, distilled, or rainwater.

Specially formulated non-clogging inks are available for tubular pointed technical pens and work well on most surfaces. They are produced in various colors--most (except blue) being suitable for diazo reproduction. They are waterproof and do not smear when dry. Always check to see if your pen uses a special ink.

Non-etching ink is suitable for drafting on tracing paper and coated and non-coated film using technical pens. They are waterproof and smudgeproof when dry, and reproduce well.

Etching ink is specially designed for coated film and can be applied to all plastic surfaces. It is fast-drying, waterproof, and lightfast, being designed for reproduction. It should only be used in acetate-resistant pens, as its function is to eat into the surface of film. For this reason it should not be used in conjunction with plastic accessories such as stencils.

There are five basic types of ink containers. Ordinary bottles and bottles with an integral filling insert to protect the nib are suitable for use with dip pens, fountain pens, technical pens with a piston plunger, and brushes.

A B C D

Bottles with an integral pipette in the cap and plastic bottles with a nozzle are designed for refilling pens such as the Graphos and technical pen cartridges--and for loading ruling pens.

Ready-filled cartridges are also available and the easiest to use.

Technical Pen and Accessories

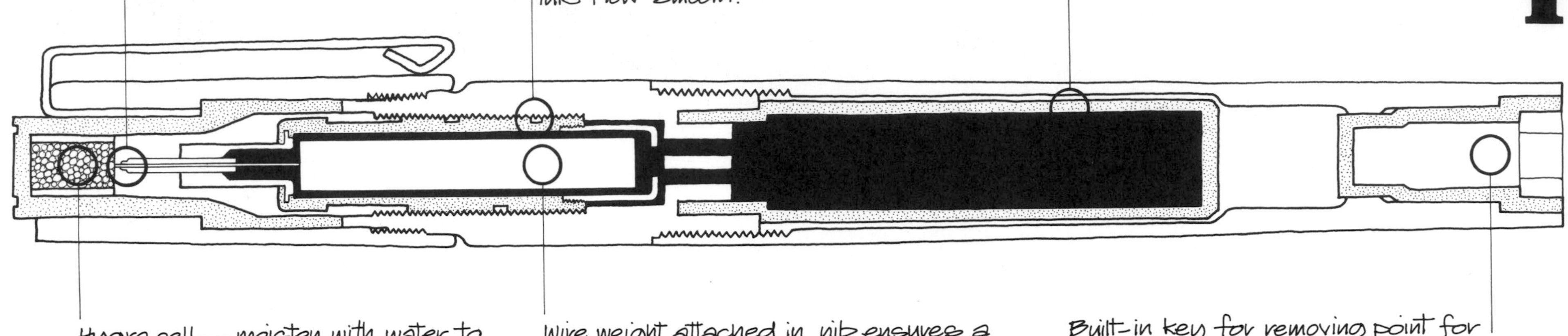

Section through a typical technical pen. The nib is a fine wire held in a tubular sleeve and attached to a plastic weight. The nib and weight move freely in the sleeve at core of pen, allowing constant ink flow around its main parts. The ink reservoir is usually a plastic cartridge which squeezes onto the barrel. In some pens a metal band around the cartridge ensures a tight fit and prevents thermal expansion when held in the hand.

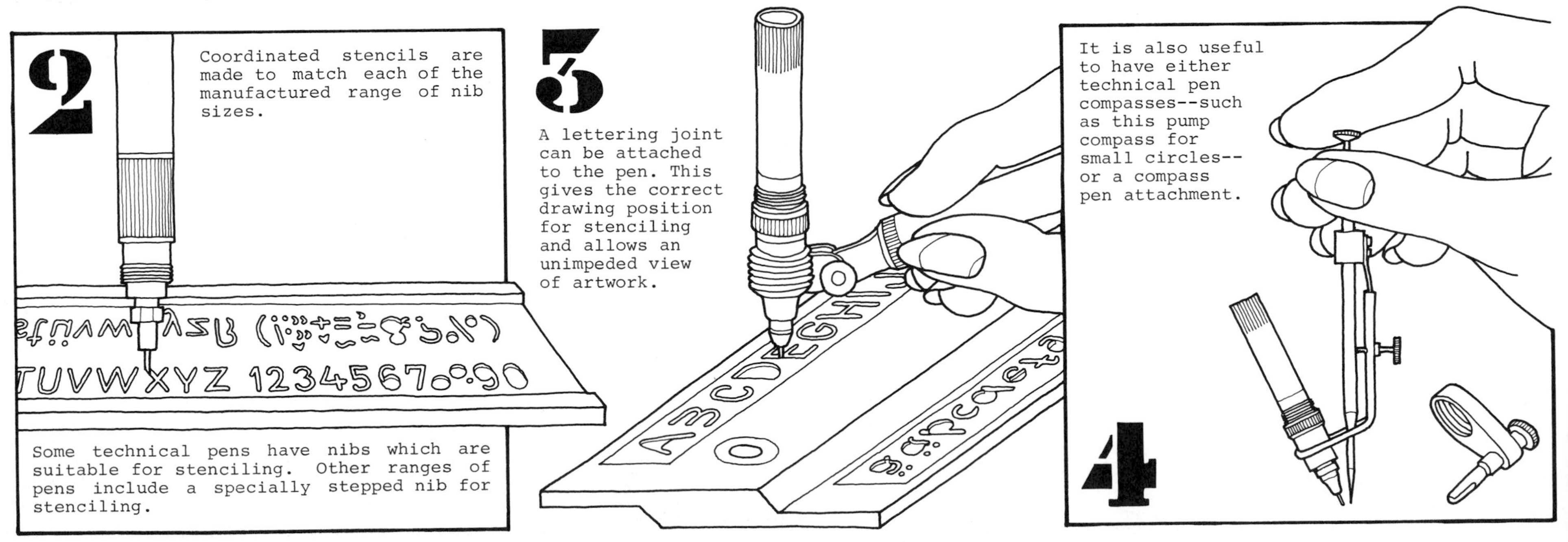

2

Coordinated stencils are made to match each of the manufactured range of nib sizes.

Some technical pens have nibs which are suitable for stenciling. Other ranges of pens include a specially stepped nib for stenciling.

3

A lettering joint can be attached to the pen. This gives the correct drawing position for stenciling and allows an unimpeded view of artwork.

4

It is also useful to have either technical pen compasses--such as this pump compass for small circles--or a compass pen attachment.

Technical Pen Maintenance

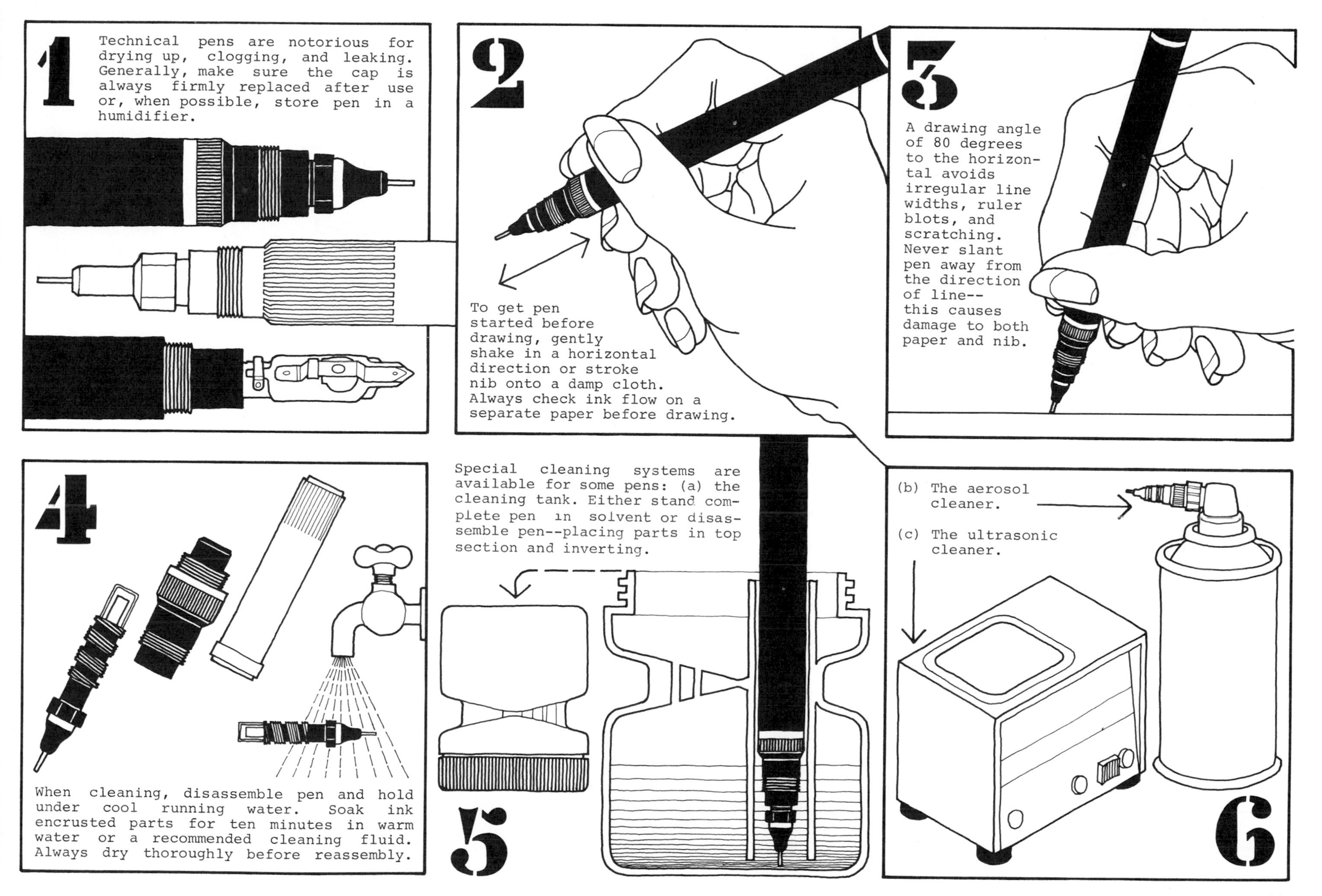

Erasing Ink Mistakes

1

The quickest way of erasing mistakes from tracing paper is to carefully scrape off the ink with a razor blade, using firm, light strokes. Finish with a soft eraser and burnish.

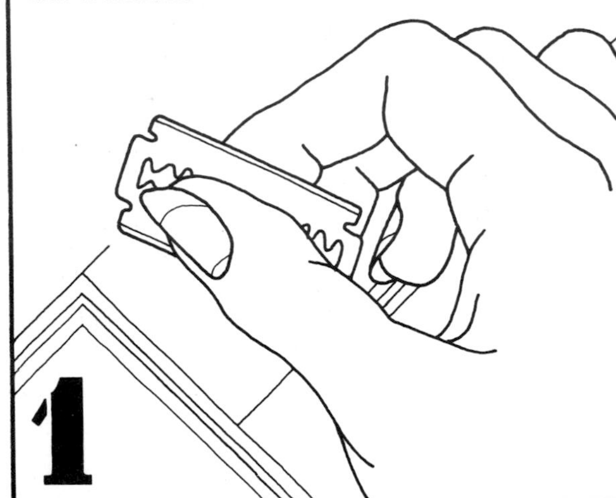

2

The pencil-shaped glass fiber eraser is accurate but abrasive. If the tracing paper surface is damaged, smooth off with a soft eraser and burnish.

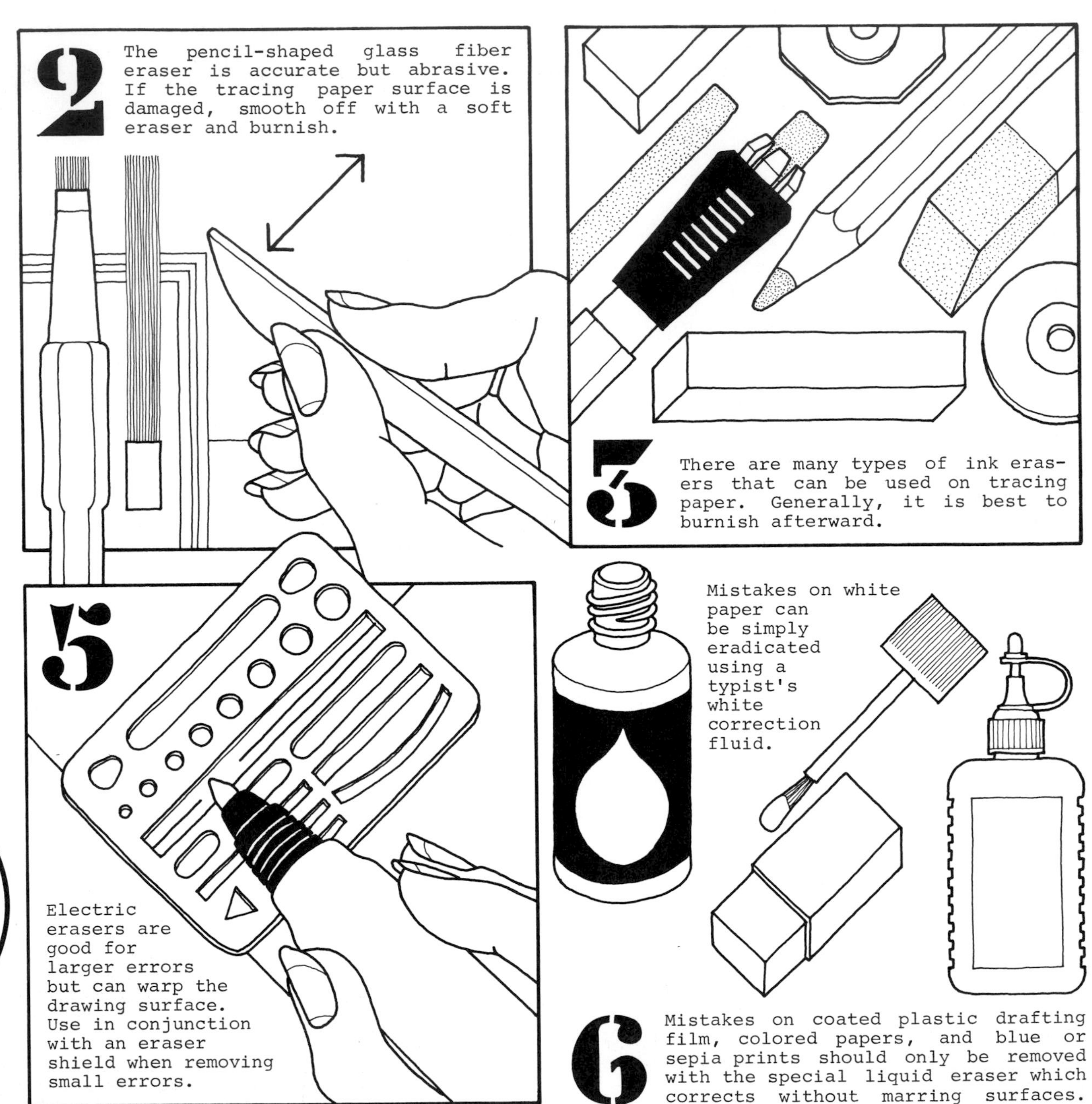

3

There are many types of ink erasers that can be used on tracing paper. Generally, it is best to burnish afterward.

4

For the best results, use a plastic eraser containing solvent in its composition which dissolves the ink into removable strings.

5

Electric erasers are good for larger errors but can warp the drawing surface. Use in conjunction with an eraser shield when removing small errors.

Mistakes on white paper can be simply eradicated using a typist's white correction fluid.

6

Mistakes on coated plastic drafting film, colored papers, and blue or sepia prints should only be removed with the special liquid eraser which corrects without marring surfaces.

Pen and Ink Hatching Techniques

One function of hatching is the convention of coding materials in technical drawings (see page 73). In the wider context of drawing and sketching, however, hatching can be either formal or free in character--depending upon your own mood or personality. Hatching is, essentially, the structuring of lines and dots into tonal arrangements which describe surface, form, space, and light.

Even or gradated surface values and textures are easily created with the three basic tubular nib sizes--although the fine nibs are liable to snap under pressure.

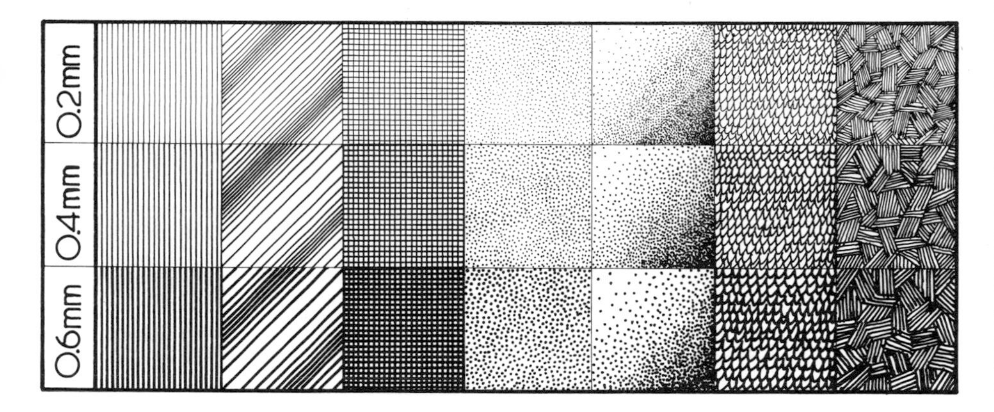

Basic forms can also be constructed using a variety of hatching systems. Such simple drawing experiments exploit light and shadow direction--an important visual clue in communicating illusions of depth in graphics.

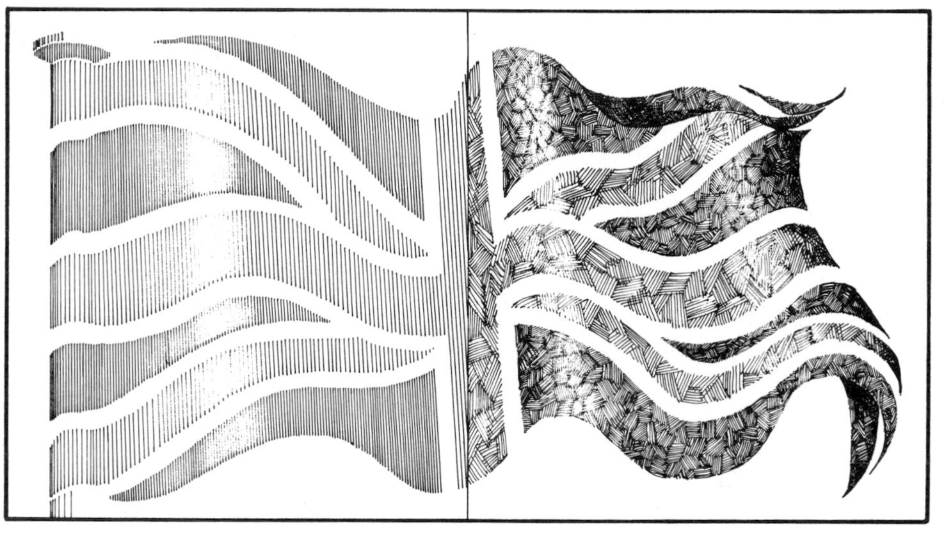

Ruled or freehand hatching techniques can be utilized to simulate the illusion of three-dimensional surfaces. When experimenting, doodle with different techniques, different nibs, and on differently grained drawing surfaces: this experience will increase a drawing ability.

Experiment with ranges of hatching in an objective sketch which records a group of objects in space.

Delay the adoption of a fixed personal hatching style until after exhaustive experimentation: stereotyped hatching can restrict design prowess by limiting the means of graphic visualization and expression.

The Graphic Depth Cues

When harnessed to the visual perception of form in space, hatching functions as a powerful ally in the graphic description of depth, for it offers a variety of techniques for simulating tonal value and surface texture. To reinforce this illusion, linear hatching should be directional when depicting three-dimensional objects--lines following the main inclination and surface direction of planes and forms. Apart from light and shadow, the other major depth cues are:

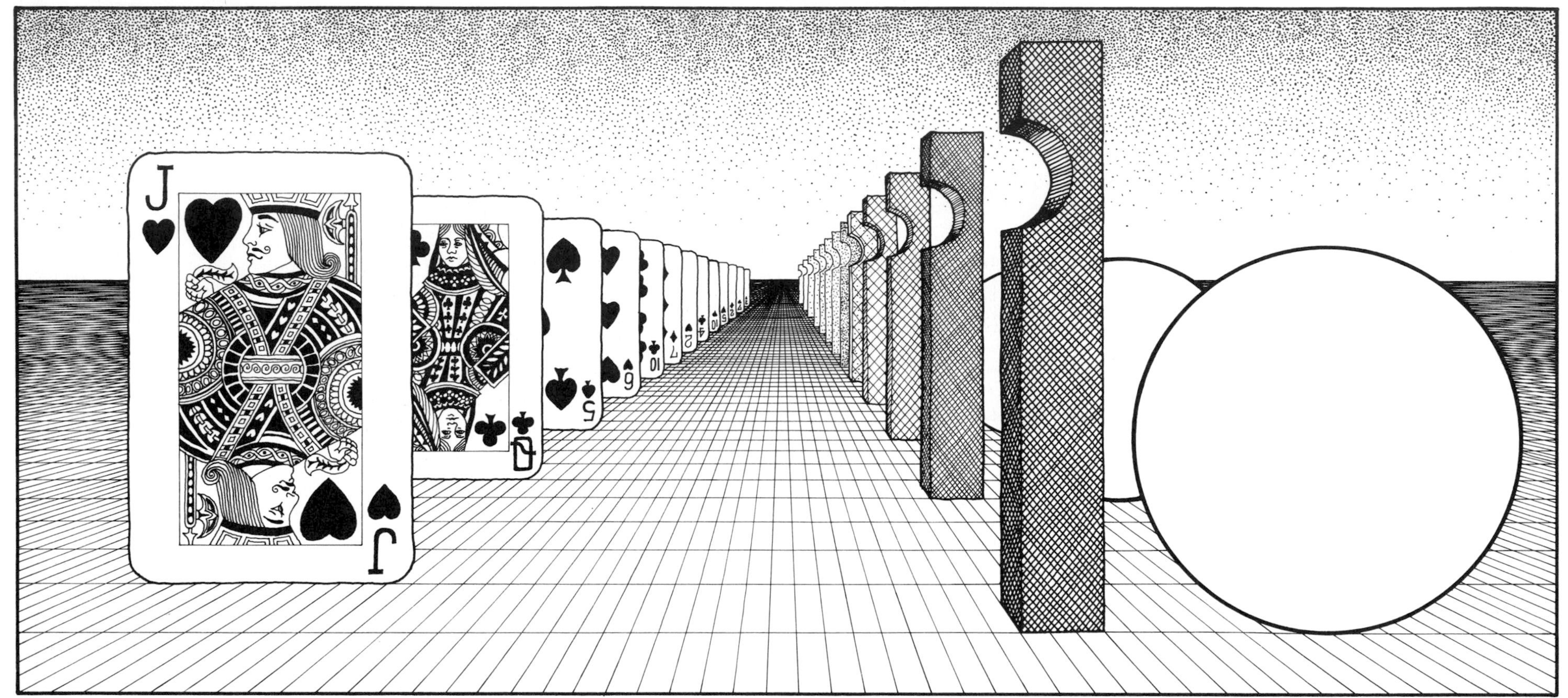

1

Texture gradients (sky mass and floor plane). Many psychologists such as J. J. Gibson have been fascinated by the perceptual depth effect of texture gradients. These also enhance depth in graphics.

Overlap. Gibson conducted an experiment using playing cards. He discovered that overlap--i.e., part of a nearer object partially hiding that of a further--to be a powerful indication of depth.

Aerial perspective. Leonardo da Vinci described the effect of aerial perspective. This refers to the graying effect of objects as they are seen at progressively distant points. Atmospherics can be graphically simulated, using dots.

Perspective. The observation that objects diminish in size in depth perception led to Brunelleschi's invention of perspective in 1417. His central vanishing point controls the relative size and position of drawn objects (see page 76).

Pen in the Design Process

A first-year student study made in technical pen of his motorcycle. His aim was to exploit both freehand and ruled hatching techniques in combination with other mediums such as aerosol spray and gouache.

Dry-Transfer Lines, Tones, and Patterns

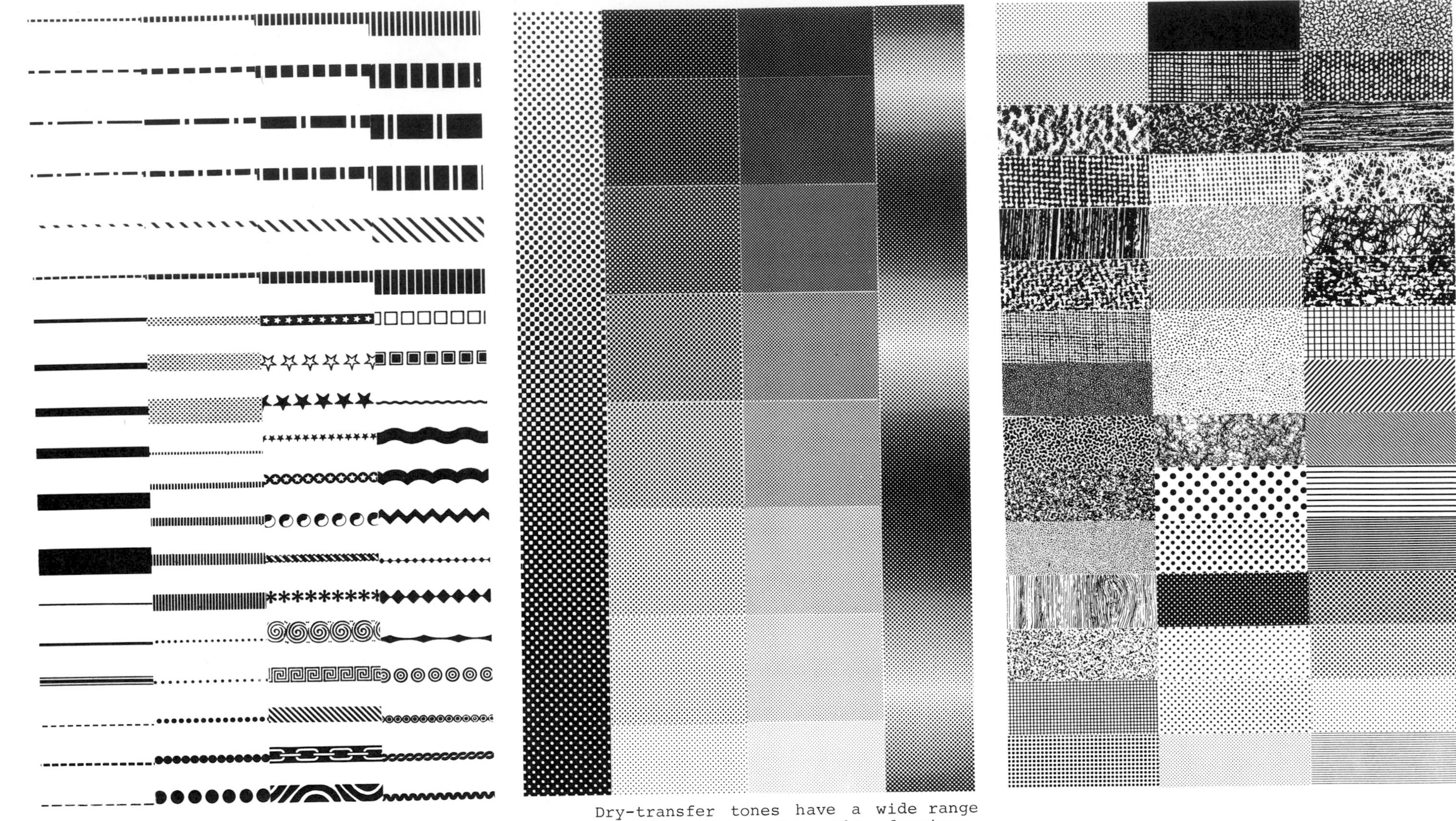

1

Dry-transfer lines are available in tape dispensers and are manufactured in several widths of solid and patterned strips. They are primarily intended to reduce the preparation time spent by graphic designers when producing advertisements, charts, diagrams, layouts, and technical drawings.

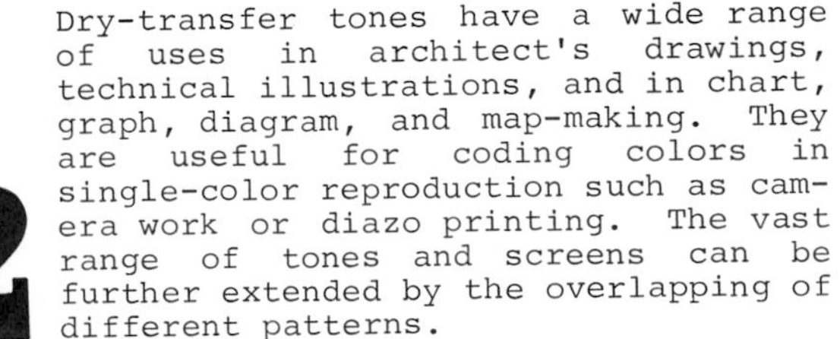

2

Dry-transfer tones have a wide range of uses in architect's drawings, technical illustrations, and in chart, graph, diagram, and map-making. They are useful for coding colors in single-color reproduction such as camera work or diazo printing. The vast range of tones and screens can be further extended by the overlapping of different patterns.

3

Dry-transfer patterns are versatile sheets of printed textures for adding shading effects and surface elaborations to illustrations, artwork, and freehand drawings for reproduction--the matte acetate surface reducing glare in photographic reprography.

How to Apply Dry-Transfer Lines, Tones, and Patterns

1 Dry-transfer lines: Using the dispenser, draw the tape across the artwork surface and press into contact. Cut the tape while lifting the dispenser--avoiding extracting further tape.

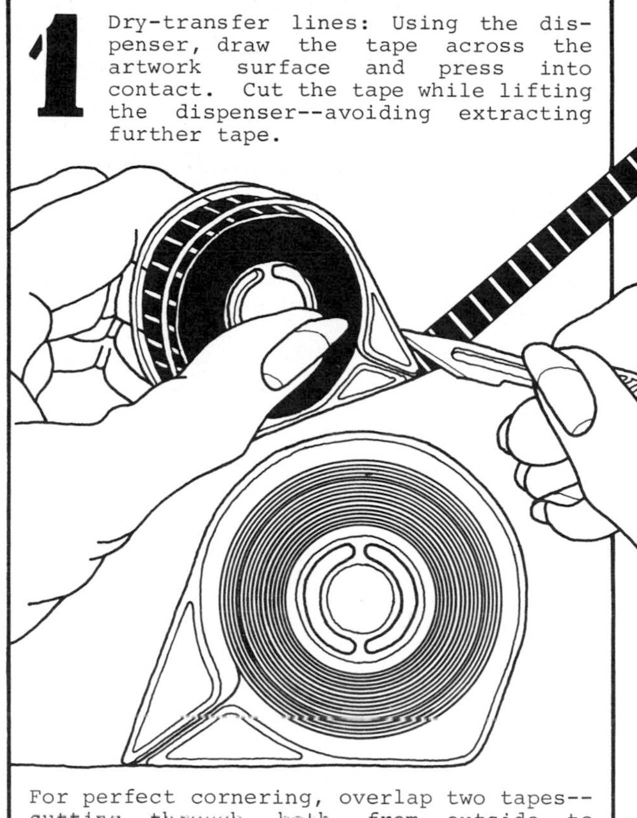

For perfect cornering, overlap two tapes--cutting through both from outside to inside corner. After removal of excess pieces, reposition tape to form a perfect miter.

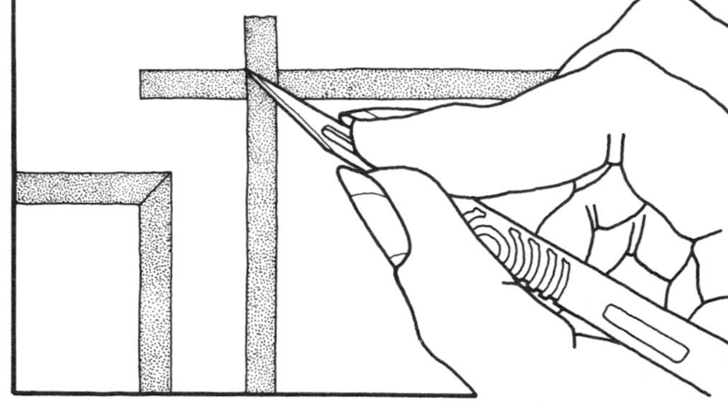

2 Dry-transfer tones: To use, position the sheet over the artwork and cut the rough shape you require with a scalpel--taking care not to cut through the backing sheet. Remove the film from the backing sheet and lay it on the art surface--the low-tack adhesion allows the shape to be repositioned, if necessary.

Once the film is in position, smooth over lightly with fingers. Then, trim around exact shape, and burnish.

3 Dry-transfer patterns: Lay the printed sheet face down over the artwork and draw directly on the unprinted surface--the textured pattern will transfer as you draw (there is even a solid black sheet available for making direct line drawings).

When the sheet is lifted clear, the transfer is complete. Single lines, detailed shapes, and large areas can be transferred--the latter requiring a broad-ended spatula.

Interaction of Mediums and Surface

Make a test sheet comprised of four or more different paper types and surfaces heat-mounted to a support board. Explore the behavior of the basic "dry" and "wet" mediums in contact with, for example, tracing paper (smooth grade), layout paper, cartridge drawing paper, and watercolor paper.

1 Various line and shading characteristics made by the different pencil graphite grades.

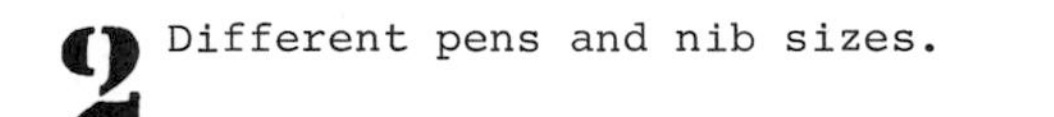

2 Different pens and nib sizes.

3 Conté crayon, charcoal, and chalk.

4 Graphite dust (collected from a pointer) and diluted ink effects from tissue paper, cotton wool, and finger applications.

5 Ink prints made from hessian, string, sliced cabbage, and the ends of wood doweling.

6 Mixed media experiments such as ink wash and pencil, pen and crayon; clear and colored wax resist under diluted ink wash; ink wash over scored and sliced paper; the "etching" effect of household bleach on permanent ink (not India ink) washes.

N.B.: The bleach should only be applied with a pointed stick or brush handle--do not use brushes, as bleach attacks bristles and hairs.

Mixed Media Drawing

The best way of experiencing the potential of mixed media is to experiment with a variety of mediums in one objective freehand drawing.

1

Ordinary well-diluted blue-black fountain-pen ink worked broadly onto a stretched sheet of drawing paper using a cloth or tissue paper as applicator. This establishes the basic tonal organization of the composition on the paper.

2

Outlines of the major forms worked in line using a bamboo pen followed by more detailed information, such as surface textures worked in a variety of pens, i.e., fine bamboo, fountain, technical, ball-point, and fine-line marker using full-strength Indian and permanent inks.

3

Tonal highlights picked out with white chalk and "etched" with diluted household bleach. The effect of the bleach is to turn darker areas of fountain-pen ink into subtle light yellows and pinks. However, use it sparingly, as it can damage the surface of the paper.

Mixed media project by a first-year architecture student.

Three Design Support Workbooks

1

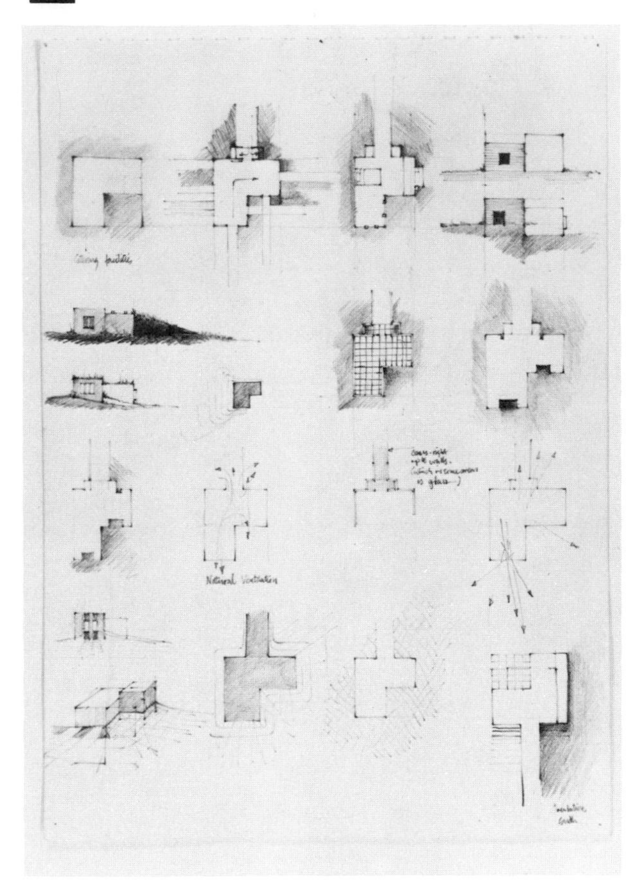

IDEAS BOOK

Ideas book: a portable pad of thin plain or graphed drawing paper useful at the outset of design. In graphically recording your initial and diagrammatic concepts along various design routes, it can be made public during critiques to explain objectives and approach to problem-solving.

SKETCHBOOK

Sketchbook: another portable pad of plain drawing paper with a stiff back support for objective freehand drawing and outdoor sketching. In documenting forms and spaces of interest, it functions as a memory store of images for future reference. Also useful for experimenting with unfamiliar mediums and techniques.

3

SCRAPBOOK

Scrapbook: a reference book in which photographs culled from newspapers and magazines are glued into collated sections. Pages could include compilations of human figures describing different poses, and various automobiles, tree types, building materials, etc., which, when required, act as a visual dictionary to inform presentation drawings.

2 COLOR: MEDIUMS AND METHODS

Colored Pencils, Pastels, and Crayons

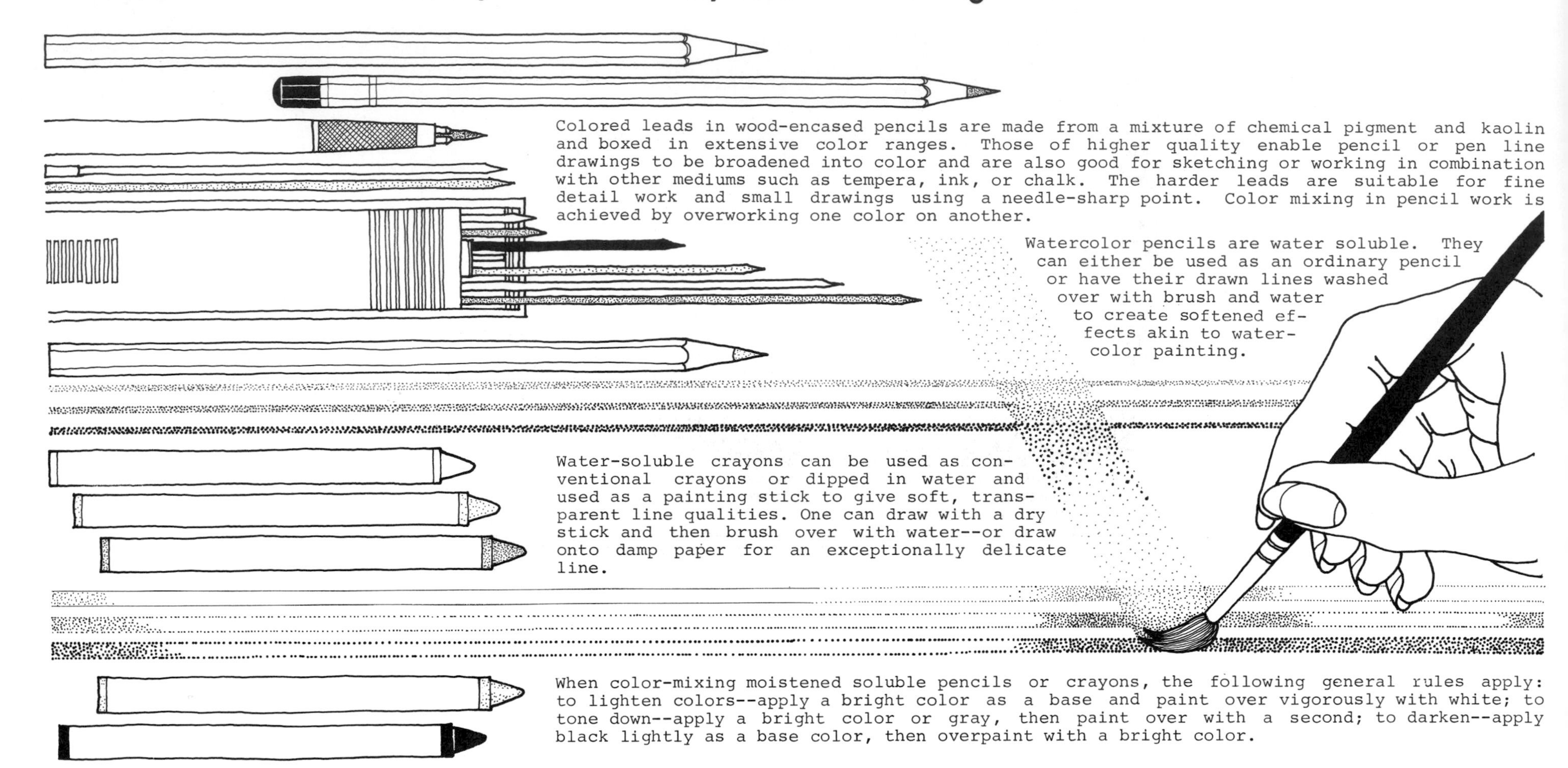

Colored leads in wood-encased pencils are made from a mixture of chemical pigment and kaolin and boxed in extensive color ranges. Those of higher quality enable pencil or pen line drawings to be broadened into color and are also good for sketching or working in combination with other mediums such as tempera, ink, or chalk. The harder leads are suitable for fine detail work and small drawings using a needle-sharp point. Color mixing in pencil work is achieved by overworking one color on another.

Watercolor pencils are water soluble. They can either be used as an ordinary pencil or have their drawn lines washed over with brush and water to create softened effects akin to watercolor painting.

Water-soluble crayons can be used as conventional crayons or dipped in water and used as a painting stick to give soft, transparent line qualities. One can draw with a dry stick and then brush over with water--or draw onto damp paper for an exceptionally delicate line.

When color-mixing moistened soluble pencils or crayons, the following general rules apply: to lighten colors--apply a bright color as a base and paint over vigorously with white; to tone down--apply a bright color or gray, then paint over with a second; to darken--apply black lightly as a base color, then overpaint with a bright color.

Pastels are chalk sticks made from powder color bound with gum arabic. Available in wide color ranges, they can be effectively used for soft, grainy artwork or worked over dry layers of tempera, gouache, watercolor, or ink. When given the choice, purchase square section crayons or pastels, as they offer both a broad and fine line width and do not roll off drawing boards.

Wax crayons are formulated from richly pigmented soft wax and, using little pressure, give dense and brilliant cover to most surfaces. Being water repellent, they are ideal for colored resist work--especially with ink and watercolor. They can also simulate scratchboard techniques; by applying a solid background using a light color and over-rubbing a second layer in a dark color, designs can be scratched through with the point of a knife. Some wax crayons are intended for dilution with white spirit and used as a paint for creating transparent layers of color. They can also be heated and, when melted, manipulated with a spatula to create relief effects.

Markers and Ball-Point Pens

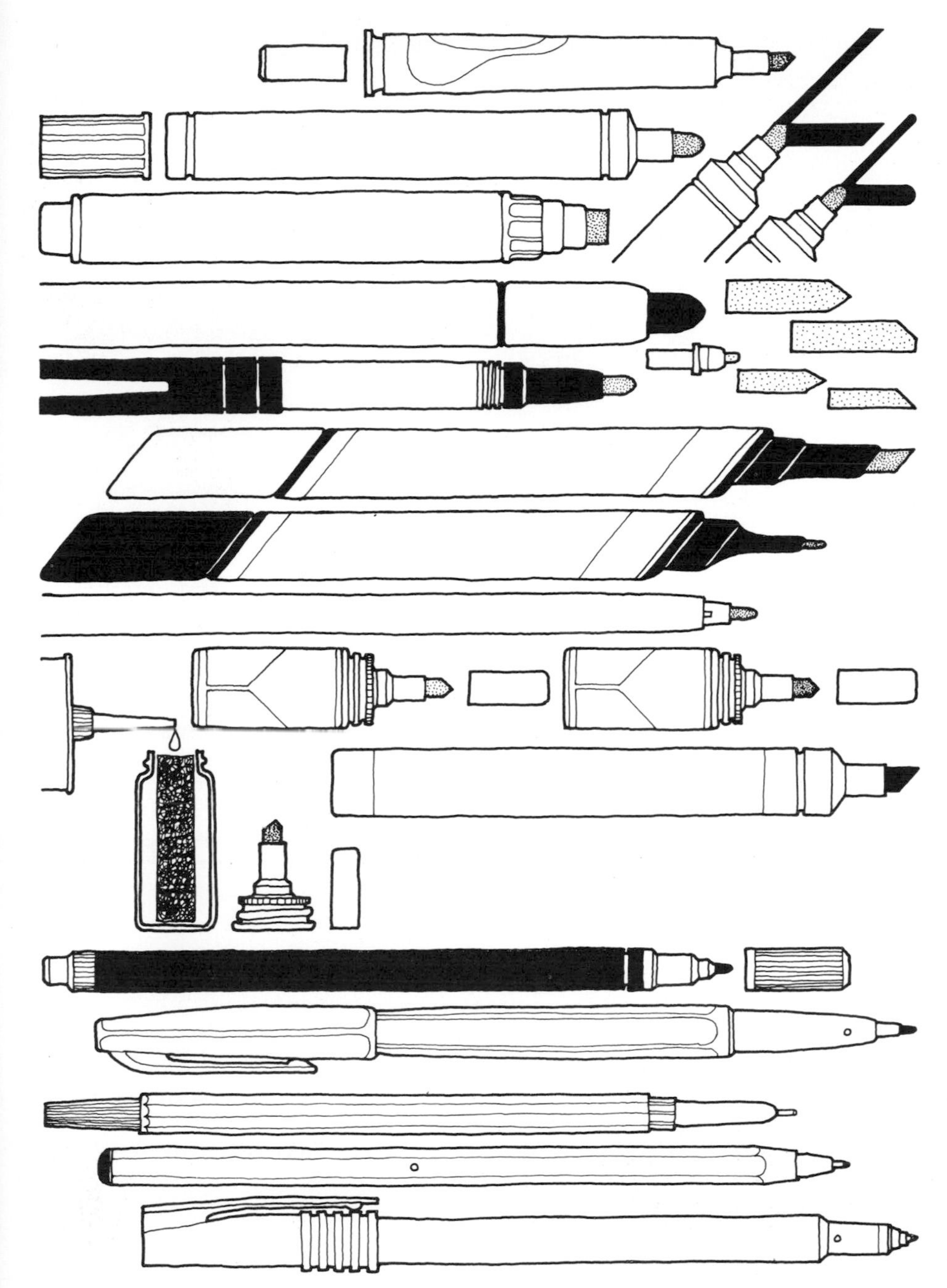

Giant markers were primarily developed to facilitate large-scale display lettering on banners and posters and for the marking of almost every conceivable surface by warehousemen and storekeepers. Giant markers can contain either soluble or colorfast inks produced in a basic color range, and are useful in design for color-coded diagramming and sketching ideas on a large scale.

Marker nibs vary: either felt composition, nylon, or fiber-tipped. There are a variety of sizes: extra-fine, fine, medium, broad, and extra-large in chisel (or wedge), round, square, and bullet (or bull-nose) points. The chisel point gives both a broad and a fine line with an oblique or square end; the bullet-shaped point gives a line with a rounded end.

There is a felt marker that is refillable and supplied with a set of interchangeable nibs. These dispense a limited range of spirit-based, permanent ink colors designed for outdoor sketching.

Studio art markers use regular felt-composition nibs which dispense either permanent oil-based or transparent water-based inks. These are marketed in an extensive spectrum of hues, tints, and shades, including a selection of warm and cold grays. If the special marker paper pads are not used, the oil-based inks tend to bleed through and across normal bonds of paper; the water-based inks do not bleed but, for softer effects, can be worked on dampened paper. Art markers are expensive but highly popular with designers, for they offer instant and constant color for preparing layouts, color overlays, sketching, and coloring drawings. Some ranges of markers are color coordinated with papers, transfer films, and printing inks to aid color matching for the graphic designer. They are used throughout the design process from idea origination to finished presentations.

Some markers incorporate a valve which releases ink only when in use. To start this type of marker, shake well and press the nib on a hard surface so that it fills with ink (do not do this with conventional markers, as it will cause nibs to spread or retract into the barrel).

Always replace the cap tightly after use, as markers will tend to dry up. Sometimes--if their tank is accessible--oil-based markers can be resuscitated by adding a few drops of lighter fuel.

Fine and extra-fine line markers have nylon, vinyl, or composite rubber tips designed for writing, drawing, and sketching in basic colors. Special function markers include permanent or removable inks for plastic film--useful for producing transparencies for overhead projectors and diascopes; transparent, luminous inks for highlighting lines of printed text; and blue, drop-out inks for non-print marks and inks for use on white boards.

There are a number of different types of ball-point pen--from the standard "ball-point" in which indelible ink is dispensed via a rolling steel ball, to pens with nylon and tungsten carbide rollers which contain water-based inks. The regular ball-point pen, which is available with medium, fine, and extra-fine line widths, has gained respectability as a drawing and sketching medium--especially useful for the rapid delineation of new ideas or even for the working of tone on finished drawings (see page 35).

Colored Pencils and Crayons in the Design Process

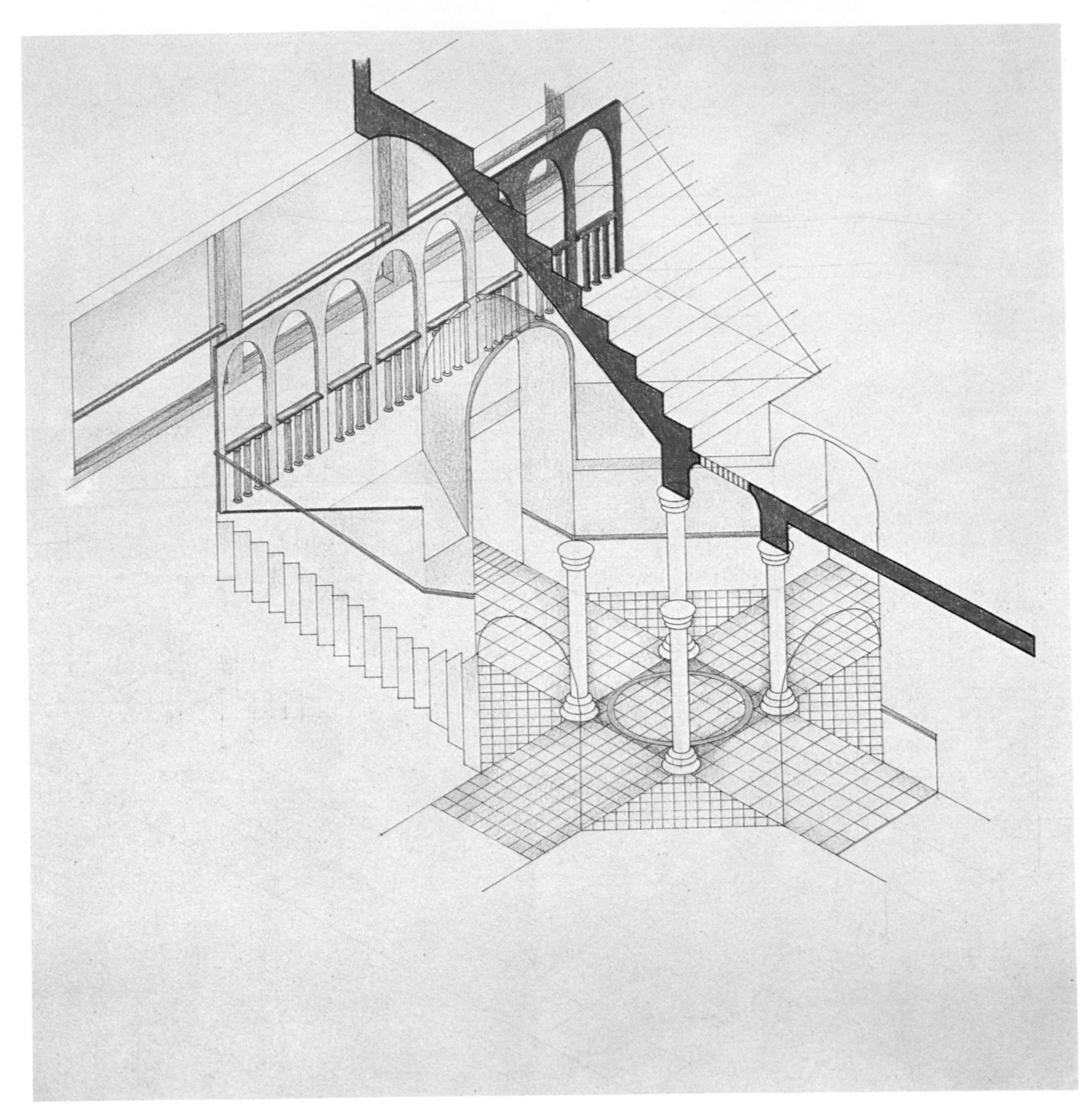

Wax resist drawing made with colored wax crayons and white candle wax on cartridge paper under a colored ink wash.

Student isometric of an interior view of a project for a leisure center. Colored pencils were applied delicately to an ink drawing worked on cartridge paper. The paper was initially given a light coat of yellow sprayed from an auto touch-up aerosol.

Markers and Ball-Point Pens in the Design Process

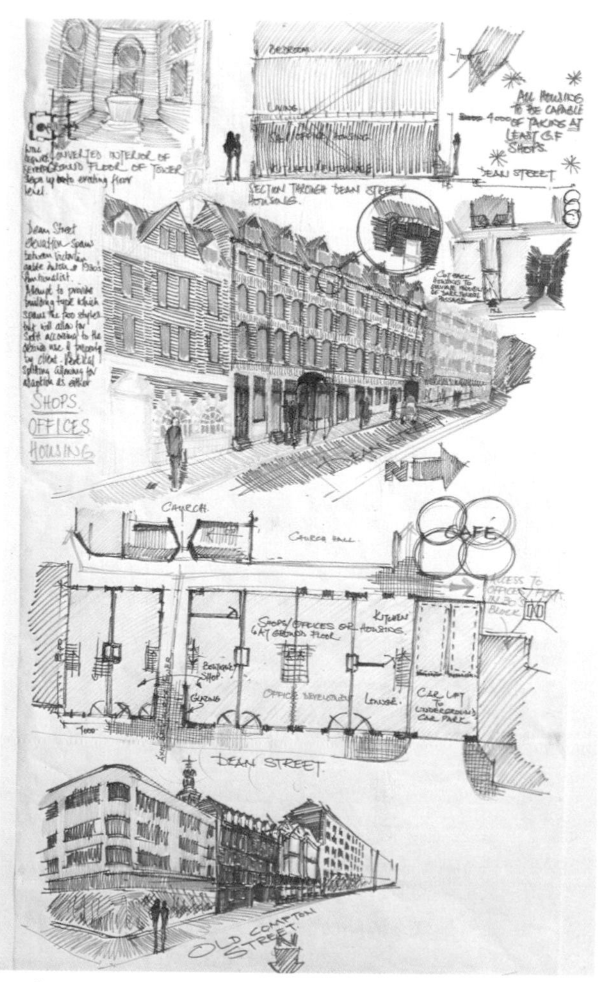

Markers are terrific for realizing new ideas in color. This trial exposure of a developing student idea for a sketch design acted both as a generative tool and as a presentation device--the roll of detail paper on which it was drawn being later hung scroll-fashion as part of a wall display.

Landscape drawing worked exclusively in ball-point pen. The sheer freedom of this medium is conducive to a vigorous buildup of lines which combine to describe shape and surface through gradated tonal sequences to a dense black.

Inks and Paints

Pigments thinned in water:

Watercolor is a transparent medium made from refined water-soluble pigments. Colors are marketed in jar, tablet, and tube and are highly suitable for more subtle renderings on paper and board--especially in conjunction with pen or pencil drawings. They are manufactured in two qualities: "artist" and "student"--the latter being cheaper and less refined.

A range of concentrated watercolors based on analine dyes are made especially for airbrush retouching on photographic surfaces and artwork on paper and art board.

Colored inks are, with the exception of black and white, based on brilliant dyes. They also contain shellac, which enables one color to be superimposed easily over another: it is this glazing ability of both watercolors and inks which produces a vibrant luminosity of color when brush- or airbrush-applied.

Tempera (poster) color and designer's gouache are full-bodied, opaque pigments for paper and board--obtainable in tubes and jars. They are all intermixable, the finer ground pigments being suitable for airbrush while the less refined version of poster color, being cheaper, is available in jars, tubes, cakes, and powder form. Showcard color extends water-based pigments into the more exotic fluorescents and metallics. Earth color is also sold in tubes, jars, and bulk form for use in fresco painting, but it can be used on paper. For extra-large artwork, use decorator's emulsion, which is sold by the gallon.

Acrylic/polymer paint represents a technological advance in the formulation of artist's color, for it is a quick-drying synthetic plastic emulsion which, since it is capable of thinned application for wash effects and can be used thickly for impasto effects, behaves both like watercolor and oil paint. Acrylic mediums are non-yellowing and will adhere to any surface. There is a special polymer paint for use on plastic film with pen or brush. It is opaque, matte, and waterproof when dry. Pens and brushes should be rinsed in water during use and cleaned in soap and water.

Pigments thinned in white spirit:

5

Oil color is mixed with linseed oil and contained in tubes. Oil paint dries very slowly, although a drier's medium can be added to speed the process. Oil paint is sold in "artist's" and "student" grades and usually worked on primed but slightly absorbent surfaces such as canvas, cardboard, Masonite, paper, and canvas board. Untreated surfaces can be primed with gesso, white thixotropic paint, or an oil-based undercoat.

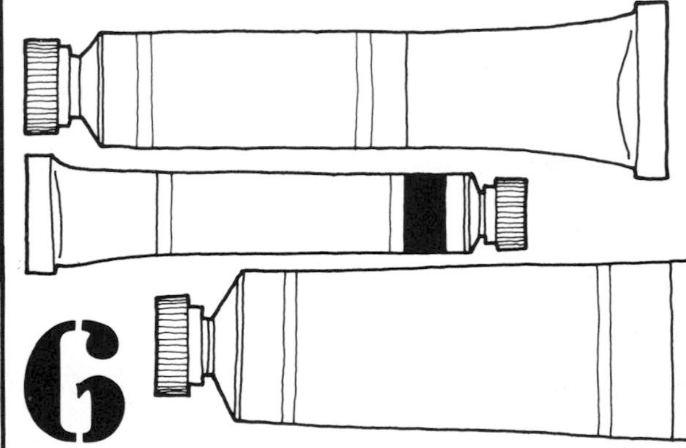

Alkyd color is another synthetic medium formulated from alkyd resins to behave like, or be intermixed with, oil paint. It has the added facility of drying quickly and resists adverse atmospheric conditions.

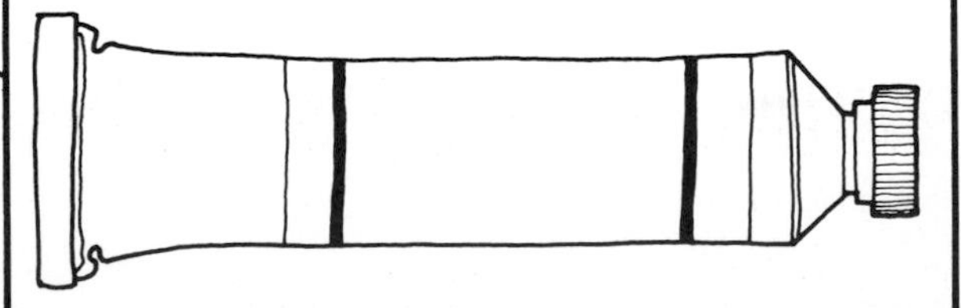

Custom varnishes and other mediums are available for each of the above pigments.

Brushes

Brushes for water-based pigments (watercolors, inks, tempera, poster, gouache, and acrylic) are manufactured in a variety of sizes and shapes. Hair and bristles are taken from the squirrel, bear, pony, ox, hog, and sable--although modern sable brushes are mainly made from weasel hair. The best red sable brushes, however, are made from kolinsky mink tail hair; being the finest, they are the most expensive, but a good investment, providing they are well maintained.

000 00 1 2 3 4 5 6 7 8 10 12 14

Size range of a typical watercolor brush: 000, 00, 1, 2, 3, 4, 5, 6, 7, 8, 9, 10, 11, 12, 13, 14.

Brush functions and shapes correspond to color-carrying capacity and mark-making ability.

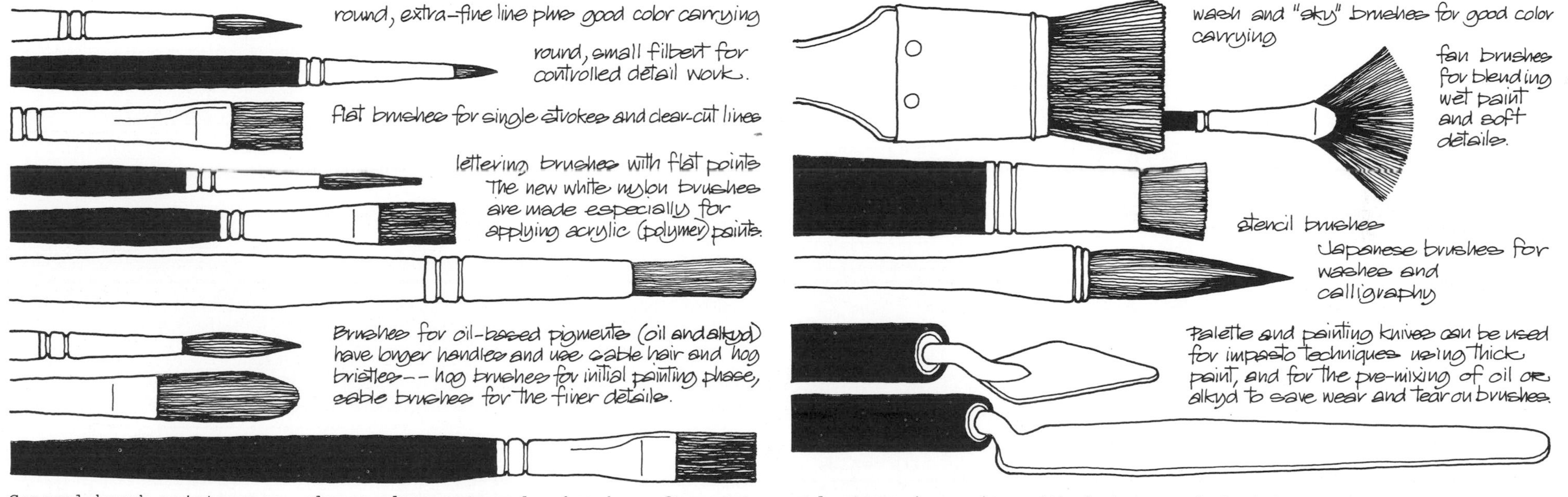

General brush maintenance: always clean watercolor brushes after use. First rinse in water, then gently work hairs or bristles into a bar of soap (not detergent). Work into a lather to release all trace of pigment, and rinse in water. Shake dry before shaping the brush head and store in a jar with hairs or bristles uppermost. Brushes used with acrylics must be washed immediately after use, avoiding contact with hot water, as it causes acrylic to harden. For oil brushes, repeat the above procedure using white spirit only.

For beginners, a suggested range of brushes would be sables--No. 2, 6, 10; hogs--flat fitch No. 14 and round fitch No. 12.

The World of Color

The colors that we see do not exist on the surface of substance, for they are manufactured in the mind's eye. Our experience of color is a sensation conveyed through the medium of energy in the form of light radiations within the visible spectrum. However, without an observer, light rays do not in themselves constitute color. It is the eye and brain of the observer that interpret the meaning of these sensory messages by a decoding process involving thousands of color receptors ("cones") located in the retina, before the color is ultimately experienced in the brain.

A color perception depends upon three important factors: first, the conditions under which the object is viewed--for example, certain colors painted under tungsten light would appear very different from those painted in natural daylight, as the two color perceptions respond to two different spectral energy distributions contained in each light source. Second, a color perception depends on the spectral characteristics of the object--the ability of its substance to absorb, reflect, or transmit light. Red paint, for instance, appears red because it has the property of absorbing from white light everything except the red component of the light. The third factor is our ability to perceive colors, i.e., the sensitivity of our personal "Technicolor processing laboratory" (the eye and brain) to create a color response.

THE THREE DIMENSIONS OF COLOR

The process of mixing patches of colored light--as in television pictures where, from combinations of red, green, and blue,it is possible to make nearly all the colors--is known as "additive" color mixture. This is distinct from the "subtractive" color mixtures which occur when we mix pigments, such as in painting or printing. Pigment colors are seen as being composed of three dimensions: hue, chroma (saturation), and value (brightness). Hue is that quality which is commonly accepted as color in defining its redness, blueness, yellowness, or greenness. Chroma refers to the intensity of a color, i.e., how much or how little gray it contains. Value describes the lightness or darkness of a color, i.e., the amount of white or black it contains. It is these three dimensional coordinates which are annotated to form the basis of color specification systems such as those by W. Ostwald and A. H. Munsell.

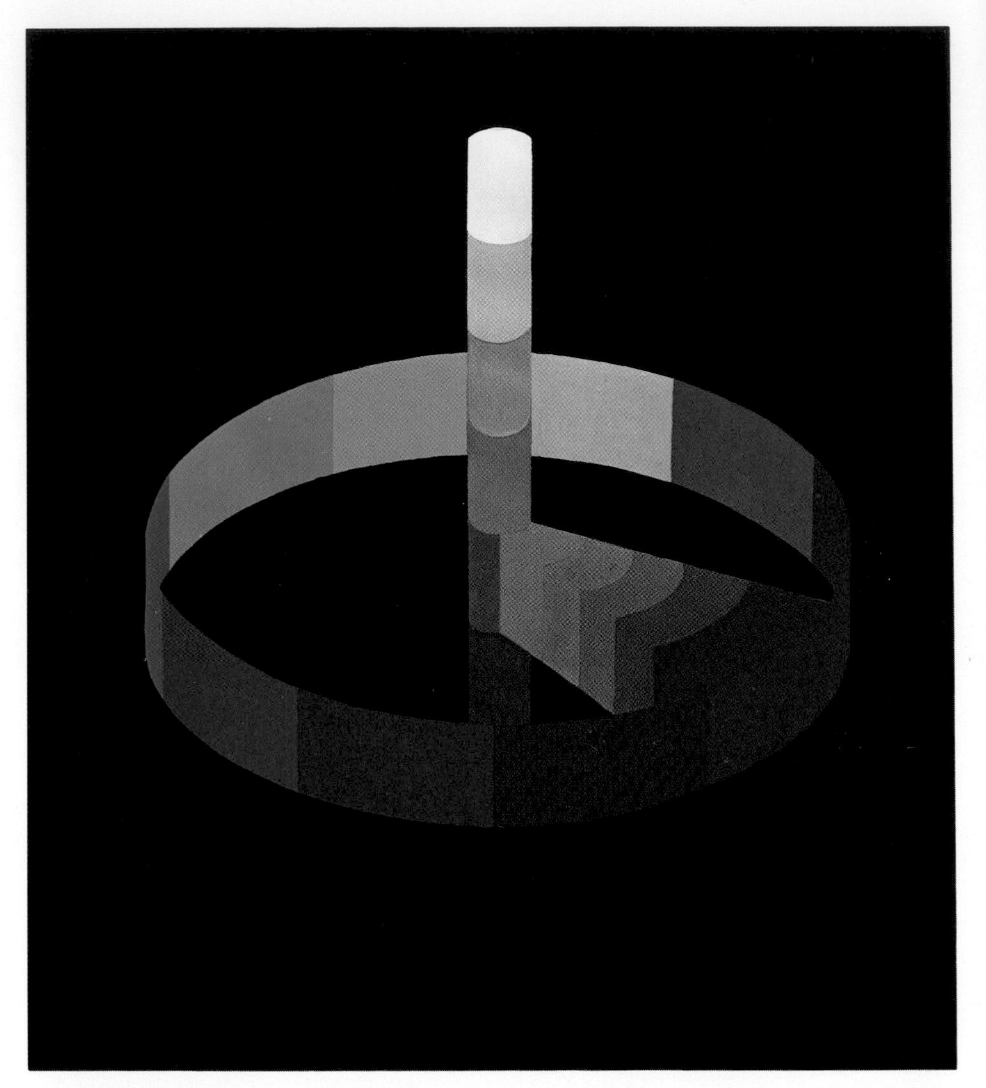

This is a conceptual diagram of the three-dimensional world of color. Its equator represents the spectrum bent into a color circle. Ten hues surround the perimeter, their levels of chroma desaturating as they encounter the gray core. Gray occupies the center of a vertical scale which determines color in terms of value. If we were to complete the color solid, the white upper pole would culminate a cone of ascending color tints (color plus white); while the black pole would terminate an inverted cone containing a descending scale of increasingly darkening shadows--or shades (color plus black).

Some Perceptual Color Effects

1

It is important to produce artwork under the type of illumination you intend it to be viewed because different illuminants--including natural daylight--emit different colors of light. Color-matching lamps which simulate daylight stabilize color perception and should be installed in design environments where correct color rendering is critical.

Here are some effects on color perception under two different light sources: those on the left were painted under tungsten light (a red-biased source), and, on the right, the same color rendered by natural daylight (a blue-biased source).

2

Apart from admixing pigments on the palette, colors can also be mixed "in the eye." One method is the use of color overlays which function as filters; another is the application of pigment in the pointilliste or divisionist technique. In the latter, different colored dots or speckles are so arranged as to cause--via their interaction--an experience of their "mix" in the eye and brain, the ultimate color experience being regulated by the distance of the viewer from the stimulus. This effect can be obtained using brushes, markers, colored pencils, and spray techniques.

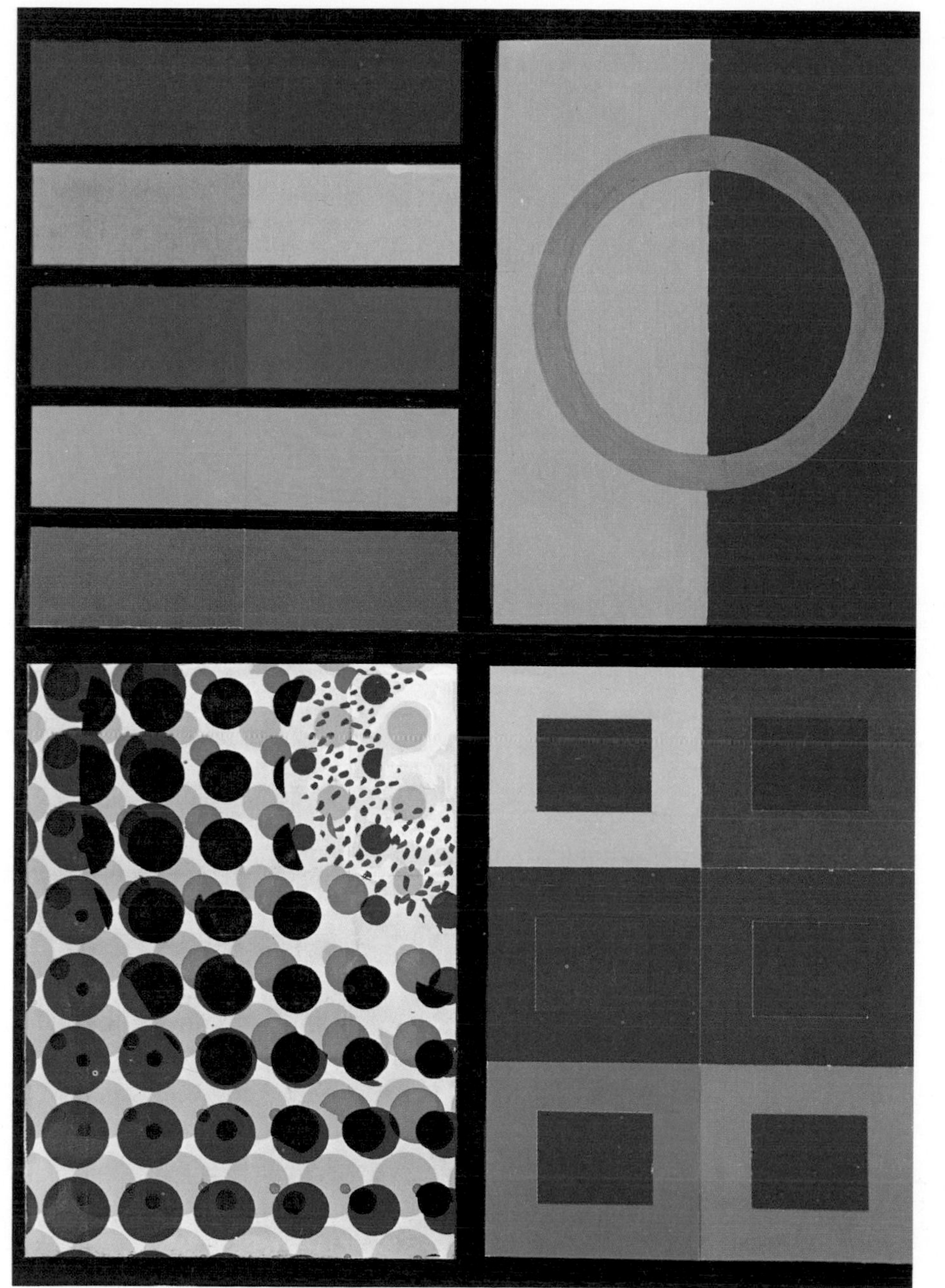

A color can never be isolated perceptually, for its experience is governed by the interaction with others viewed in the same field. This classic illustration demonstrates the dynamic nature of color. By holding a pencil between the red and green sectors, a change in hue will be detected in the gray circle. This phenomenon is called "simultaneous contrast"--an effect demonstrating another way in which the appearance of colors can vary, and caused by our visual system accentuating differences between adjacent colors.

Temperature is a further color sensation, certain hues such as red, orange, and yellow being identified as "warm," and others--green and blue--being identified as "cool." Also, different colors are said to occupy different spatial positions--the "warm," long-wavelength colors appearing "nearer" and "larger," while the "cool," short-wavelength colors recede. However, these experiences are relative, for, depending on the chroma and value of the hue in question (plus its interaction with others), a red, for example, can be made to appear both "cool" and "recessive."

Recent research questioning common stereotypes has also found that a red is not necessarily a more stimulating color than green. The excitation level of a color, it suggests, is more related to variations in chroma and value than differences in hue.

Basic Mixing Equipment and Painting Techniques

1

There is no need to purchase expensive palettes for mixing water-based pigments. Watercolor, ink, gouache, and tempera can be mixed in six-, nine-, or twelve-compartment aluminum baking trays or on a sheet of glass. Wide-necked jam jars or plastic drinking cartons suffice for holding water--one for mixing with paint, and one for cleaning brushes.

Gouache is intended to be applied as an opaque skin of flat pigment. To achieve this opacity, it should be mixed to a consistency resembling that of cream. By contrast, inks and watercolors are designed for transparent rendering in which the amount of admixed water--together with the color of the paper, or the underpainting--controls the ultimate color impression.

N.B.: Gouache tends to dry a lighter version of its color when wet. For this reason, it is a good idea to check a color on a scrap of paper before any major application. For the same reason, always mix enough paint to cover the area required and, if any overpainting is necessary, wait until the initial rendering is completely dry before proceeding.

Glazing: A technique used for achieving color luminosity whereby a layer of dry pigment is covered by a translucent layer. Successive layers produce subtle effects--each modifying the color impression of the last. This effect can be achieved using oil, acrylics, and all water-based pigments, but it is especially effective when ink or watercolor is rendered over full-bodied layers of tempera or gouache.

2

Scumbling: A dry brush loaded with opaque pigment worked over a dry base layer of another color. This technique is used mainly with full-bodied paints to achieve a softening, textural effect. A similar effect can be achieved with watercolors by working the flat of a loaded brush across the surface of textured paper to express its tooth.

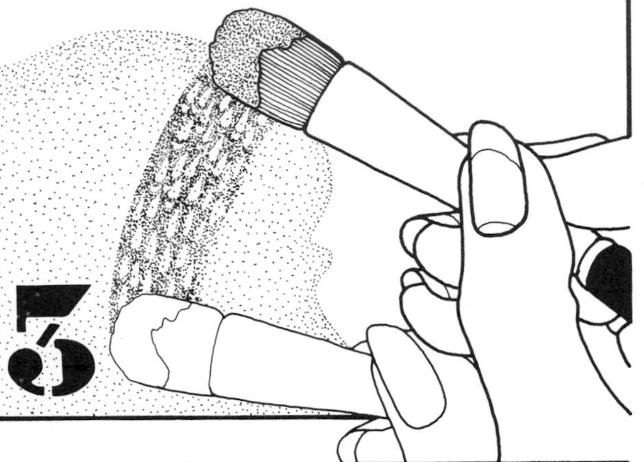

Impasto: The application of thick, full-bodied pigments to create a physically textured surface. This technique is best attained with oil paint--and also with acrylics and gouache, which can be stiffened with proprietary pastes. Impasto also refers to the buildup of thick layers of pastel and to the texture achieved by applying melted wax crayons with a painting knife.

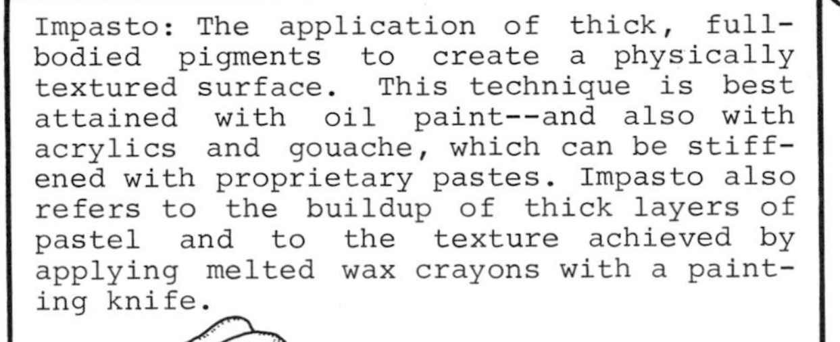

4

Wet-in-wet: A further subtle effect is the controlled introduction of diluted paint into a still-moist application of water or pigment. The resultant "feathering" is especially useful on more atmospheric artwork. This is a technique associated with all kinds of paint, and can also be accomplished by working water-based colored pencils on moistened paper.

5

How to Stretch a Sheet of Paper

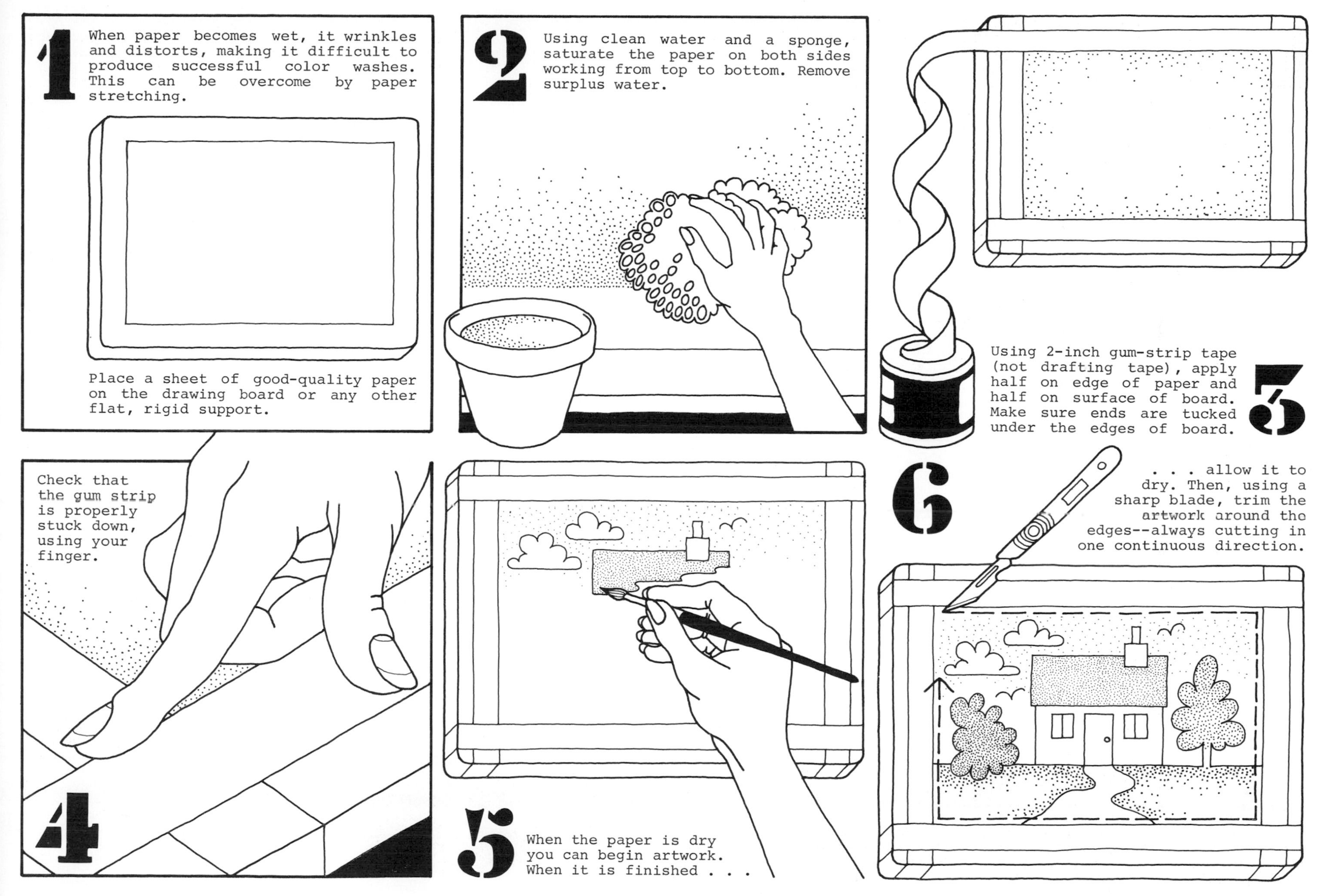

Inks in the Design Process

Elevation showing two faces of an infill design for a town house. Several methods of translucent ink rendering such as washes and glazes--using brush and spray--combine with watercolor and an ink line on a textured watercolor paper.

Paints in the Design Process

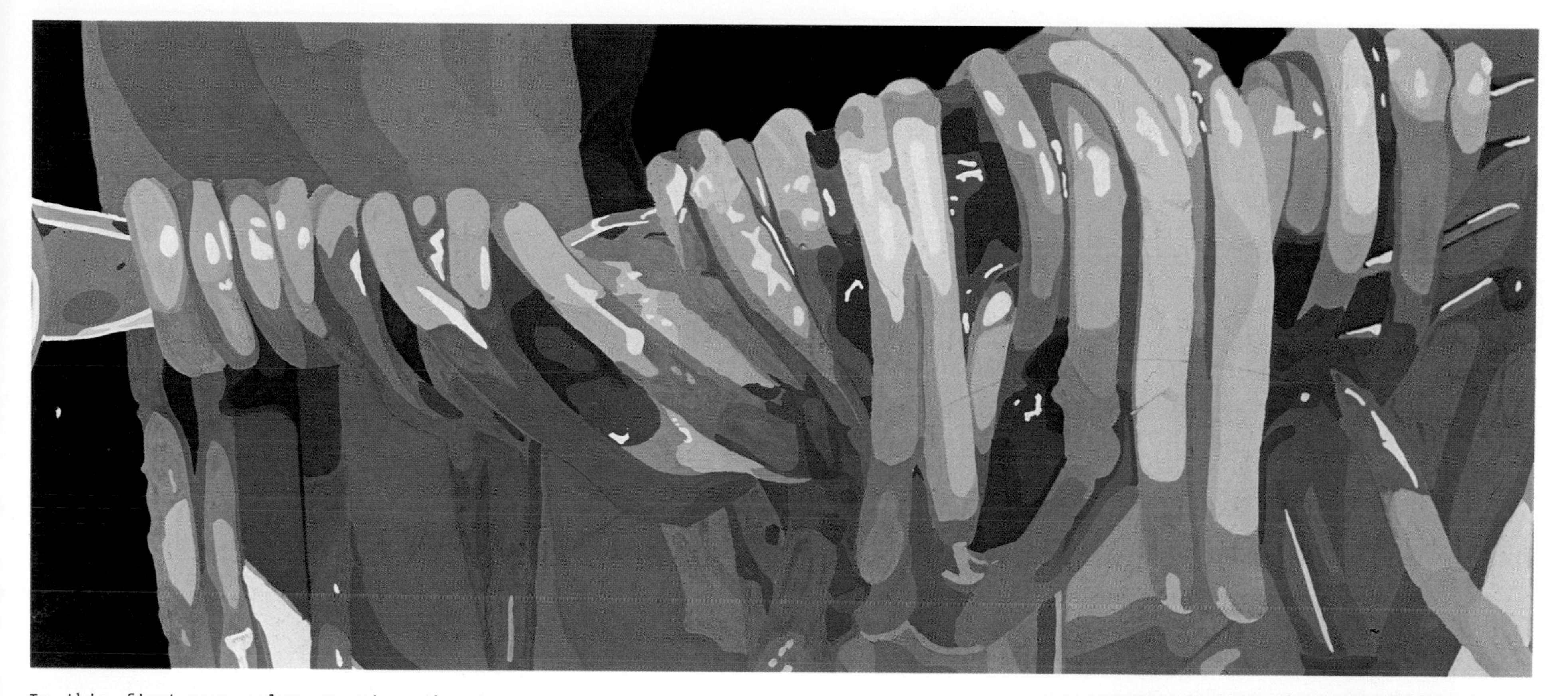

In this first-year color exercise, the student translated the patches of color seen in a section of a magazine illustration into carefully matched mixtures of gouache--each applied in a layer thick enough to obliterate the cartridge paper support.

Perspective of a proposed design for an Oxford college extension. A diluted color wash was rendered over a pencil drawing worked on a tinted, textured watercolor paper. In such applications, the color of the paper plays a major role in modifying the color of translucent layers of pigment.

How to Apply a Color Wash

1

Watercolor washes are usually applied to pen or pencil outline drawings on stretched paper or art board. Transparent washes are made from water tinted with a small amount of watercolor, ink, tempera, or gouache. A more traditional wash is made from Chinese stick ink gently worked into water to the required intensity. Check the mix on a scrap of paper. (N.B.: Chinese stick ink when bottled in liquid form is marketed as "India" ink.)

2

Before application, the board should be set at an angle of 45 degrees. Make sure enough wash is mixed at the outset--then fully load a large sable brush, taking care to avoid drips.

3

Apply the wash smoothly and evenly--working the horizontal pool of pigment left and right down the section to be colored. Refill the brush quickly mid-wash to avoid tidemarks.

4

Complete the wash in the right-hand corner of the artwork and withdraw the brush. Shake dry before using it to mop away the surplus pool of wash. Successive washes can be applied after the last is dry.

5

Sedimentary washes can be produced by crumbling an aspirin into the initial mix. Textured washes can be achieved by using heavily textured papers or the sprinkling of fruit salts over a freshly applied wash.

6

Graduated washes can be achieved by: (a) progressively diluting a rich initial mix as the wash descends, or (b) by the progressive addition of pigment to the initial mixture.

Spray Wash Techniques

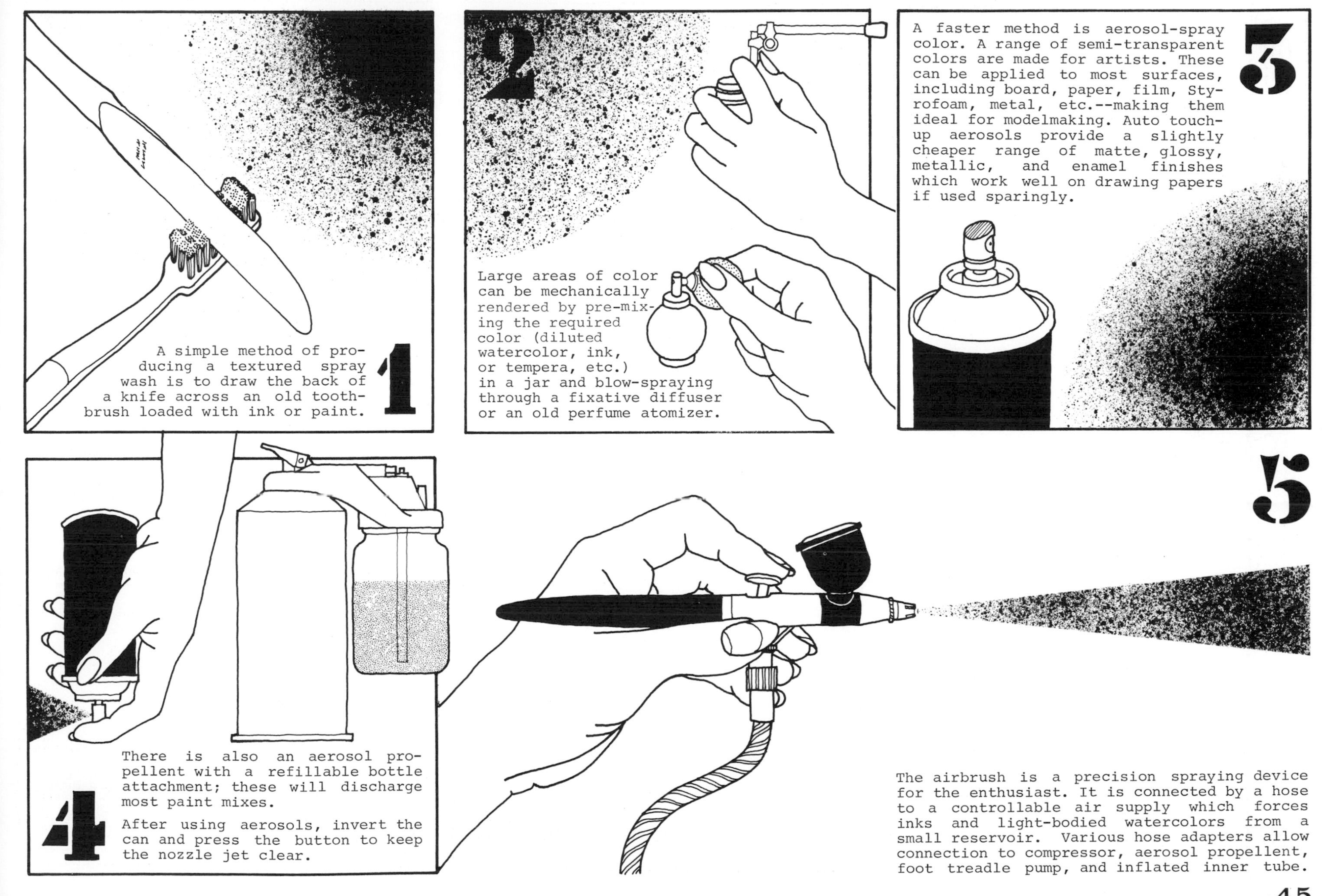

A simple method of producing a textured spray wash is to draw the back of a knife across an old toothbrush loaded with ink or paint.

Large areas of color can be mechanically rendered by pre-mixing the required color (diluted watercolor, ink, or tempera, etc.) in a jar and blow-spraying through a fixative diffuser or an old perfume atomizer.

A faster method is aerosol-spray color. A range of semi-transparent colors are made for artists. These can be applied to most surfaces, including board, paper, film, Styrofoam, metal, etc.--making them ideal for modelmaking. Auto touch-up aerosols provide a slightly cheaper range of matte, glossy, metallic, and enamel finishes which work well on drawing papers if used sparingly.

There is also an aerosol propellent with a refillable bottle attachment; these will discharge most paint mixes.

After using aerosols, invert the can and press the button to keep the nozzle jet clear.

The airbrush is a precision spraying device for the enthusiast. It is connected by a hose to a controllable air supply which forces inks and light-bodied watercolors from a small reservoir. Various hose adapters allow connection to compressor, aerosol propellent, foot treadle pump, and inflated inner tube.

Aerosol in the Design Process

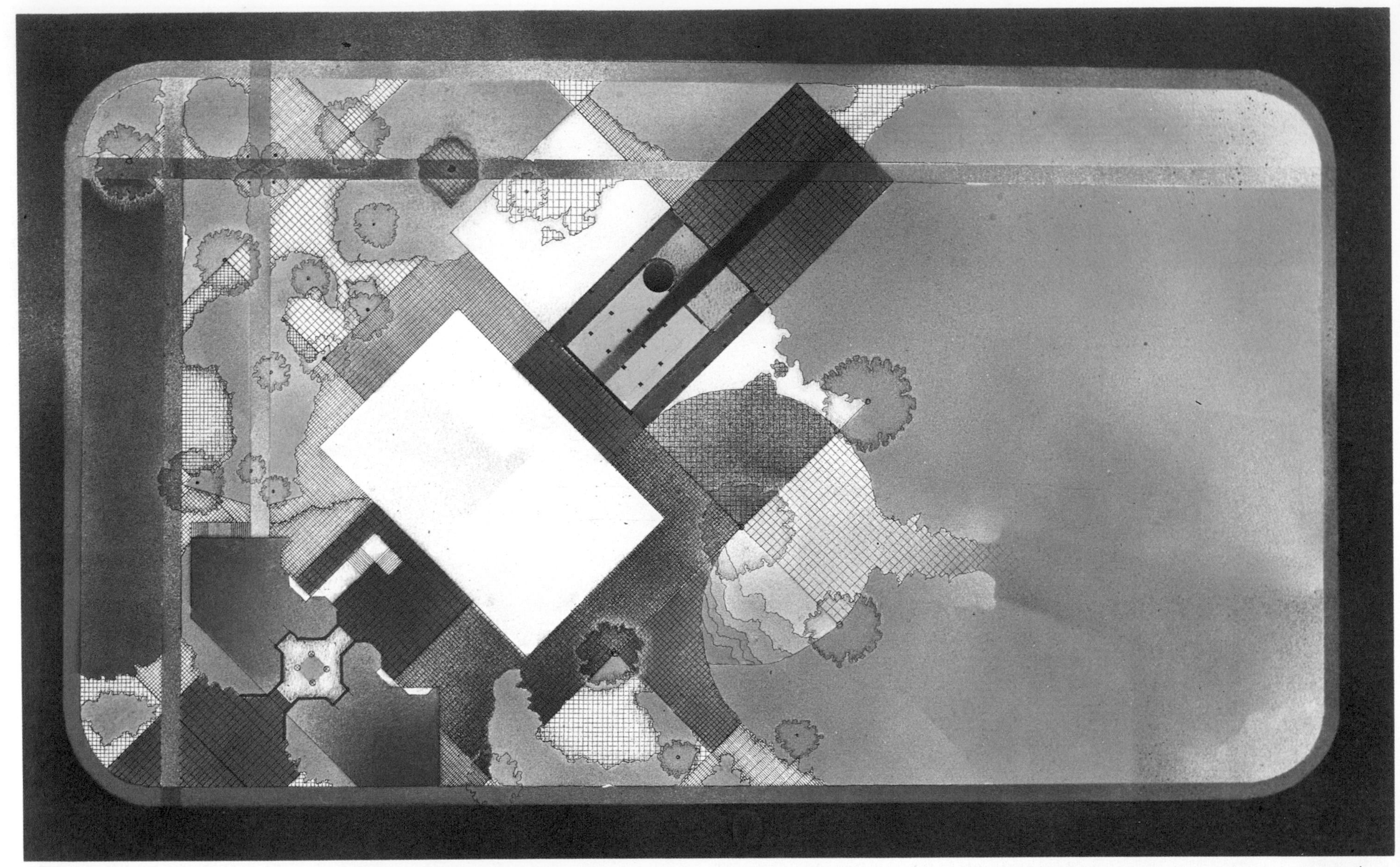

Site Plan: student presentation painting produced with a basic color range of auto touch-up aerosols. During the spray operation, basic paper cut-out stencils were temporarily held down with a pliable Plasticine-like adhesive; for the more tricky, curved areas the pliable adhesive was itself used as a mask--being molded into position with a spatula and easily removed after spraying. Highlights were later applied using a white crayon.

Airbrush Experiment and Aerosols on Models

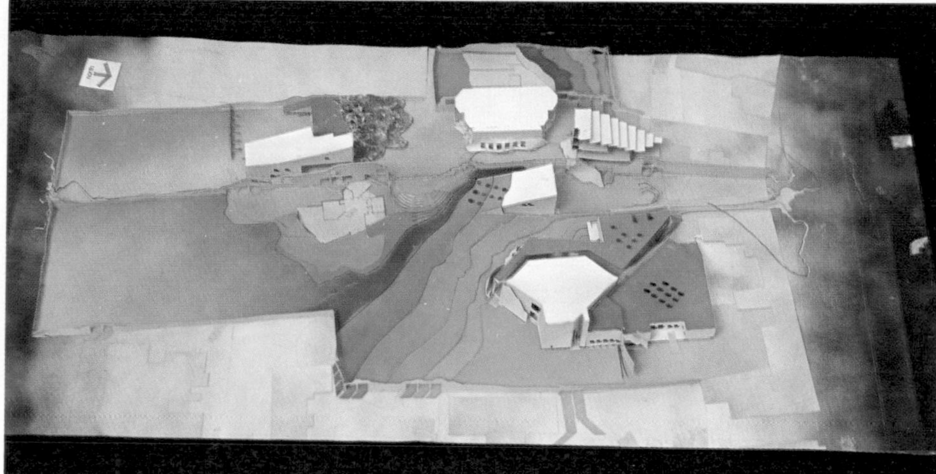

A student model of a design for a community school built at 1/16" = 1'-0" (1:200) scale in thin card. It functioned both as a design tool and a presentation aid, and, in its latter phase, was "reassembled" during the critique to explain, first, the internal planning of each unit and, later, overall external relationships. Prior to assembly, a variety of matte and gloss aerosol auto colors were applied to individual components of card in order to emphasize the arrangement of designed units, access routes, and site landscaping, together with the layout of peripheral existing housing. Aerosols were used because they provide a fast means of achieving color on models--successive sprayed layers creating both powerful and subtle effects.

Section of a large, experimental airbrush painting by Paul Proudman employing the frisket film masking technique. The medium used was ink on card--highlights were later brush applied using gouache.

N.B.: Invest in a double-action rather than single-action airbrush. The air supply on double-action airbrushes is controlled by depressing the button; color is introduced by moving the button backward. This two-stage operation allows much more control than single-action brushes in which finger action controls only the air volume (a wheel or other adjustment is necessary to change the spray size). Hold the brush as you would a pen, with the first finger on the double-action lever; use it as you would a hand brush--making strokes. The different widths of strokes and shading are obtained with the backward movement of the lever and, at the same time, by the distance the brush is held from the work. When spraying larger areas, avoid arcing over the surface but maintain a regular distance between brush and artwork.

Some Airbrush Tips for Beginners

1

The pressure of most compressed air units can be economically regulated at the source. Generally, the following pressure guides operate: inks and watercolors, 15-20 lbs; tempera/gouache, 20-25 lbs; enamels, 35-40 lbs. However, whichever pressure works best with your colors is the one to maintain, as variation will spoil the quality of the spray.

2

Detrimental pressure variations can be experienced with aerosol propellents, which tend to frost up when subjected to temperature changes. This can be avoided by immersing the can in cool water.

Always ensure that you have sufficient air supply to finish a job--keep a spare can of propellent in reserve.

3

Apart from air compressors, some designers find the tire inner tube to be the smoothest source of air. However, if you decide on this source, purchase a complete second-hand assembly, i.e., inner tube, tire, and wheel hub. Also, fit a moisture trap to ensure that any condensation inside the tube is filtered before it can ruin fine spray work.

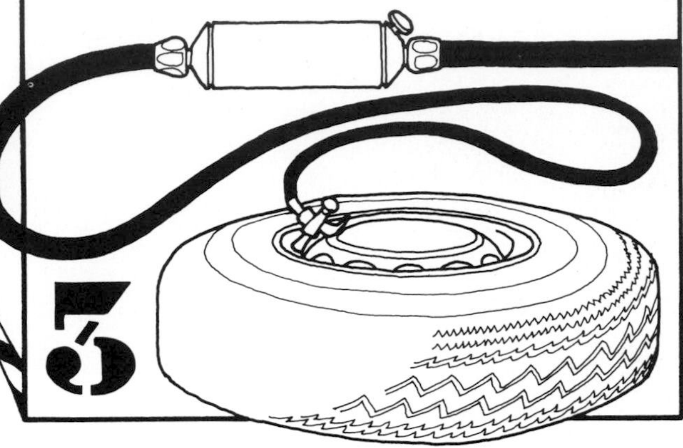

4

If the brush spits and splatters, it may mean that the ink is impure. It is always wise to use colors formulated for use in airbrushes; if not, thoroughly mix colors with a palette knife to the consistency of milk and strain through coarse muslin. A good method of transferring inks from bottle or palette to reservoir is to use an eyedropper, available from drugstores.

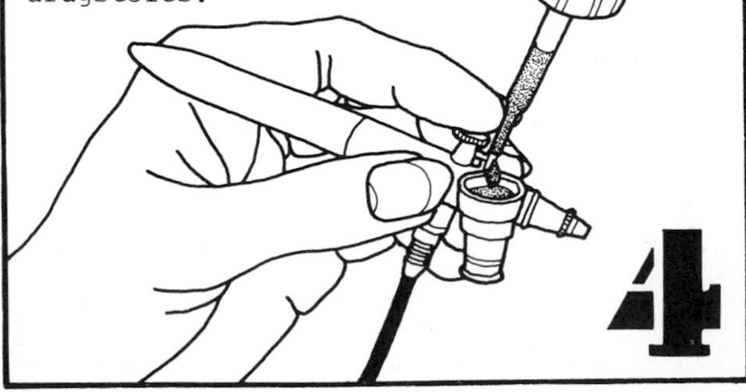

5

Take great care not to damage the airbrush needle. Examine the tip if your spray pattern seems erratic--it may be bent. A desk clip is supplied with most brushes; this should be attached to the worktop within easy reach so that, when not in use, the vulnerable airbrush is secure.

6

To clean the needle after using water-based colors, remove and wipe across the moistened palm of your hand; after using oil-based colors, use appropriate thinners--never use a cloth. When cleaning the brush, follow the instruction manual carefully, as the different kinds of colors are handled differently.

Keep a record of all the color mixes and achievement of effects (even the failures), for in this way your knowledge and experience of airbrush techniques is developed.

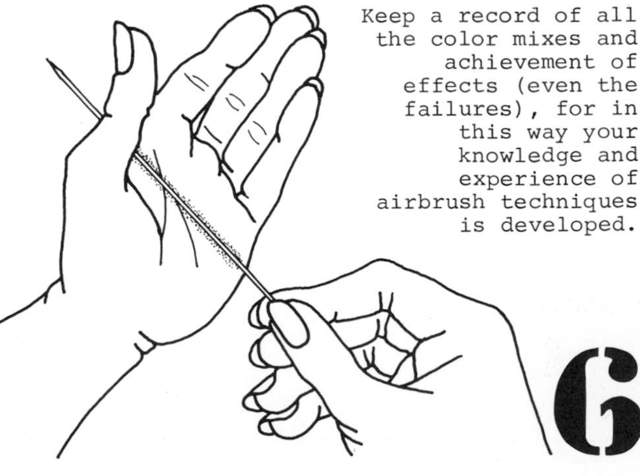

Masking Techniques for Spray Work

1

Before rendering, the artwork should be completely masked--exposing only the section to be sprayed. After application, this area is covered up and successive areas exposed as the spray process proceeds.

All spray artwork should be preplanned in sketch form--usually darker colors being sprayed first, followed by a progressively lightening sequence of color until completion.

2

The cheapest masking method is the cutting of stencils from thin cardboard. Use coins to weight the edges to avoid spray bleeding under the template.

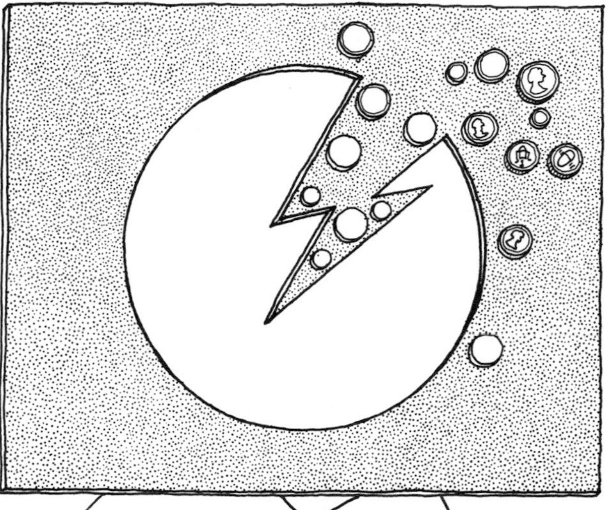

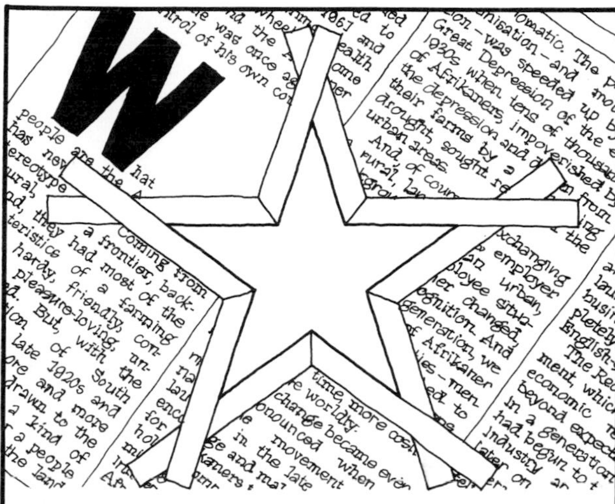

3

Masking tape and newsprint is a common method. Always check first that the tape peels away easily without spoiling the paint or paper surface.

4

For small, complex details, resists such as liquid frisket or rubber cement can be brush-applied and finger-rubbed away afterward. The pliable, Plasticine-like adhesives are also useful and reusable for this purpose.

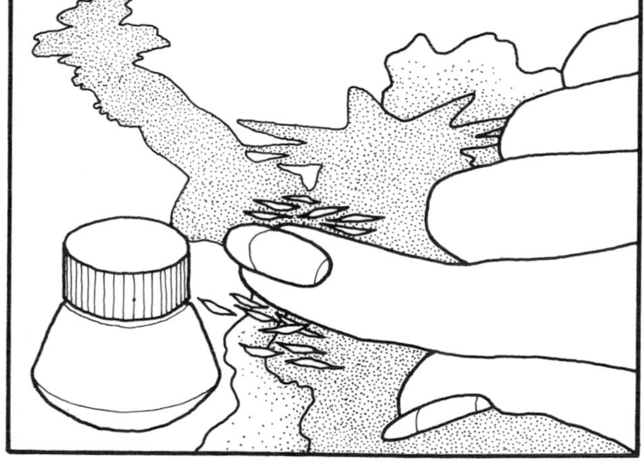

5

Frisket film is a self-adhesive low tack transparent mask; frisket paper is a clear, waterproof tissue used as a mask with rubber cement. A sheet is applied to cover entire artwork. Exposed areas are then progressively cut away with a scalpel or swivel knife and replaced after each spray operation.

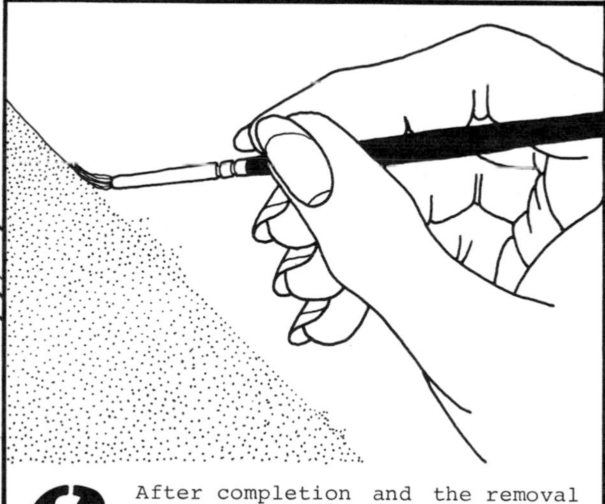

6

After completion and the removal of the mask material, highlights can be touched in and any blurred edges sharpened using a brush with tempera or gouache.

The Potential of Collage

Collage is the simple but exciting technique of constructing graphics, using torn or precision-cut paper together with other materials glued onto a backing sheet. Graphics can be created totally from collage materials or be simply the addition of shaped paper to block in large areas of color or texture--or to highlight sections of a painting or line drawing.

All kinds of material are potential raw material for this process. A visit to any stationers, hardware store, or do-it-yourself store will reveal an extraordinary variety of papers, cards, boards, and plastics; colored sticky labels, dots, lines, and tapes; tissue and crepe papers, metal foils, wires, cables, balsa wood, veneers, and cork; pieces of mirror, ceramics, and glass mosaics; Styrofoam and plastic tiles; fabrics, ribbons, and string, etc.

Apart from scissors, special studio knives and scalpels with interchangeable blades are useful for cutting intricate shapes in paper, film, light cardboard, and many other collage materials.

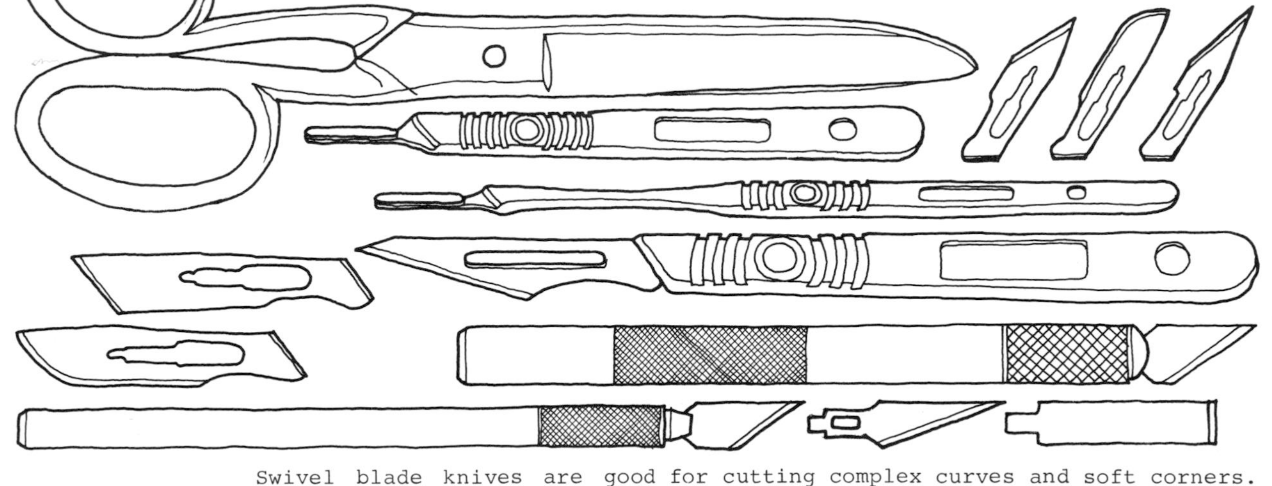

Swivel blade knives are good for cutting complex curves and soft corners.

Plastic and metal burnishers for transferring pressure-mounted dry color sheets and instant lettering.

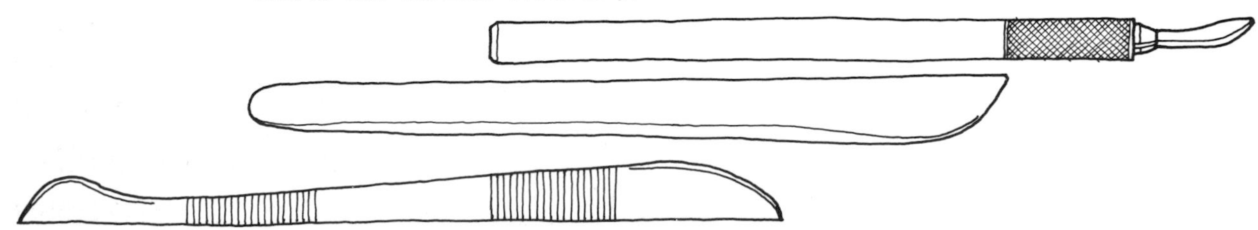

Site perspective incorporating various fabrics, papers, wool, cotton, and string glued to a baseboard.

Paper Adhesives

1

Rubber cement is ideal for collage work and for mounting artwork. It is a strong, clear latex-based adhesive that sticks all types of lightweight papers without wrinkling. Rubber cement comes in cans or jars and is applied with a brush, spatula, or a strip of card. It spreads smoothly without pulling or shrinking, allowing papers to be pulled apart and repositioned if necessary. Surplus cement can be removed easily without damage to artwork by a gentle rubbing with the fingertips or by using a rubber cement "pick-up."

2

Spray-mount adhesives are colorless and diffused from aerosols. For immediate positioning, it is necessary only to evenly spray one surface---the controlled adhesion permitting the repositioning of paper. The spray gives a thin film of glue, which means the adhesive will not squeeze out of the edges of mounted papers. It is recommended for collage and mounting artwork, photostats, and sticking paper to acetates. There is also a colorless photomounting aerosol spray for the permanent mounting of photographs, art, and display work. Only on big sheets requiring maximum strength need both surfaces be sprayed.

3

Polyvinyl acetate (PVA) is a white plastic non-toxic adhesive which is marketed in stick, paste, and liquid form and contained in various dispensers including "lipstick" and roll-on cartridges, refillable "pens" for dispensing dots, and jars and tubes. Although PVA adhesives glue many different materials such as paper, board, fabric, Styrofoam, etc., they tend to "dry out" and be impermanent.

4

The golden gum-based glues and the white starch-based pastes are general-purpose office and studio adhesives. They are usually bottled and dispensed using an integrated brush or spatula affixed to the underside of the cap--some jars combine an external nozzle-spatula.

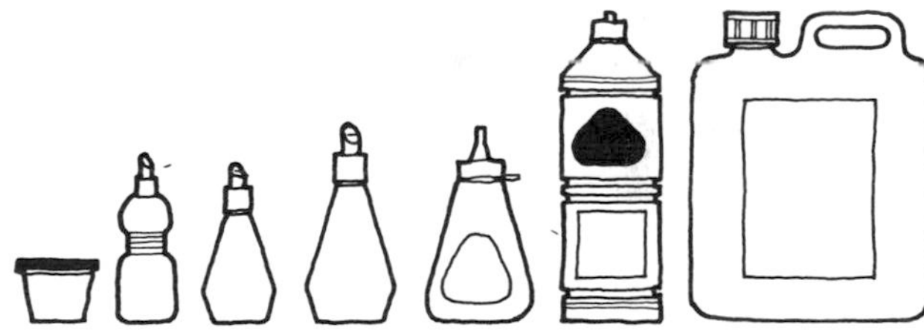

5

Other adhesion methods include double-sided tapes and pressure-sensitive tabs and dots. These are useful for the temporary mounting or positioning of artwork or paper stencil templates in spray work.

6

A do-it-yourself paste is simply mixed from flour and water or from wallpaper paste. Both are useful in papier-mâché work in which newspaper or newsprint is saturated with either solution and formed--layer by layer--into self-supporting reliefs or wire supported forms which, when dry, become rigid and can be painted or color-sprayed.

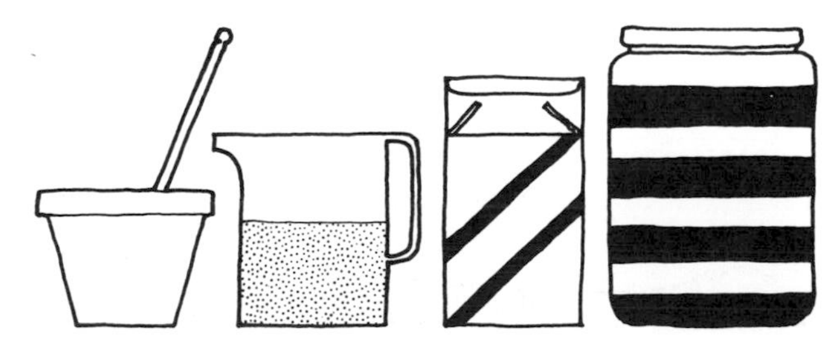

How to Apply Color Overlay Sheets

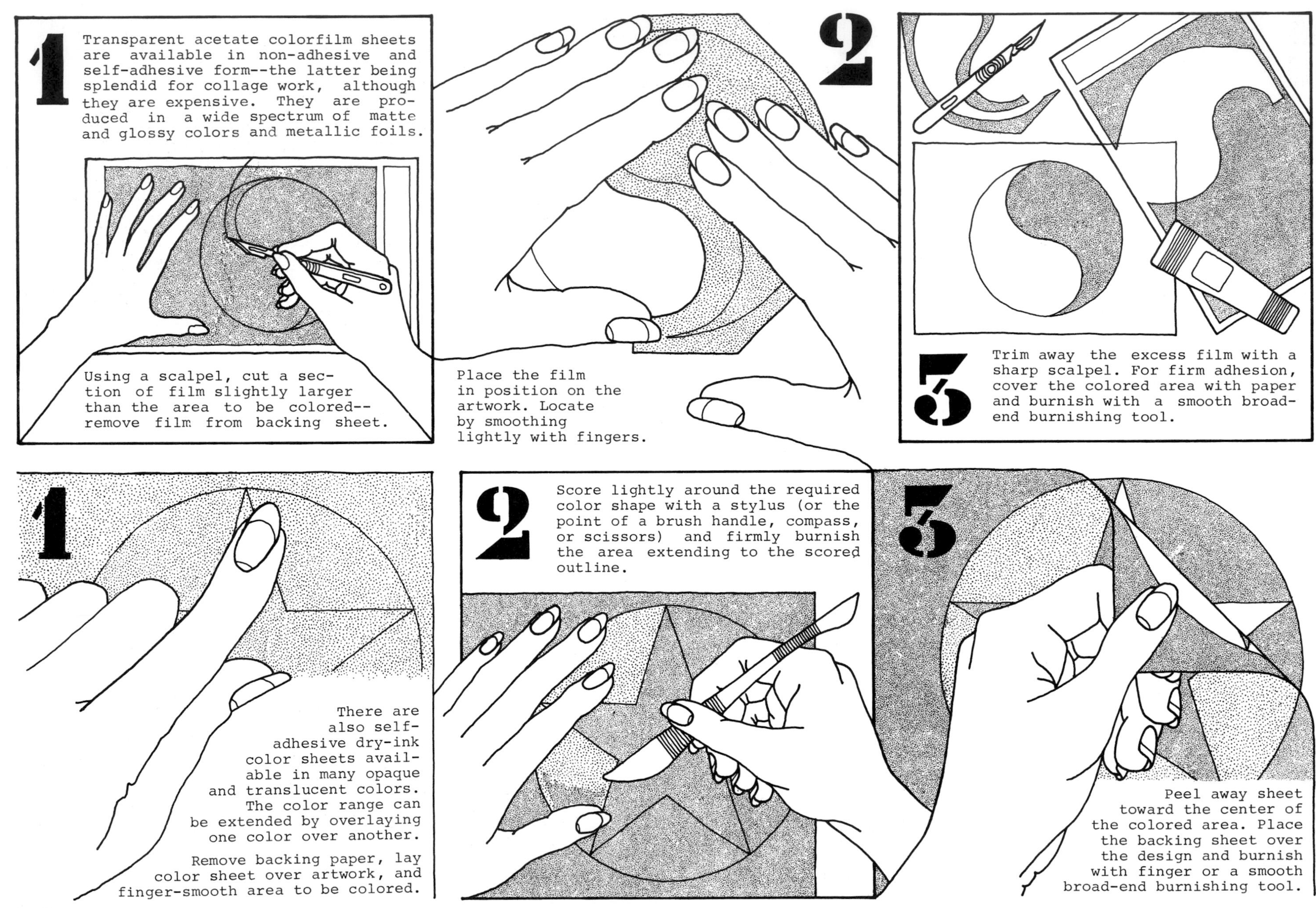

Photomontage and Photo-Transfer Color Techniques

1

Photomontage is the process of assembling selected color or monochrome magazine photographs into the construction of a new image. Designers commonly use this technique to superimpose drawings of projected buildings--or photographs of models of buildings--onto photographs of an existing site--especially in sensitive environments. Photographs of trees, skies, automobiles, figures, and furniture, etc. can also be introduced into line drawings as a means of strengthening visuals or simply as a speedy method of graphic communication. Images used in this way should be chosen for their compatibility with the presentation style and should be in scale with the intended graphic space.

1

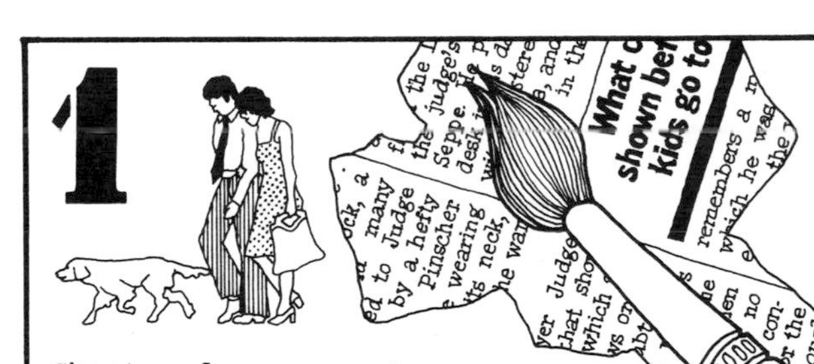

Sheets of pressure transfer figures--trees, automobiles, and architectural elements--are marketed, but an inexpensive and effective method is the photo-transfer process using appropriate newspaper or magazine photographs--color photographs on less glossy paper work best.

Place the selected photograph facedown on scrap paper and paint liberally with a solvent. Solvents include white spirit, nail polish remover (acetone), methylated spirits, and silk screen cleaning or printer's ink solvents.

2

The importance of scale in graphics cannot be overstressed. For example, the position of each of the identically sized figures conveys a totally different impression of the room scale.

2

Transfer image facedown to artwork and carefully work completely over the required image area with a soft, blunt pencil such as a 6B. Gently peel away original image paper--the ink will have been transferred to the artwork.

3

Isolated cut-out photographs of figures correctly located and affixed to a line drawing both adds a sense of scale and humanizes the interior space.

3

Experimental color photo-transfer image. As not all the ink is transferred, the resultant image is soft and the colors subtle.

How to Silk-Screen Print

1

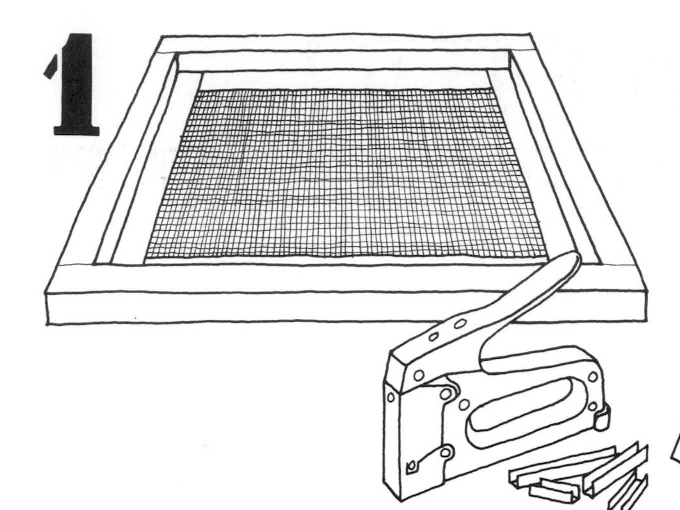

A simple frame can be made from wood or a discarded picture frame. The screen can be cotton organdy, nylon, or other fine mesh fabrics stretched drum-tight over the frame and stapled on all sides.

2

Professionals use various stencils including photographically applied gelatins, but stencils adequate for basic designs can be made from ordinary paper. Cut stencil to desired shape; place on sheet of scrap paper.

3

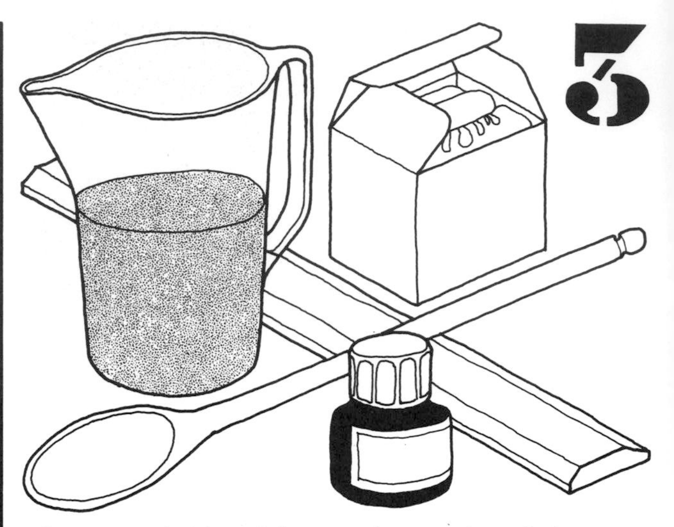

Screen printing inks can be purchased in permanent, water-based, or acrylic form, but a good do-it-yourself ink is made from adding colored ink to a thick mix of wallpaper paste. A plastic ruler will double for a squeegee.

4

Lay the screen carefully over the stencil and squeegee some ink through to make stencil adhere to back of screen. It will stick there for large numbers of prints.

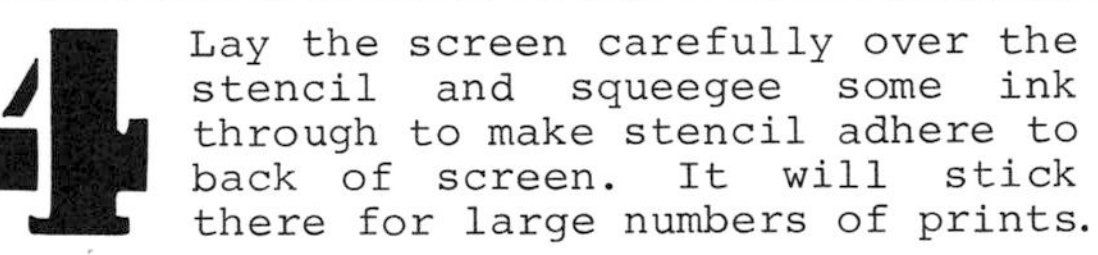

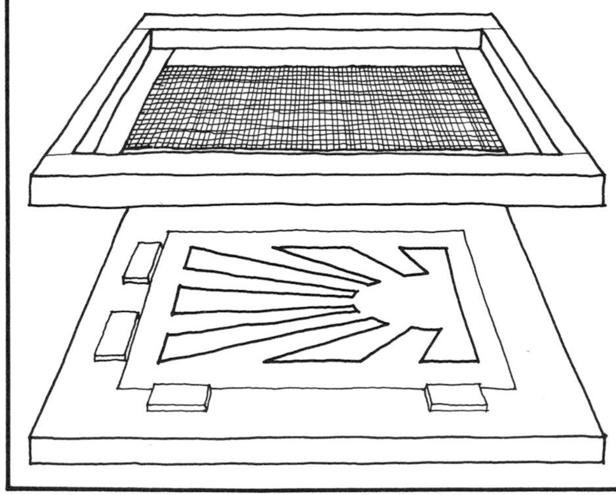

5

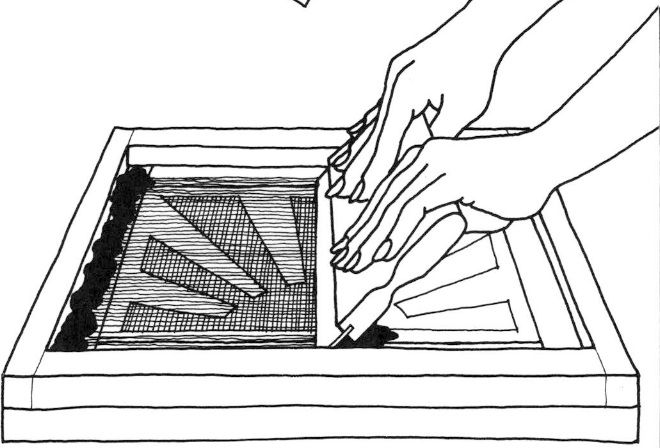

Put a generous line of ink along short end of screen. Hold screen firmly over printing paper. Place squeegee behind ink and drag evenly across screen--keeping squeegee at 45 degrees in direction of pull.

6

Lift screen and peel away successive prints after each pull--working quickly to avoid mesh clogging. To clean water-based inks, hold screen under running water. If clogged lay screen on blotting paper and press water through mesh with squeegee. Use appropriate solvents for permanent inks.

3 ORTHOGRAPHIC AND PERSPECTIVE DRAWING

Drawing Boards

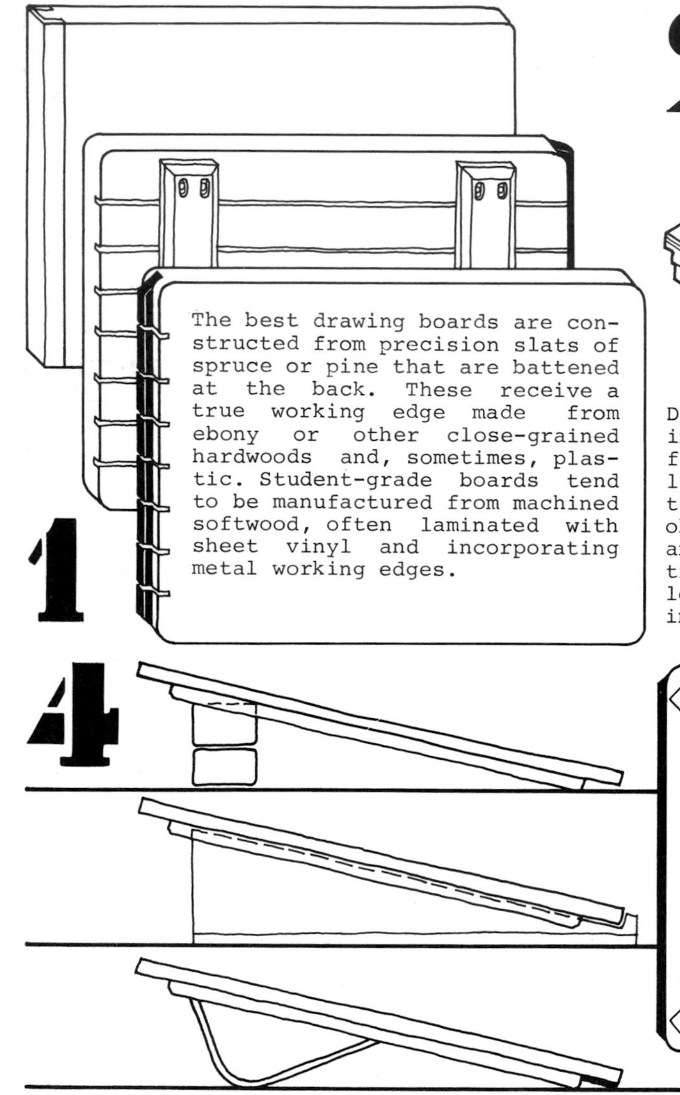

1

The best drawing boards are constructed from precision slats of spruce or pine that are battened at the back. These receive a true working edge made from ebony or other close-grained hardwoods and, sometimes, plastic. Student-grade boards tend to be manufactured from machined softwood, often laminated with sheet vinyl and incorporating metal working edges.

2

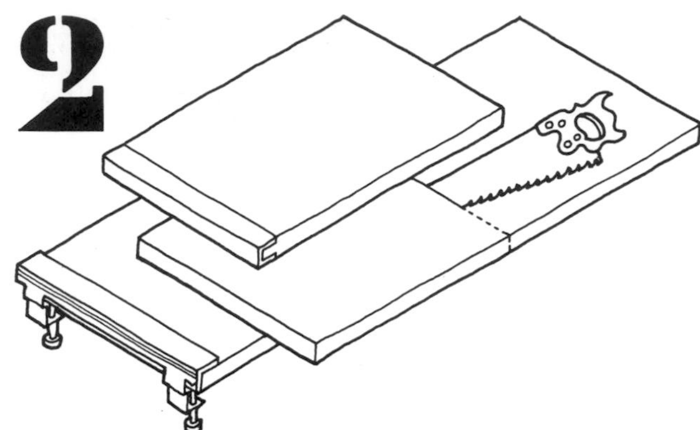

Do-it-yourself boards for sketching, stretching paper, or home use can simply be made from 3/4-inch (19 mm) plywood or blockboard lipped with U-section aluminum or strips of timber. Two general-purpose boards can be obtained by purchasing a Masonite flush door and sawing it in half. A detachable metal true edge for T square work is available in lengths up to 60 inches (1525 mm), for clamping to the sides of plain boards and tables.

To enhance and protect the drawing surface of wooden boards, many designers apply a smooth paper base sheet under the drawing paper. Two kinds of drawing-board covering can also be purchased. One is a strong, flexible film of cellulose acetate bonded to a paper base; another is a sheet of vinyl plastic which is affixed to the board with double-sided tape; both are colored green to reduce eyestrain. When transporting boards, protect the ebony edge with a taped-on strip of corrugated card.

3

4

Apart from an attachment which permanently fixes the drawing board to bench tops but allows incline adjustment, the cheapest method is to prop up the board on a double stack of bricks--each pre-painted to contain dust. Other methods include the purchase of custom timber supports or the special metal brackets which are screwed to the back of the board.

5

The best methods of fixing drawing paper to boards are those that do not impede the movement of the T square. For sheets slightly smaller than the board, corner strips of drafting tape are adequate; for sheets of a similar size to the board, drawing board clips can be used. Avoid using pushpins on wooden boards, as they will irrevocably damage the surface, and never use pins in plastic supports, unless they are of the "self-healing" type.

6

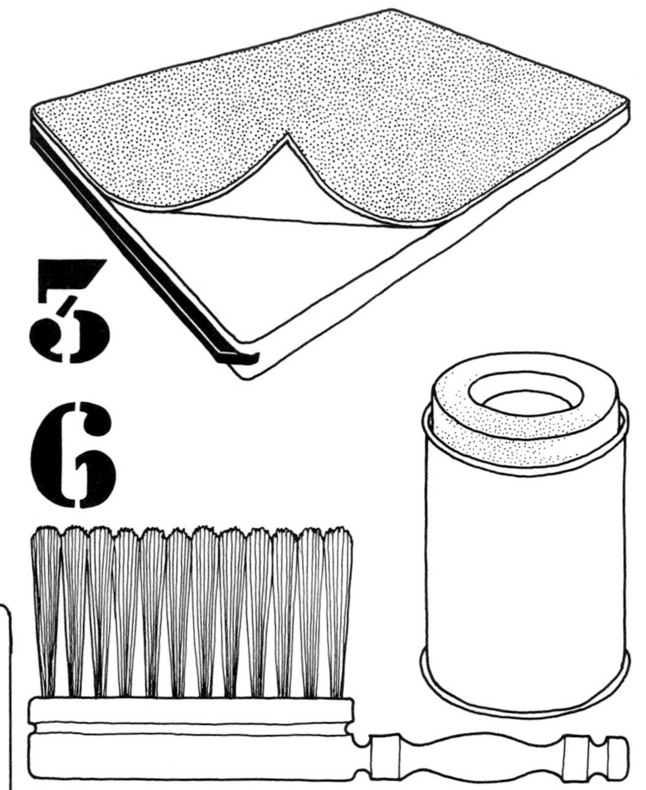

At the outset of the drawing operation, it is important to work with clean hands and equipment--using a drafting brush or a 2-inch (50 mm) household paintbrush to keep the drawing surface free from dust and eraser particles. Pounce powder is sometimes used to prepare paper surfaces prior to drawing in ink. This is sprinkled over the paper and rubbed with a felt pad--usually incorporated on the can--then dusted off before commencing to draw.

T Square and Drawing Machines

1

When engaged with the working edge of drawing boards, the T square provides an accurate right angle. The best T squares are made from hardwoods, such as mahogany, fitted with ebony or PVC drawing edges--some designers preferring the visibility allowed by clear plastic. Others are made with aluminum stocks fitted with stainless-steel blades.

Before purchasing, check for any deviation from the true by carefully looking along the working edge. Another check is to draw a line on the drawing board, reverse the T square to the opposite side of the board, and check the alignment of the line with the inverted true edge.

The underside of the blade should be of a polished finish to facilitate movement over the drawing surface; occasional wiping with a cloth moistened with methylated spirit should keep this clean. Traditional T squares incorporate a hole in the blade for hanging when not in use.

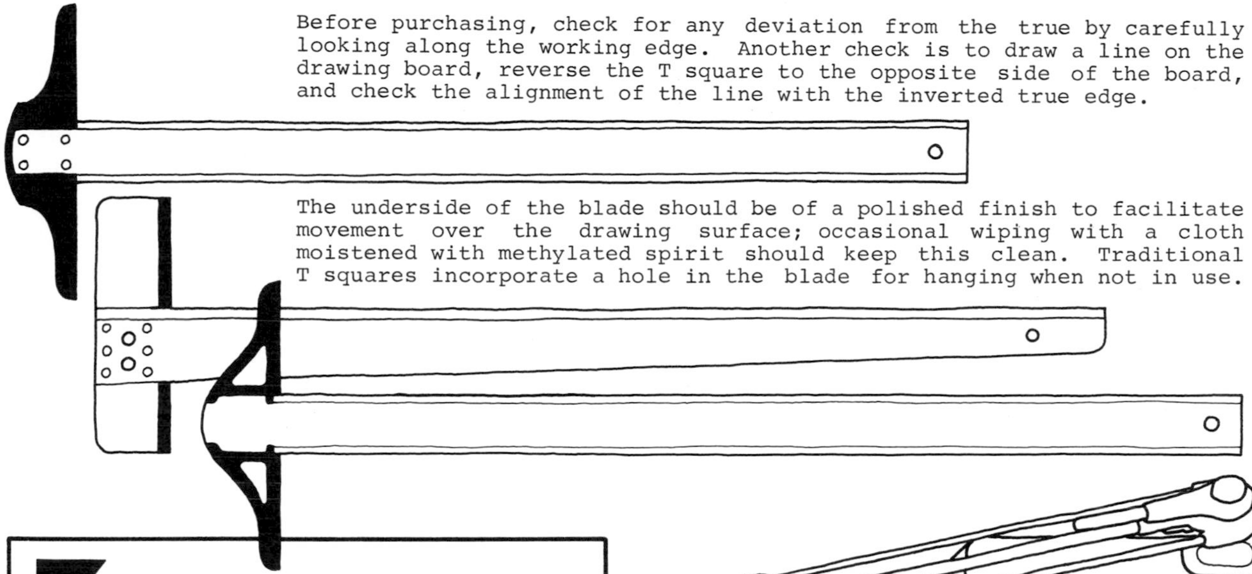

2

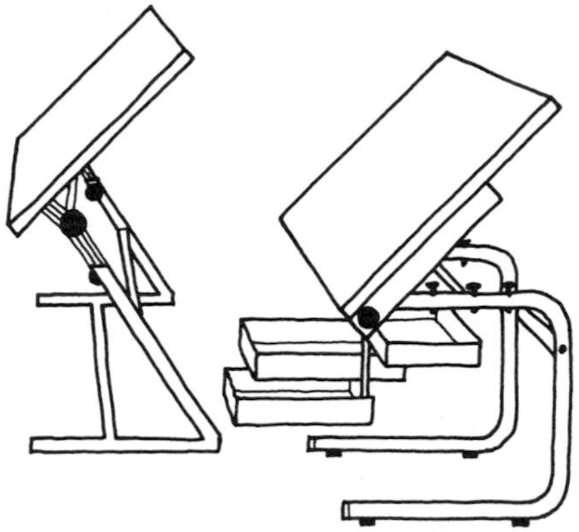

Apart from an attachment which permanently fixes a drawing board to bench tops, allowing incline adjustment, there are many types of timber and metal freestanding drawing stands supporting integral boards--some of which incorporate storage compartments--and with either parallel-motion ruling units or drafting machines.

3

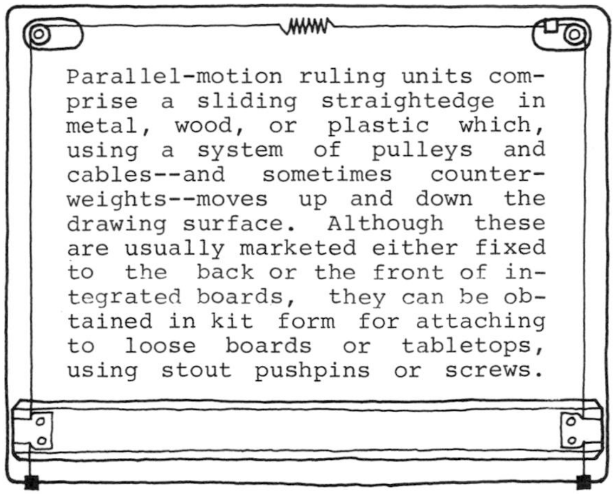

Parallel-motion ruling units comprise a sliding straightedge in metal, wood, or plastic which, using a system of pulleys and cables--and sometimes counterweights--moves up and down the drawing surface. Although these are usually marketed either fixed to the back or the front of integrated boards, they can be obtained in kit form for attaching to loose boards or tabletops, using stout pushpins or screws.

4

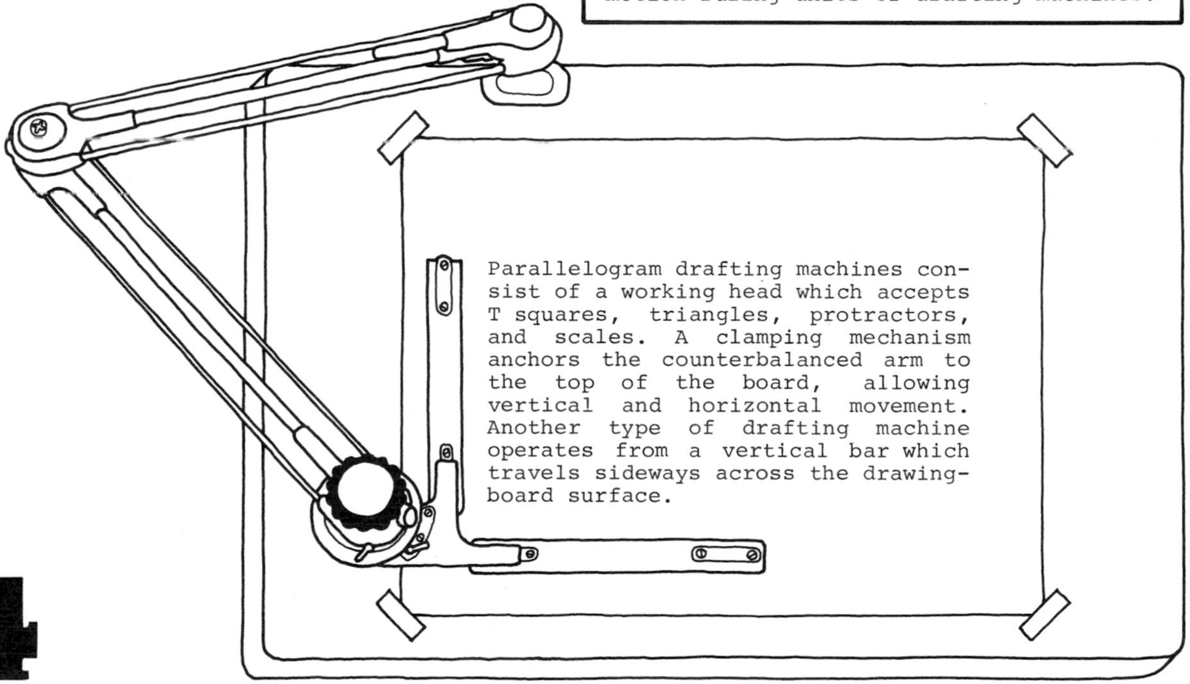

Parallelogram drafting machines consist of a working head which accepts T squares, triangles, protractors, and scales. A clamping mechanism anchors the counterbalanced arm to the top of the board, allowing vertical and horizontal movement. Another type of drafting machine operates from a vertical bar which travels sideways across the drawing-board surface.

Basic Drawing Guides and Instruments

1

The adage that the "workman is only as good as his tools" applies also to the designer and his drawing instruments. A basic range of equipment should be selected with care, checked for compatibility with technical pens and pencils, and be well maintained.

To avoid smudging during drawing, always select guides with working edges which are beveled or stepped. All true working edges should be protected when not in use and never used as cutting edges. Equipment that has a sliding action on drawing surfaces is likely to get dirty and, therefore, should be occasionally wiped clean with a little methylated spirit or lighter fluid on a cloth.

2

Triangles (set squares) are used for drawing vertical and inclined lines. Several kinds are available made from wood, nickel-silver steel, and clear or tinted acrylic. However, the plastic versions are best--provided they are not used with spirit ink markers--as they allow visibility of the work underneath.

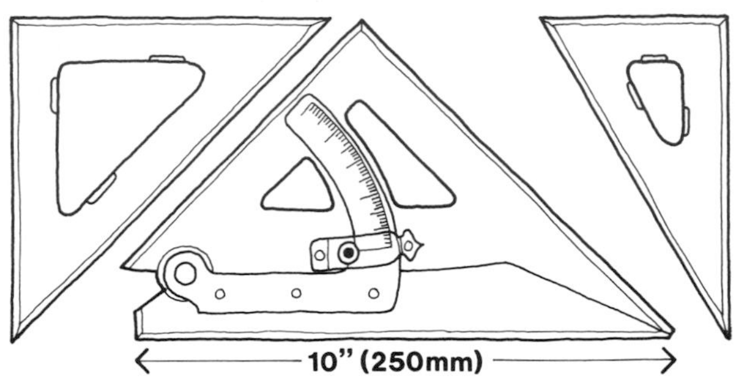

It is a good idea to buy a 6-inch (150 mm) version of the 45/90-degree and 30/60-degree fixed triangle for general-purpose work, but for architectural drafting invest in an adjustable triangle made from clear acrylic.

3

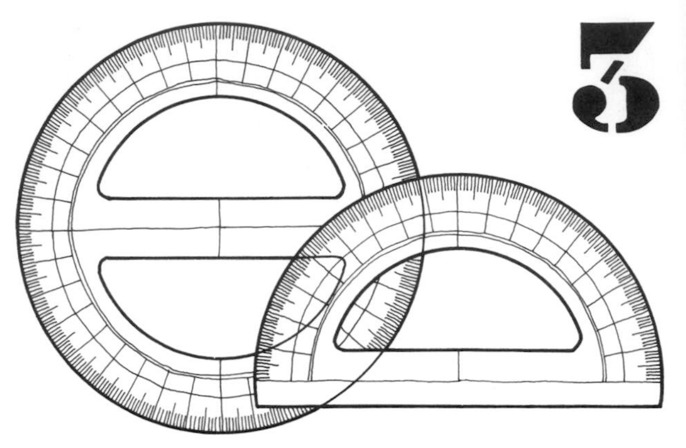

Protractors are basic instruments which enable the determination of unknown angles in a drawing. They are produced in circular and semicircular forms and made of clear plastic.

4

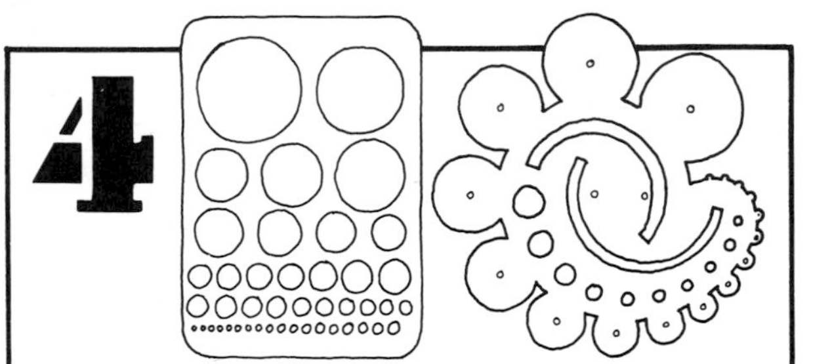

A circle template or radius aid will come in useful for drawing small circles of various radii. Two types are common in "positive" and "negative" form.

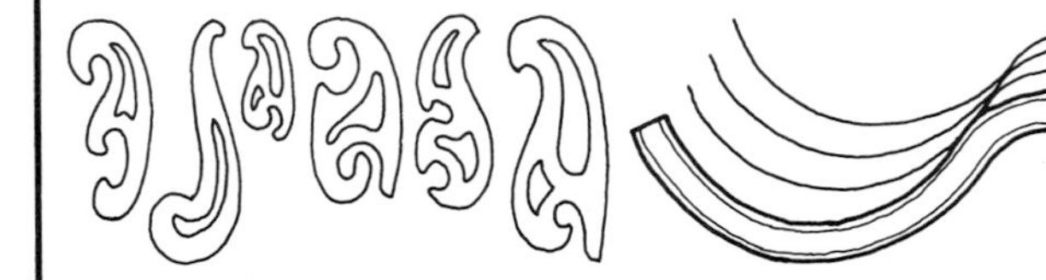

There are also two types of curved templates. One is the French curve, available individually or in sets of up to eight pieces. Short lengths of different curves can be combined to draw curves not contained in the set, but the flexible curve rule or "lead snake," which has a stepped ruling edge, is more useful--retaining its shape in most configurations.

5

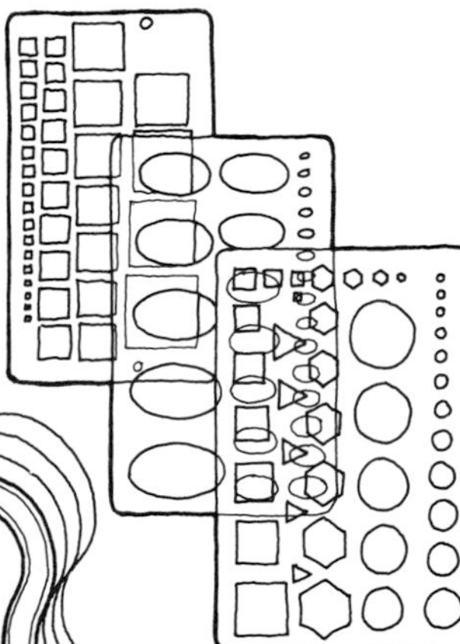

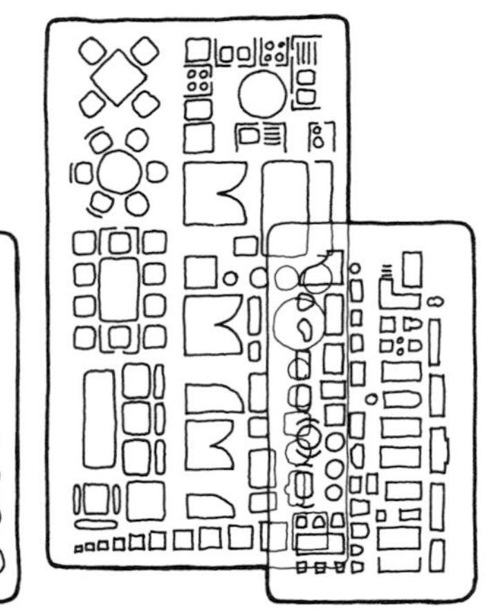

There is a myriad of metal and plastic templates marketed which enable the designer to quickly draw smaller ranges of geometric shapes. There are also wide ranges of templates which enable the rapid delineation of architectural symbols. However, these should only be purchased when there is a particular need for them.

6

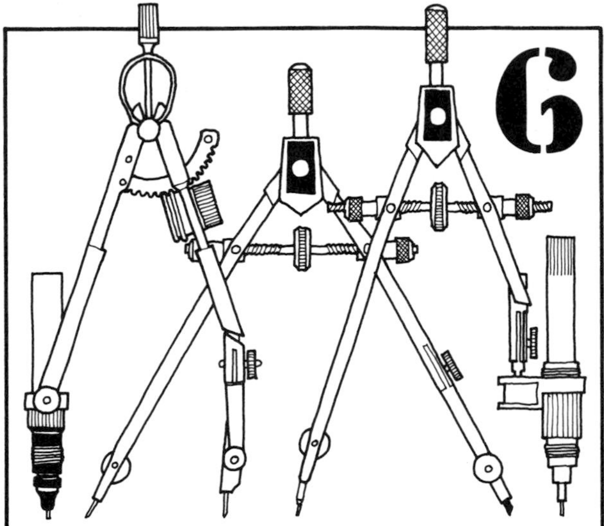

The compass extends the ability to draw accurate arcs and circles beyond the radii offered by templates. It is wise, therefore, to buy a reasonably large version, making sure that it is adaptable to your drawing instruments. The best type have screw adjustments and adaptors for incorporating technical pens and leads; these are included in the boxed sets, but can be purchased individually.

Scales, Tapes, and Full-Scale Mock-Ups

1 The scale enables dimensions to be either read, transferred, or converted from or between drawings. They are made from stable materials such as kiln-dried wood or unbreakable plastic--or a combination of the two. Two general types in common use are open divided scales and fully divided scales.

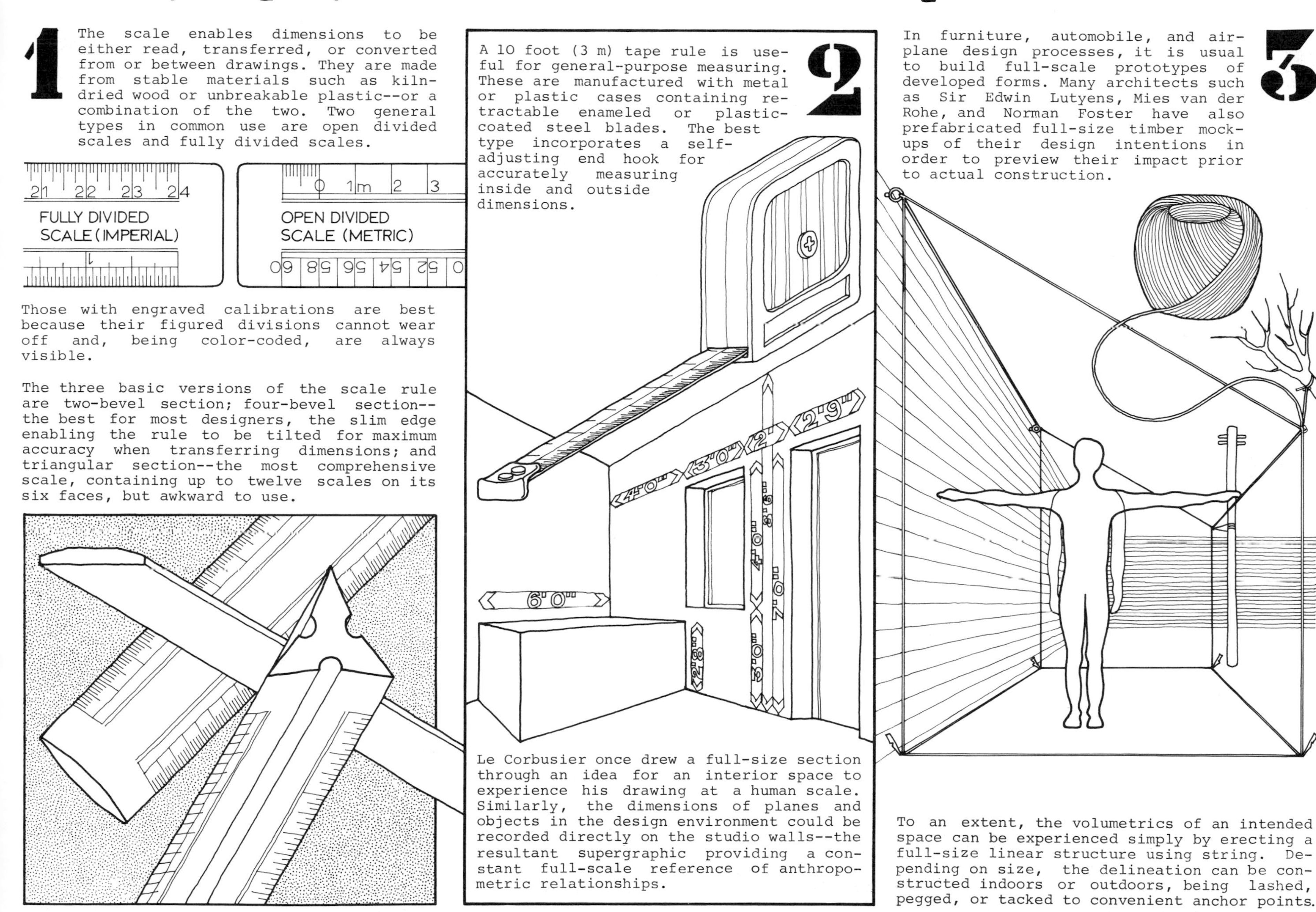

Those with engraved calibrations are best because their figured divisions cannot wear off and, being color-coded, are always visible.

The three basic versions of the scale rule are two-bevel section; four-bevel section--the best for most designers, the slim edge enabling the rule to be tilted for maximum accuracy when transferring dimensions; and triangular section--the most comprehensive scale, containing up to twelve scales on its six faces, but awkward to use.

2 A 10 foot (3 m) tape rule is useful for general-purpose measuring. These are manufactured with metal or plastic cases containing retractable enameled or plastic-coated steel blades. The best type incorporates a self-adjusting end hook for accurately measuring inside and outside dimensions.

Le Corbusier once drew a full-size section through an idea for an interior space to experience his drawing at a human scale. Similarly, the dimensions of planes and objects in the design environment could be recorded directly on the studio walls--the resultant supergraphic providing a constant full-scale reference of anthropometric relationships.

3 In furniture, automobile, and airplane design processes, it is usual to build full-scale prototypes of developed forms. Many architects such as Sir Edwin Lutyens, Mies van der Rohe, and Norman Foster have also prefabricated full-size timber mock-ups of their design intentions in order to preview their impact prior to actual construction.

To an extent, the volumetrics of an intended space can be experienced simply by erecting a full-size linear structure using string. Depending on size, the delineation can be constructed indoors or outdoors, being lashed, pegged, or tacked to convenient anchor points.

Functions of Orthographics and Perspectives

1

The plan functions as a horizontal slice made through a designed form at approximately eye level. It affords the designer--and his audience--an aerial view of the dimensioned arrangement of both contained and surrounding space.

2

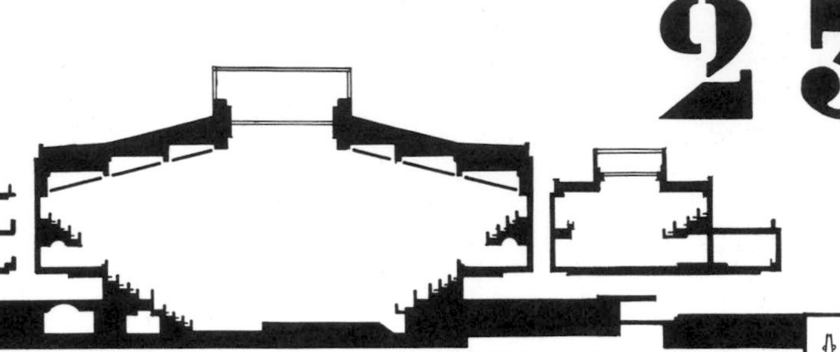

The section is a selective crosscut made vertically through the substance and hollowness of form. It is made in order to experience the outer profile of form or its internal workings. When applied to architectural concepts, sections, like plans, function as cutaway graphics but allow a horizontal view of the shape of interior and exterior space.

3

Elevations, like plans and sections, are graphic abstractions. They are non-spatial paraline drawings in which planes are represented to the same scale, regardless of their position in space. In design, elevations function to assess or convey the all-around massing and silhouette of a designed form and, together with sections, are used as a check on the planning stage.

4

Selecting scale for an orthographic drawing is one means of regulating the distance between the designer's eye and the size or degree of complexity of a concept. For example, plans, sections, and elevations are usually drawn at 1/4" = 1'-0" or 1/8" = 1'-0" (metric equivalents 1:50 or 1:100), but a scale of 1/2" = 1'-0" (1:20) allows details to be focused.

Increasingly, larger buildings and building complexes can be shrunk along decreasing scales of 1/16" = 1'-0" (1:200) or 1:500. Thus, in selecting a scale, the designer not only regulates the distance of an idea from his eye but also regulates its graphic size so that it fits within the confines of his drawing board.

5

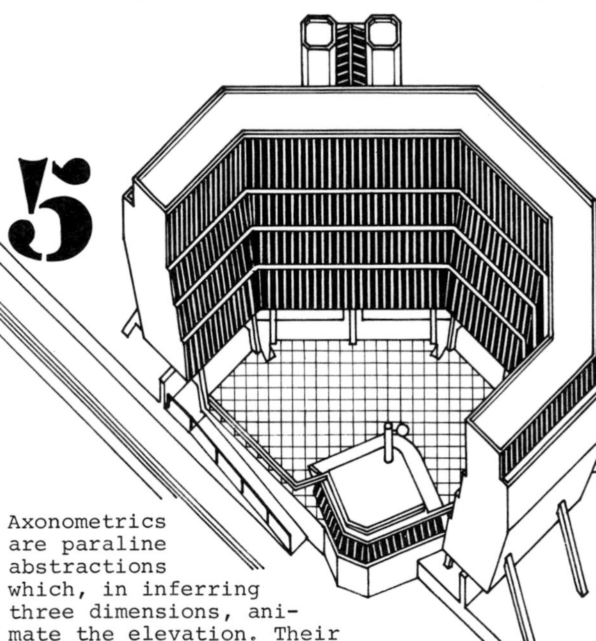

Axonometrics are paraline abstractions which, in inferring three dimensions, animate the elevation. Their configurations force the designer's view of his concept upward into a hovering position, affording exterior views and glimpses of interiors. In such drawings all lines are to scale regardless of depth, and all parallel lines remain parallel.

6

Unlike axonometrics, perspective coordinates recognize the diminishing size of objects in space and allow them to be represented at eye level. Interior and exterior views of building designs can be graphically simulated, and when applied sequentially, the changing impression of movement toward, around, and through design concepts can be communicated.

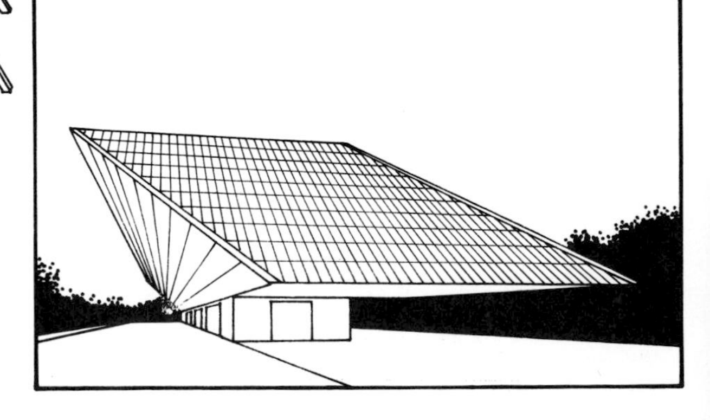

Functions of Diagrams

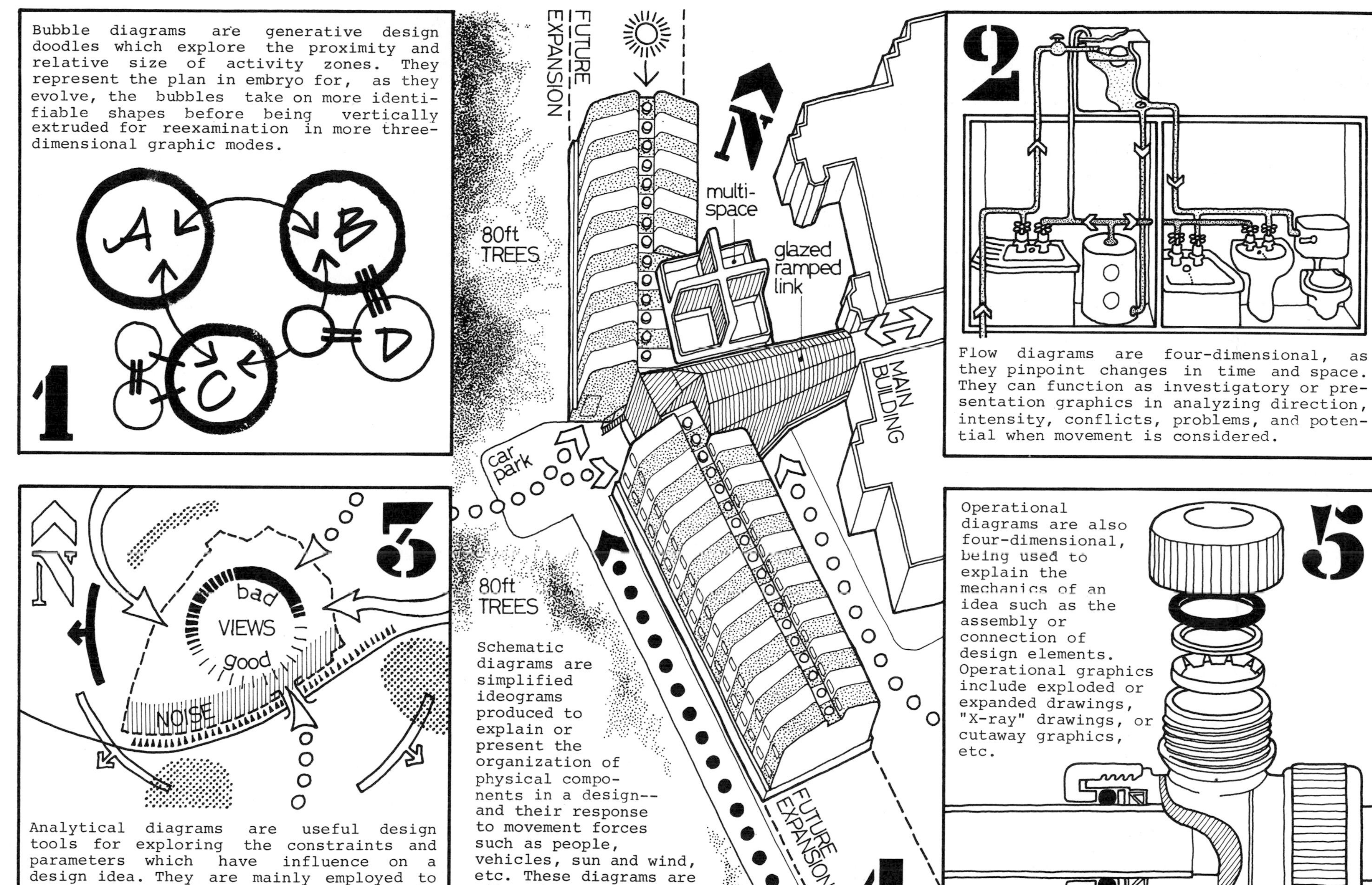

Bubble diagrams are generative design doodles which explore the proximity and relative size of activity zones. They represent the plan in embryo for, as they evolve, the bubbles take on more identifiable shapes before being vertically extruded for reexamination in more three-dimensional graphic modes.

Flow diagrams are four-dimensional, as they pinpoint changes in time and space. They can function as investigatory or presentation graphics in analyzing direction, intensity, conflicts, problems, and potential when movement is considered.

Analytical diagrams are useful design tools for exploring the constraints and parameters which have influence on a design idea. They are mainly employed to study existing conditions, such as in site surveys (see page 62).

Schematic diagrams are simplified ideograms produced to explain or present the organization of physical components in a design--and their response to movement forces such as people, vehicles, sun and wind, etc. These diagrams are often shown as axonometrics annotated with graphic symbols.

Operational diagrams are also four-dimensional, being used to explain the mechanics of an idea such as the assembly or connection of design elements. Operational graphics include exploded or expanded drawings, "X-ray" drawings, or cutaway graphics, etc.

How to Use an Analytical Diagram

1

Many design clues can be found at the setting for a proposed building. For example, decisions concerning its potential location, orientation, formal arrangement, color, and fabric might be partly informed by a simple sequence of analytical diagrams which convey useful information quickly collected in situ.

The various kinds of information might be color-coded and superimposed in one diagram or, alternatively, worked individually to the same scale on transparent material and later superimposed to achieve a synthesis of data.

2

A simple record of the location and function of existing building materials situated on and around the site area could offer important clues to a future selection and juxtaposition of materials and finishes--together with the informed introduction of color.

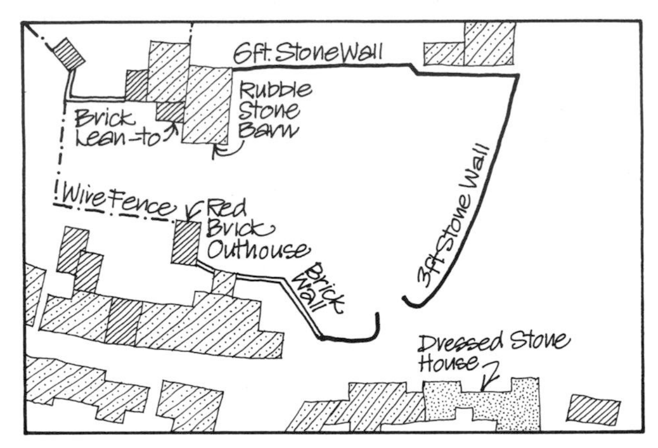

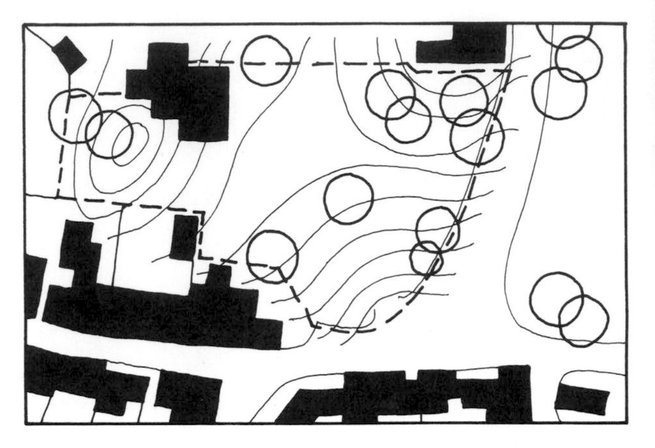

3

A topographical documentation--using a simple contour plan and sections--of the site area will be useful when planning the massing and spatial organization of the new design. This analysis could also include relationships between man-made and natural forms.

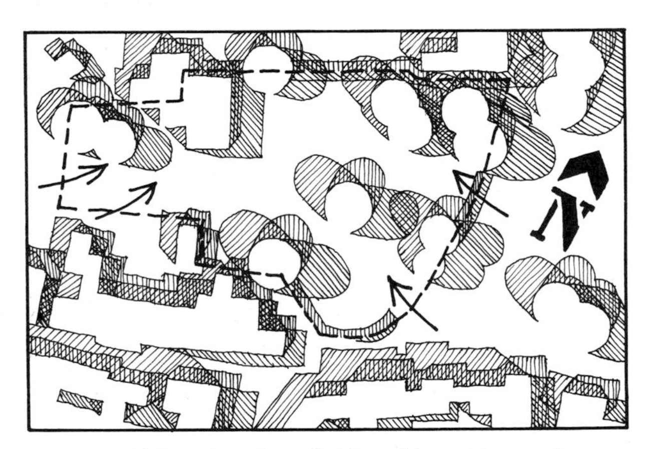

4

Make a note of the direction of prevailing winds and record or predict sun and shadow patterns at several points in the day cycle; this should pinpoint exposed and sheltered zones on the site. Such information will aid decisions on location, orientation, and relationships between "open" and "closed" parts of the new design.

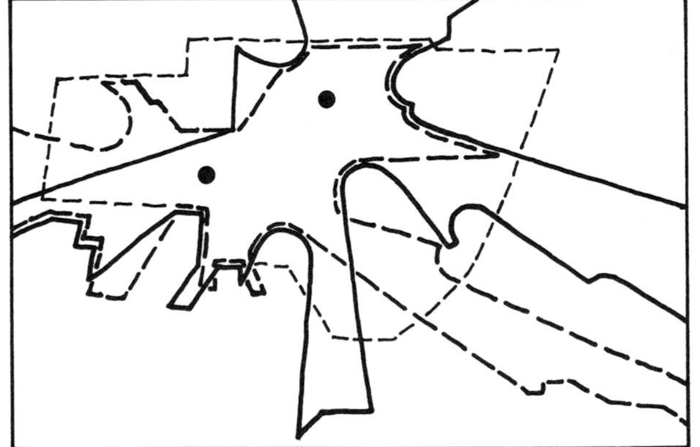

5

Orientation of a building design may also be influenced by visual links from the site. The direction and quality of views can be documented by drawing a line around the limits of vision from a series of vantage points from within the site. The resultant "bubbles" can then be supported with sketches or photographs which convey the nature and functions of each view (see page 94).

6

Further analytical diagrams might explore existing or potential access points, services, etc., or be used to isolate any other particular aspects of a site in question. Beyond their function as a design tool, the diagrams could later be presented in report or wall-display format in order to communicate the range of influences on your problem-solving route.

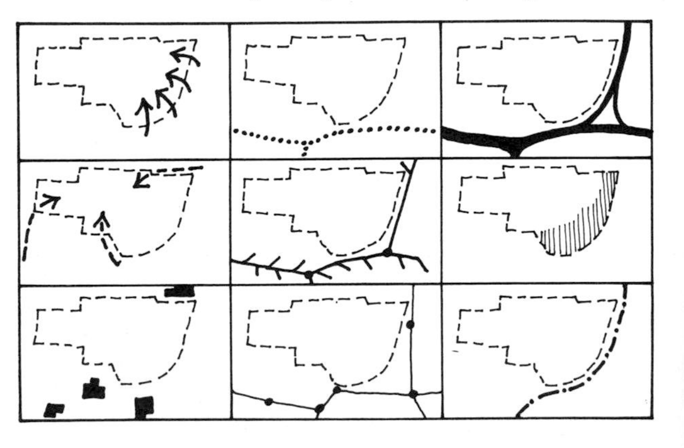

The Plan

1 The plan is a conceptual, horizontal cut through a building concept which, in slicing walls at a height which accounts for windows and doors, graphically explains solid-void and interior-exterior relationships. Although plans are two-dimensional images, a strong impression of depth can be implied through the adoption of a simple hierarchy of technical pen or lead line weights.

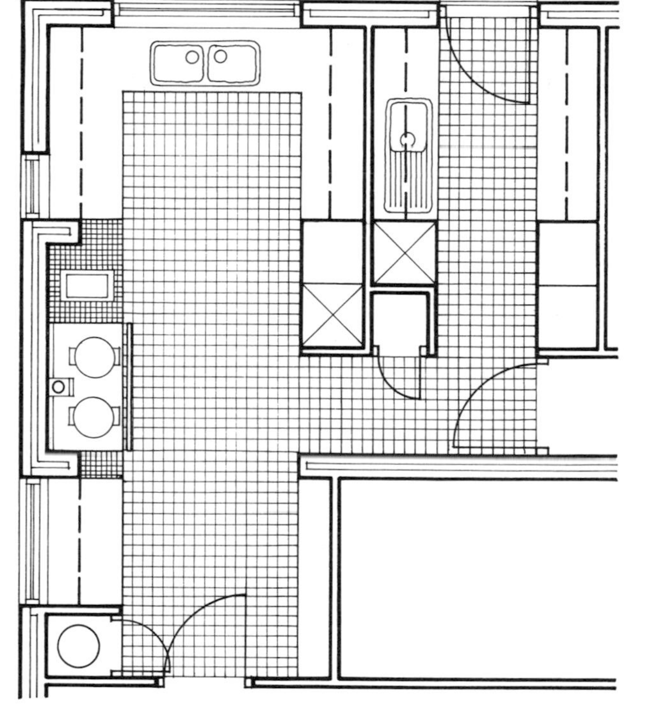

This floor plan enlists a system of descending ink line weights. The thickest, darkest lines denote the areas which have been cut, i.e., the sliced wall projections which would, in a real view, be nearest the eye. An intermediate line weight defines objects such as furniture contained within and below the level of the cut. A fine line describes floor-surface treatments--the plane farthest from the point of view--and other details at intermediate levels. N.B.: Any information included above the level of the cut should be delineated with a broken line.

2 Beyond simple structures of line weights--which respond to degrees of depth or degrees of importance in information--ascending or descending systems of tonal value or color intensity may be introduced. This opens the door to the potential of all forms of mediums in the creation of informative graphics in design communication.

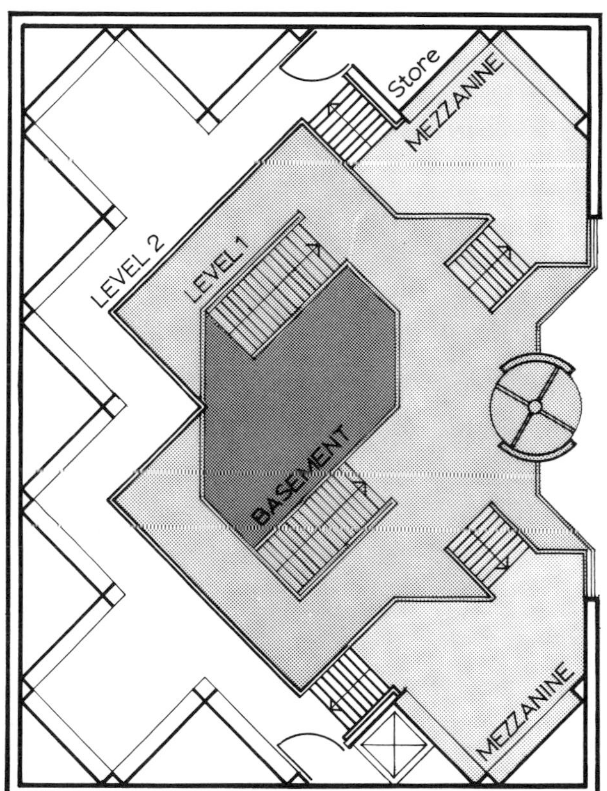

This plan uses a basic range of lines and dry-transfer tones; others might utilize hatching, pencil tones, washes, dry-color films, collage, inks, or paint. Color in plans can be objectively rendered to describe materials, or in abstraction--to communicate aspects of spatial function.

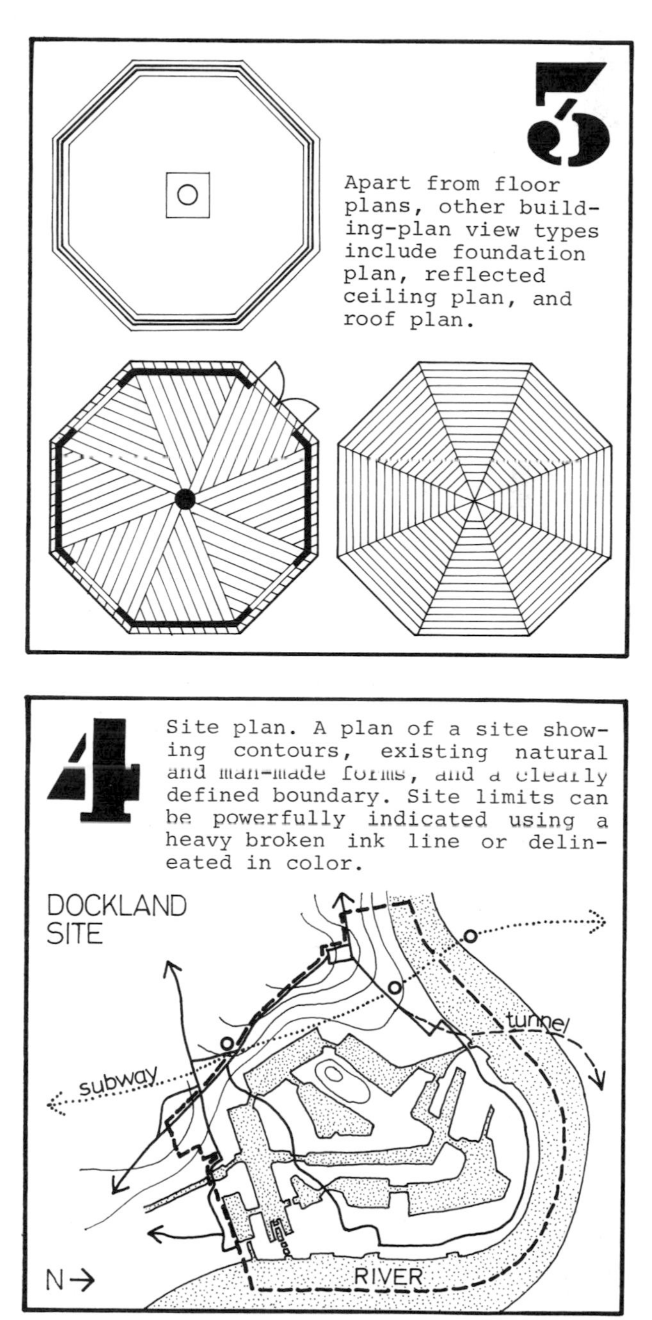

3 Apart from floor plans, other building-plan view types include foundation plan, reflected ceiling plan, and roof plan.

4 Site plan. A plan of a site showing contours, existing natural and man-made forms, and a clearly defined boundary. Site limits can be powerfully indicated using a heavy broken ink line or delineated in color.

The Site Plan

1 When communicating the relationship between a proposed building and its setting, the amount of time spent in its execution--as with any drawing--dictates the amount of information and degree of detail. For example, when working against a pressing deadline, only the most important zones of form and space need be established. This can be achieved through a hierarchical deployment of ink or graphite line weights which delineate a descending order of priorities.

2 With more time at one's disposal, more visual detail can be added to increase the degree of information. For example, site topography, landscaping, and an indication of materials can be included to good effect. N.B.: It is usual to show the roof plan of proposed buildings in site plans, but if you need to convey interior-exterior relationships, it can be "removed" and the same degree of detail applied to internal finishes.

3 Longer time spans will allow an indulgence in simulated realism--extended by the simple 45-degree projection of vertical planes into a planometric oblique. Planometrics provide a simulation of an aerial view which some designers successfully adopt, especially when communicating with laypersons. This degree of detailed drawing should occasionally be experienced, as its objectivity informs a future, more selective drawing perception and helps to avoid the sterility of a drawing-board stylism.

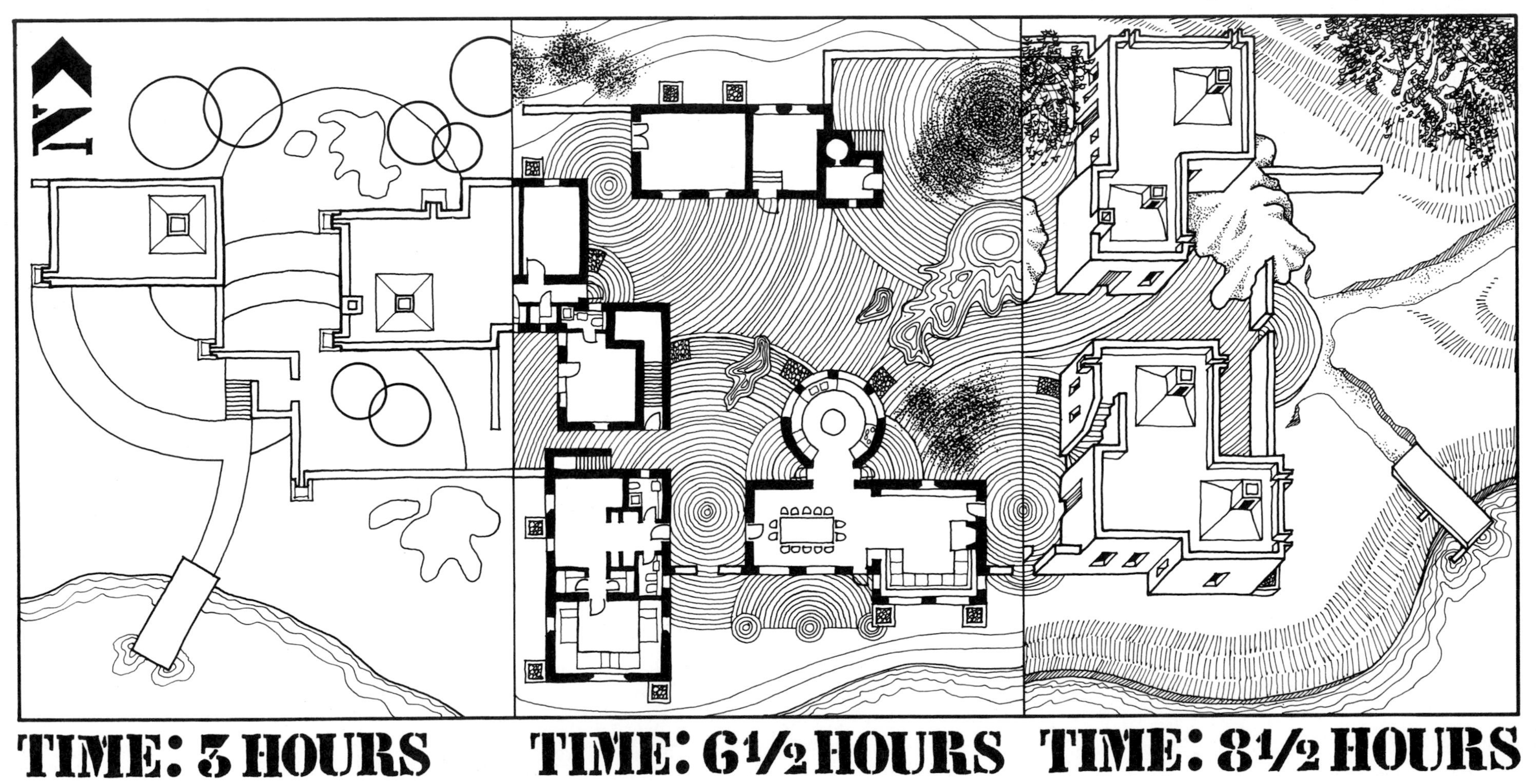

TIME: 3 HOURS　**TIME: 6½ HOURS**　**TIME: 8½ HOURS**

How to Use an Analytical Plan

1

An additional function of the plan view is as a useful vehicle in the study and communication of more subtle or complex relationships of a design scheme. Spatial and functional patterns together with other design mechanisms can be quickly and analytically described--the process underlining the formation of a basic interior-design philosophy.

Beyond the examples shown here, other analytical plans might investigate alternative layouts, changing zones of texture and color, and relationships between natural and artificial illumination, etc. This kind of plan can be a precision or freehand graphic, but draw from a wide range of media: those in color utilizing a color code; those in monochrome, a tonal code. In either case, a simple explanatory key provides the plan with instant meaning.

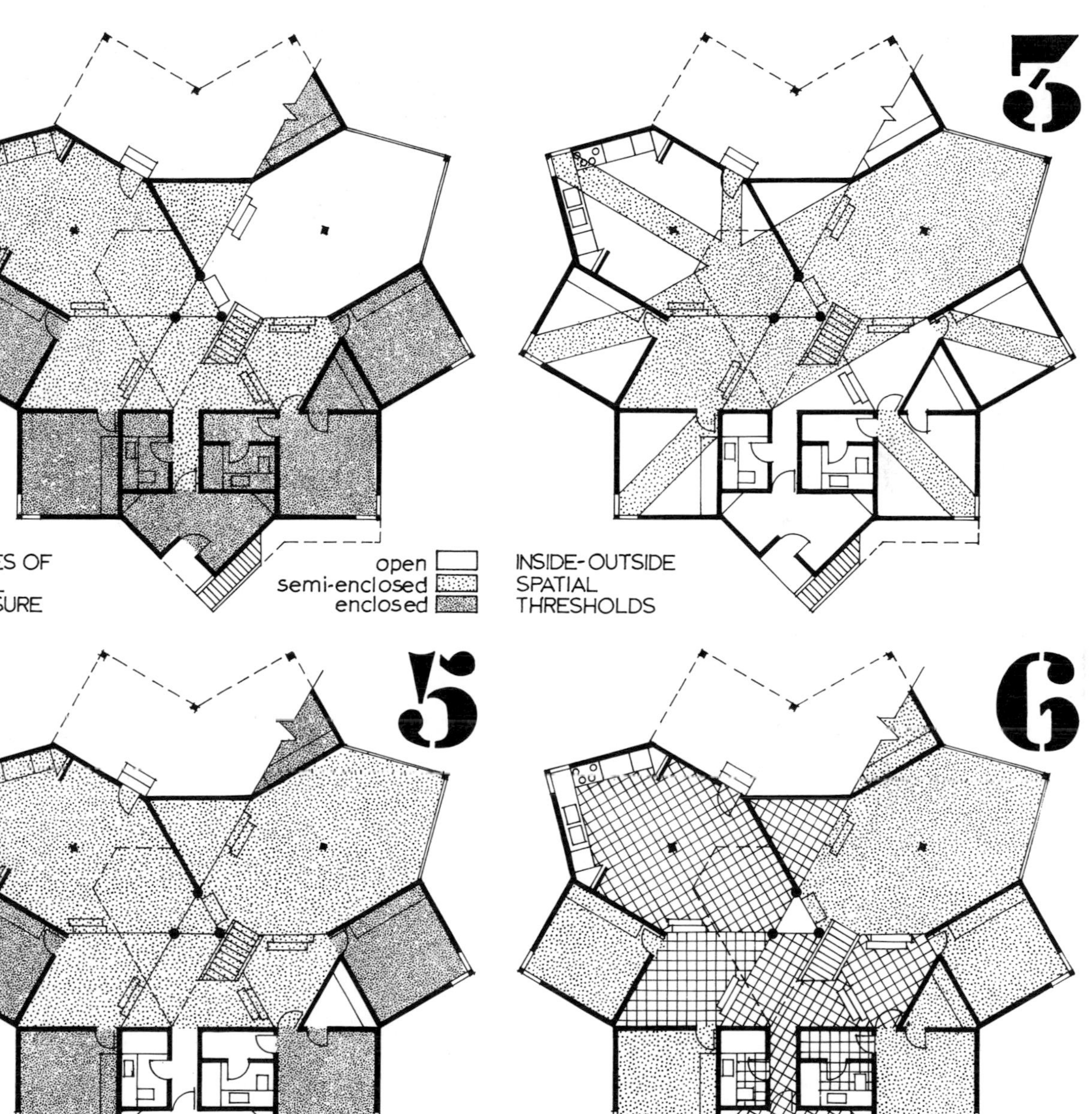

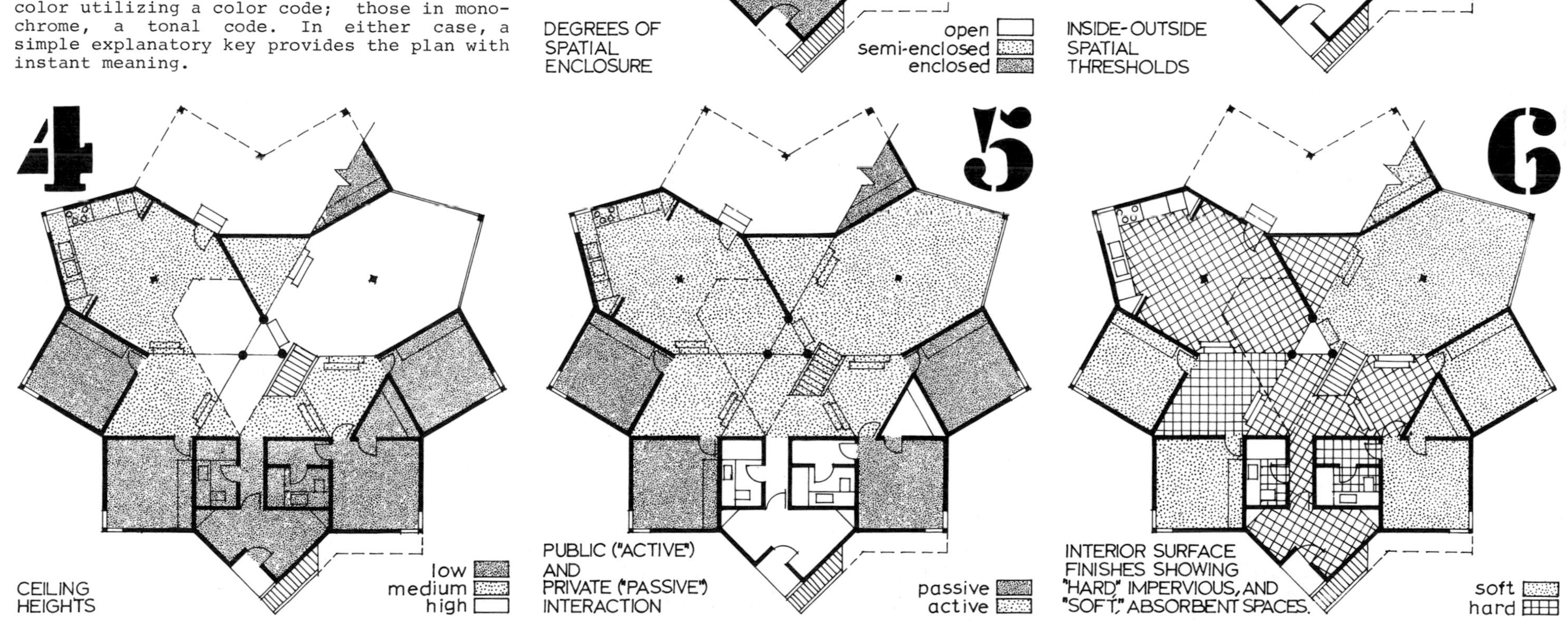

Elevations in the Design Process

1

The elevation is usually drafted into design currency in order to gain views of the exterior faces of design concepts in flux. However, in realizing graphically the external features of an architectural form, the function of elevational representation can be misconstrued as a kind of wrapping which parcels design ideas. For example, their exclusive use in fenestration design can reinforce a schism between "inside" and "outside." The elevation should, therefore, be used in conjunction with other orthographic views and, in presentation, give visual access to both exterior and--via more major openings--to interior space.

2

Like their other orthographic counterparts, elevations are simple to construct: all planes parallel to the drawing surface and perpendicular to the observer's line of vision retaining their true size, scale, shape, and proportion. They can be quickly projected on translucent paper using the plan drawing as an underlay.

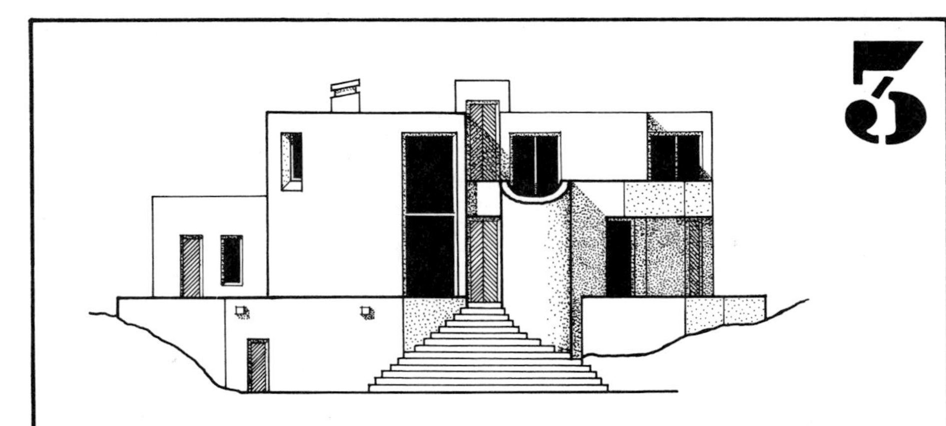

As elevations make no reference to the diminishing size of progressively distant planes, they challenge the designer to create illusions of depth through other means. Beyond the introduction of line weights (heavier nearer the eye, lightest farthest away), elevations attract tonal modulation and shadow projection to describe the effect of light on the shape and finish of surfaces. They are also highly responsive to descriptive color renderings in wash, spray, and collage form.

Presentation elevations provide an excellent opportunity for testing the impact of newly designed forms on the nature of their immediate environments. The inclusion of surrounding landscape features, people, existing built forms, and a sky elevate this orthographic beyond the starkness of those in glorious isolation on the sheet. The contextual elevation also reflects a degree of environmental sensitivity in the designer and produces more readable images for those uninitiated in orthographic communication.

The Planometric

1 Tests have demonstrated that lay people find great difficulty in "reading" orthographics--seeking insight concerning the designers' intentions in their preference for models and perspectives. Plan drawings, on the other hand, are found to be the most difficult to comprehend but, paradoxically, the planometric, i.e., a simple projection of the plan, elevated them to a much higher level of spatial meaning.

2 The planometric is achieved by extruding graphically all vertical planes to scale at 45 degrees to the left or the right of the plan--in a direction complementing the best angle of view. This simple method of projection is particularly useful for conveying a more overall glimpse of clusters of buildings, being drawn---depending upon the nature of the information--with or without rooftops.

3 The introduction of shadows reinforces the illusion of its three-dimensional appearance. These are also simple to construct, their coordinates being a further 45-degree projection of the form, but in a direction complementary to the established angle of view. When adding shadow tones, remember that the planes which cast them will also be in shade. N.B.: Shadows cast in this drawing are purely schematic and do not respond to the sun's azimuth or altitude.

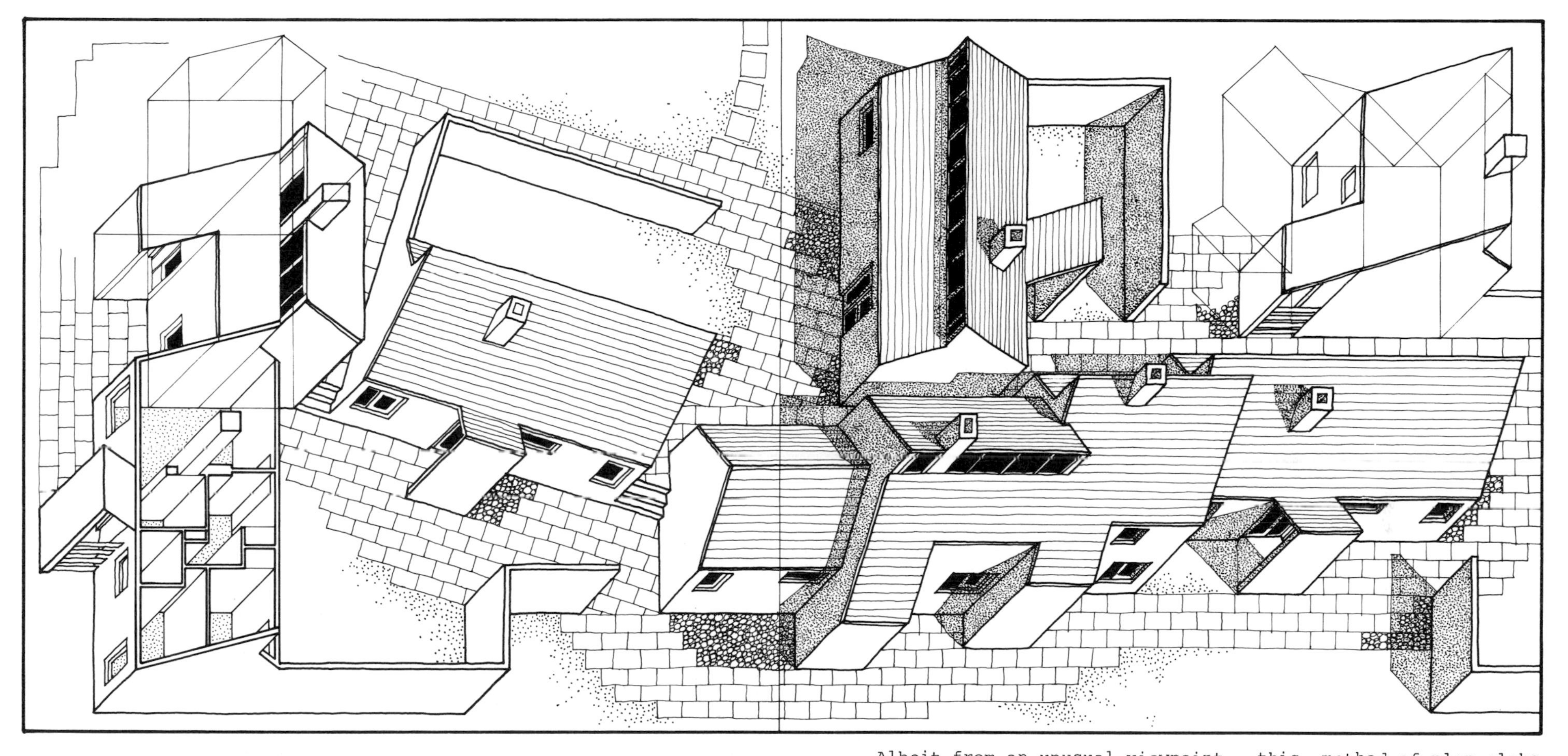

4 Albeit from an unusual viewpoint, this method of plan elaboration provides a stance that encourages some awareness of the space between architectural forms. Such an awareness is important, for the spaces defined by related groups of buildings---as in the urban environment---are as positive a design consideration as the spaces they contain. N.B.: The planometric is responsive to color rendering--being applied in "wet" or "dry" mediums to describe either natural or schematic finishes.

The Cross Section as a Design Tool

1

Within an evolving design sequence, the use of generative sections enables the designer to monitor the changing relationships between the positive and negative space of developing ideas.

At the presentation stage the point of incision at which this design surgery is made differs in response to the kind of information being communicated. For instance, in sections examining constructional methods, the incision can be staggered to take account of as many different details as possible; in a design section the cut usually describes one plane--its location representing the best possible vantage point from which to inspect the solid and void of a cutaway concept. In either case, the position and trajectory of the sectional cut are shown on accompanying plans.

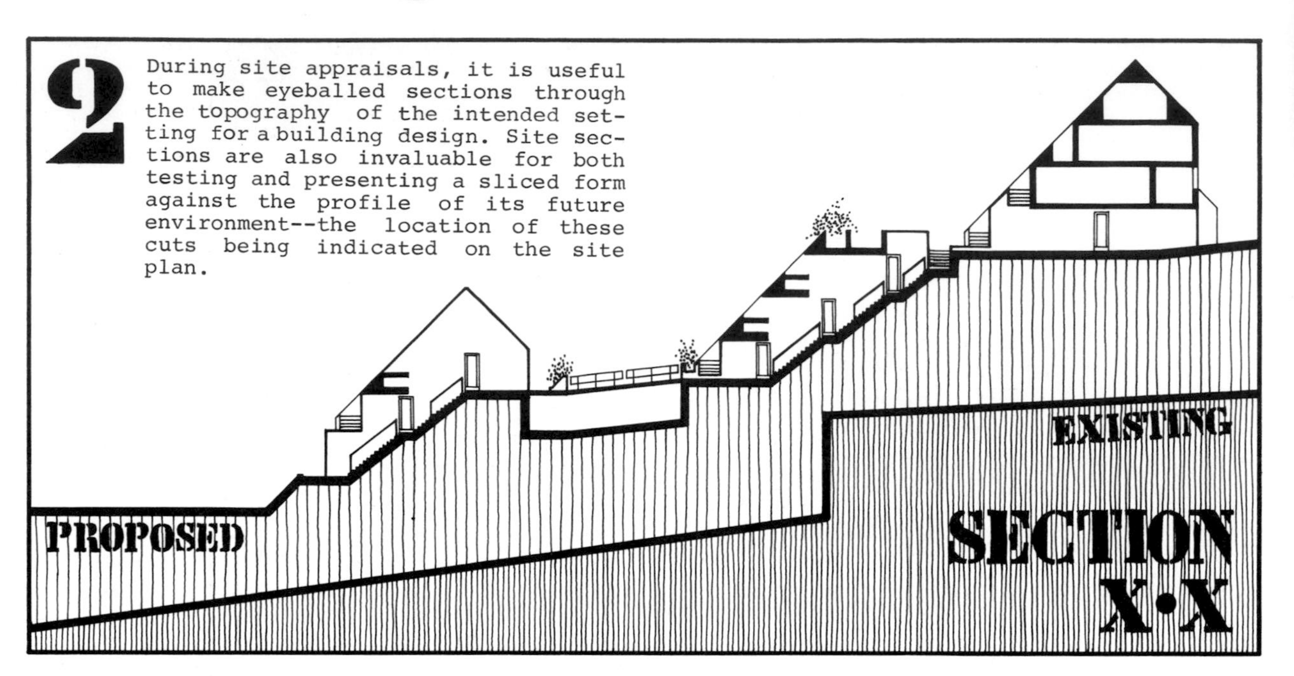

During site appraisals, it is useful to make eyeballed sections through the topography of the intended setting for a building design. Site sections are also invaluable for both testing and presenting a sliced form against the profile of its future environment--the location of these cuts being indicated on the site plan.

There are various degrees of visual information which can be incorporated into building sections:

a) Section showing only solid-void relationships.

b) Section including information in elevational form behind the line of incision.

c) Section incorporating single-point perspective view of the interior space.

B

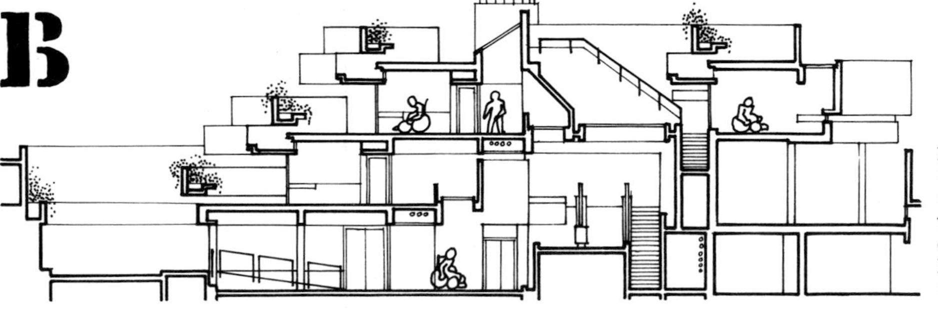

N.B.: The inclusion of figures in sections enhances impressions of scale; inclusion of differing line weights--using the heaviest to describe the cut through the building and its base--enhances impressions of depth.

A

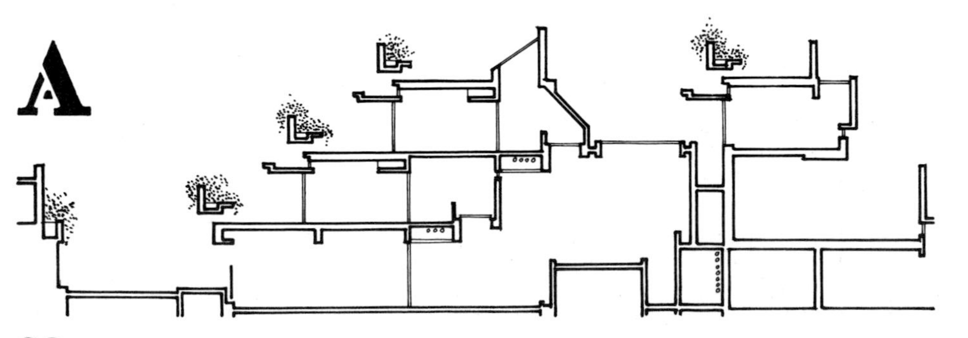

C

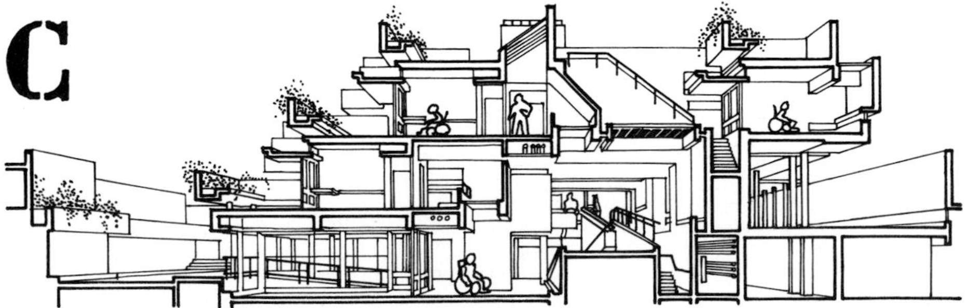

The Design and the Production Drawing

The drawings used by the designer to communicate ideas to others differ from the more private, generative, and developmental graphics used along the process of design. At a public level of communication, two basic kinds of drawing convey different forms of information to different recipients.

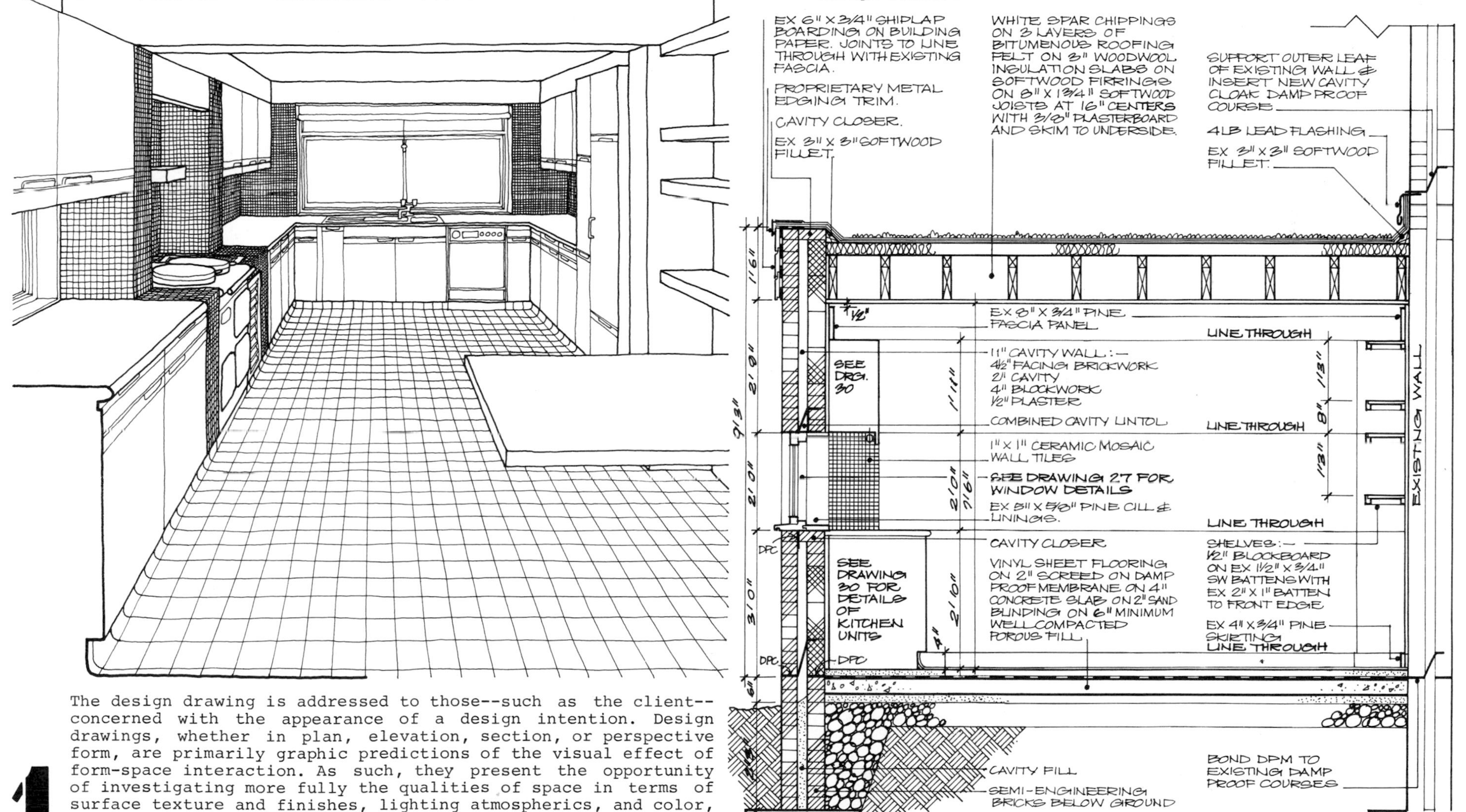

1 The design drawing is addressed to those--such as the client--concerned with the appearance of a design intention. Design drawings, whether in plan, elevation, section, or perspective form, are primarily graphic predictions of the visual effect of form-space interaction. As such, they present the opportunity of investigating more fully the qualities of space in terms of surface texture and finishes, lighting atmospherics, and color, etc. In conveying these impressions to those concerned, many designers see them as vehicles for selling ideas.

2 The production, or working, drawing is concerned with how a proposed built form is to be constructed. It involves a language of graphic codes, symbols, and conventions through which the designer conveys his detailed, finalized intentions to the builder or contractor. A full set of production drawings coordinates component, assembly, and locational graphics which combine to communicate a total picture of the mechanics of a design scheme.

Viewing Concepts Within Axonometrics

1

Axonometric (paraline) drawings function primarily as containers for brand-new ideas. They are used by designers to graphically witness the birth of design conceptions previously visualized in the mind's eye. They are also used to communicate design solutions in conjunction with plans, sections, and elevations.

Each type of axonometric projection represents a slightly different design stance--the choice of container (or view) relating to the nature of the designed form. They also represent a single, three-dimensional glimpse of a developing idea--their box-like frameworks being sympathetic to cubic forms. More fluid, organic ideas, on the other hand, may be better physically visualized in responsive mediums like clay.

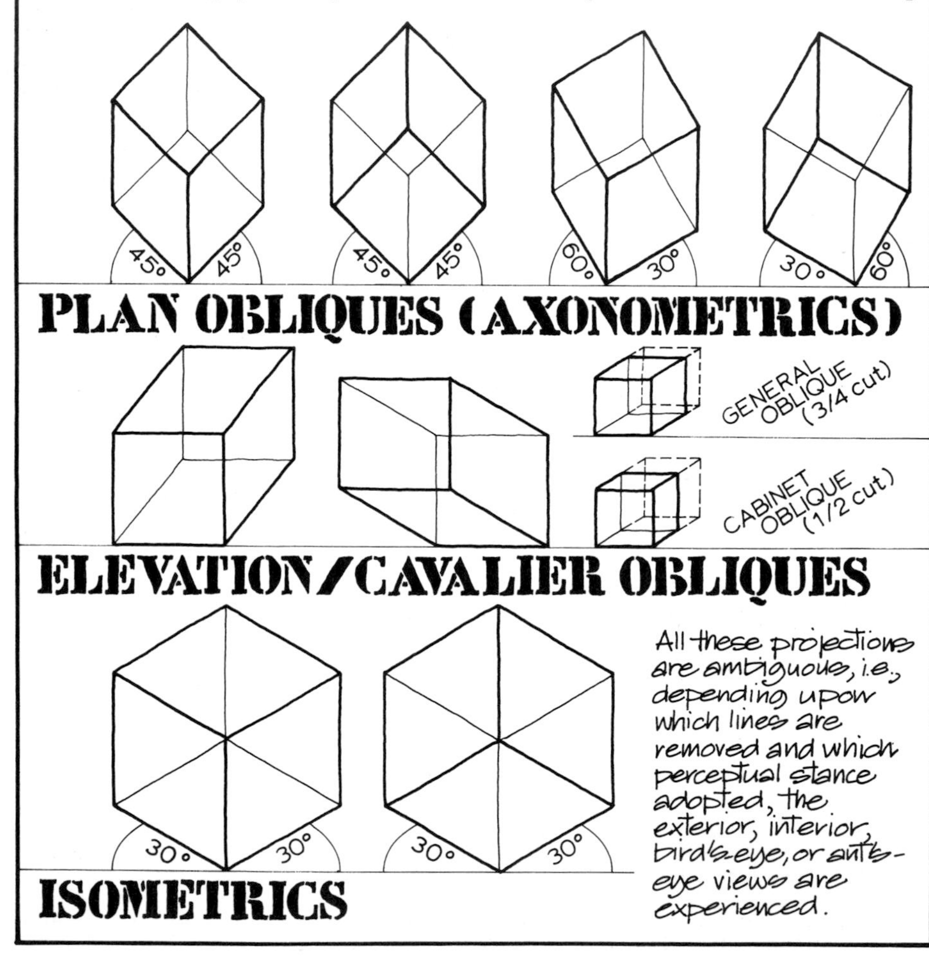

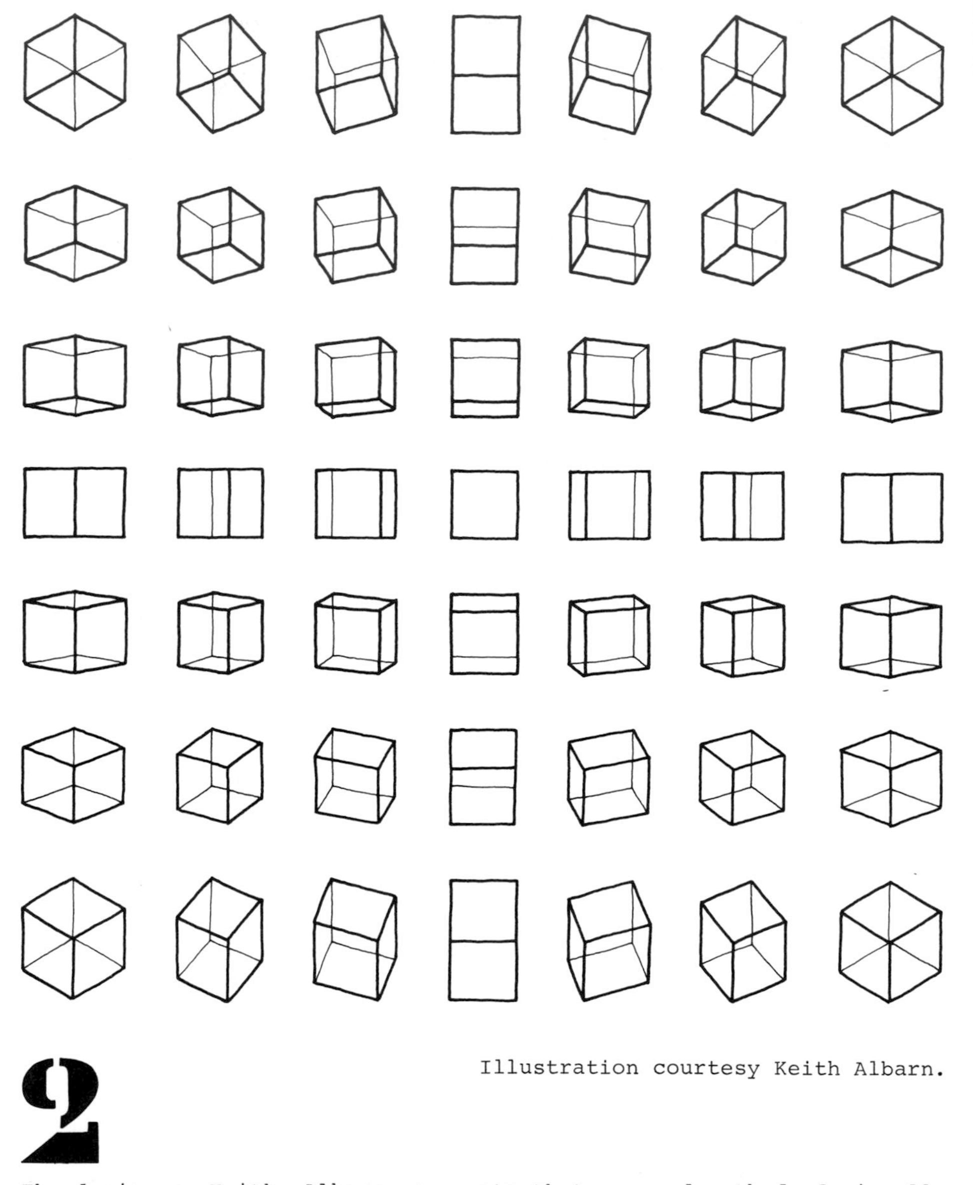

Illustration courtesy Keith Albarn.

2

The designer Keith Albarn suggests that a good method of visually testing the totality of design concepts is to subject them to an extensive sequence of orthographic views. In this manner, a new idea is rotated, i.e., seen four-dimensionally, and, therefore, visualized more completely before further development of ideas.

Functions of Axonometrics

1

When someone is asked to draw a cube, he tends to respond by showing it in axonometric form. Similarly, the axonometric is usually employed for the designer's first graphic glimpse of the three dimensions of an emergent idea.

Beyond the design stage, however, axonometrics are useful in conveying a more total--if somewhat distorted--view of a design proposal.

2

Axonometric views are quicker to construct than isometric views. For example, a plan drawing can be placed under translucent material and traced before projecting its walls to scale for an interior or exterior view. When constructing isometrics the plan has to be redrawn--possibly after some trial roughs to determine its composition on the sheet.

3

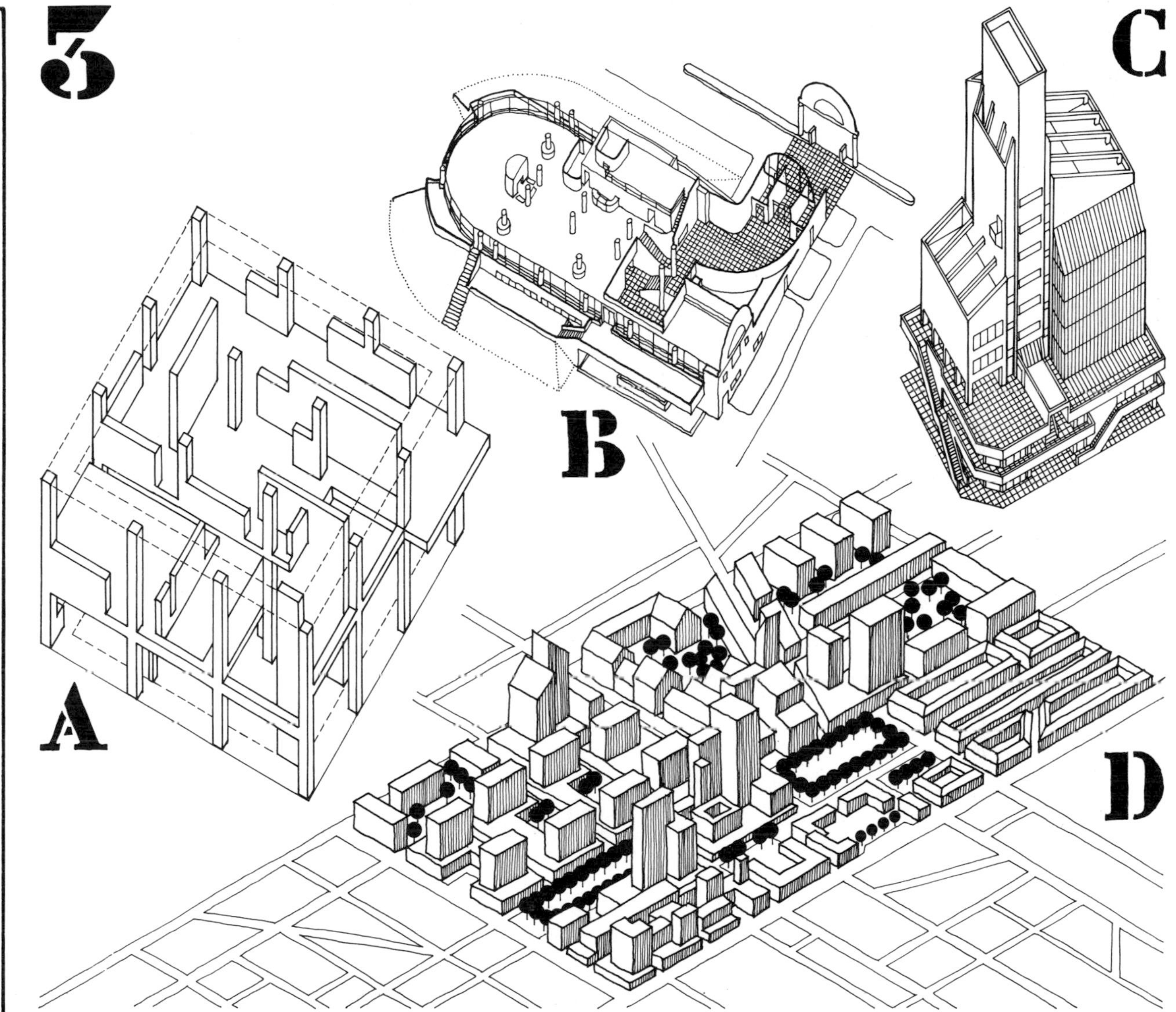

Axcnometrics showing a cutaway skeletal construction (a) and an interior design treatment (b) together with an external view of a complete architectural form (c). The most complex arrangements of cubic forms can be quickly constructed axonometrically to create the most ambitious-looking graphics--further enhanced by the addition of tone and color.

An isometric projection of a design scheme for a city section (d) demonstrates the strength of this form of drawing vehicle when conveying wider contexts of design.

Planning Orthographic Sheets and Display Layouts

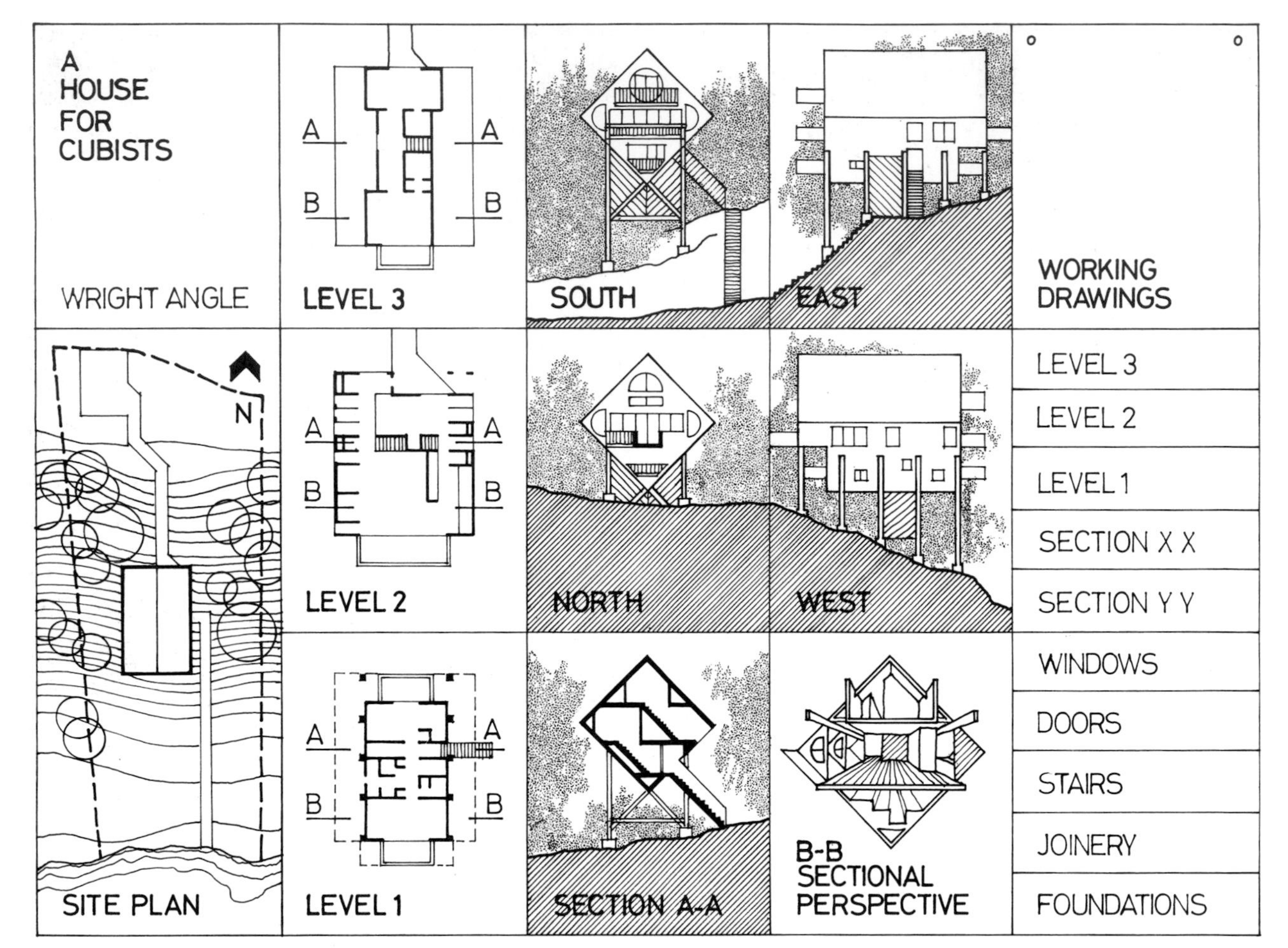

1

The layout of orthographic drawings is important in communication, for in the translation of design concepts, plans, elevations, and sections have to be mentally and visually coordinated by the recipient. In order to pre-plan the composition of a set of orthographics, adopt a structure of invisible lines--a simple grid which will help determine total layout and, within it, the composition of individual sheets. Organize sheet layouts so that site plan relates to building plans--the latter being stacked in the order reflecting that of the building and with all levels clearly indicated. Similarly, elevations should be grouped to respond both to plan displacement and to the sequence of their own importance--the direction of each elevational face being clearly labeled. Sections make up a further component in the set. These may incorporate interior perspective views or be combined with other three-dimensional graphics such as exterior perspectives or axonometrics; however, the line of sectional cuts should be carefully annotated on the plans. If the display is of design drawings and construction details are required, these could be stacked or overlapped to make up a final component in the layout (see page 119 for tips on presenting ideas).

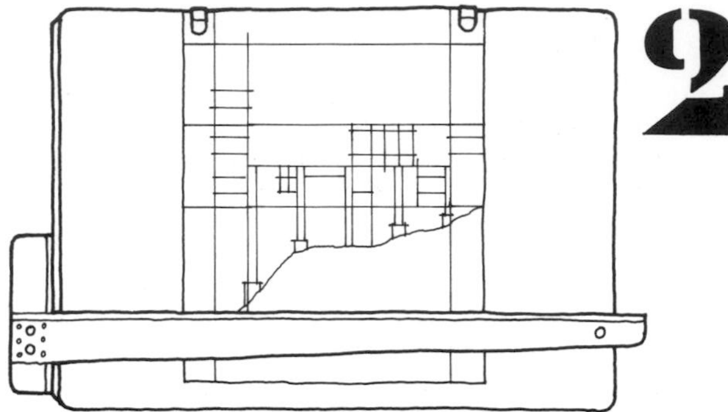

2

As each design project creates different demands on both mediums and layout, the pre-planning of presentation layouts can never occur too early in the design process. Awareness at the drawing-up stage means that individual layouts can respond both to the requirements of a total format and to the nature of each graphic and its relationship to the sheet. Each drawing should also be pre-planned lightly in pencil so that it is satisfactorily established prior to the introduction of more irrevocable mediums.

If the drawing is to be inked, select a range of line weights and redraw the pencil drawing completely in the thinnest nib size. Progressively add each ascending line thickness to the drawing, always working inside the initial fine-line framework to preserve the original dimensional accuracy.

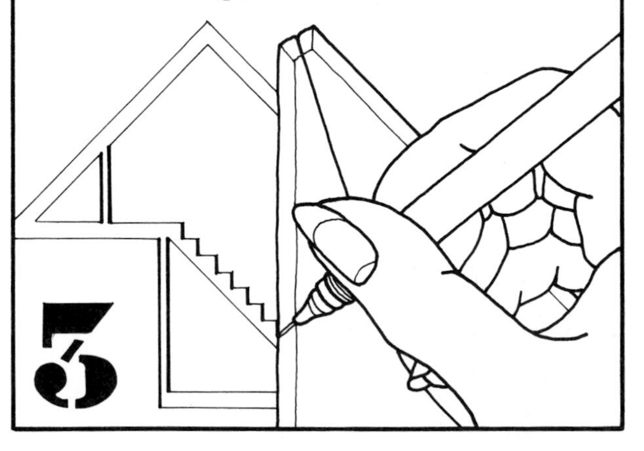

3

Some Orthographic Codes and Symbols

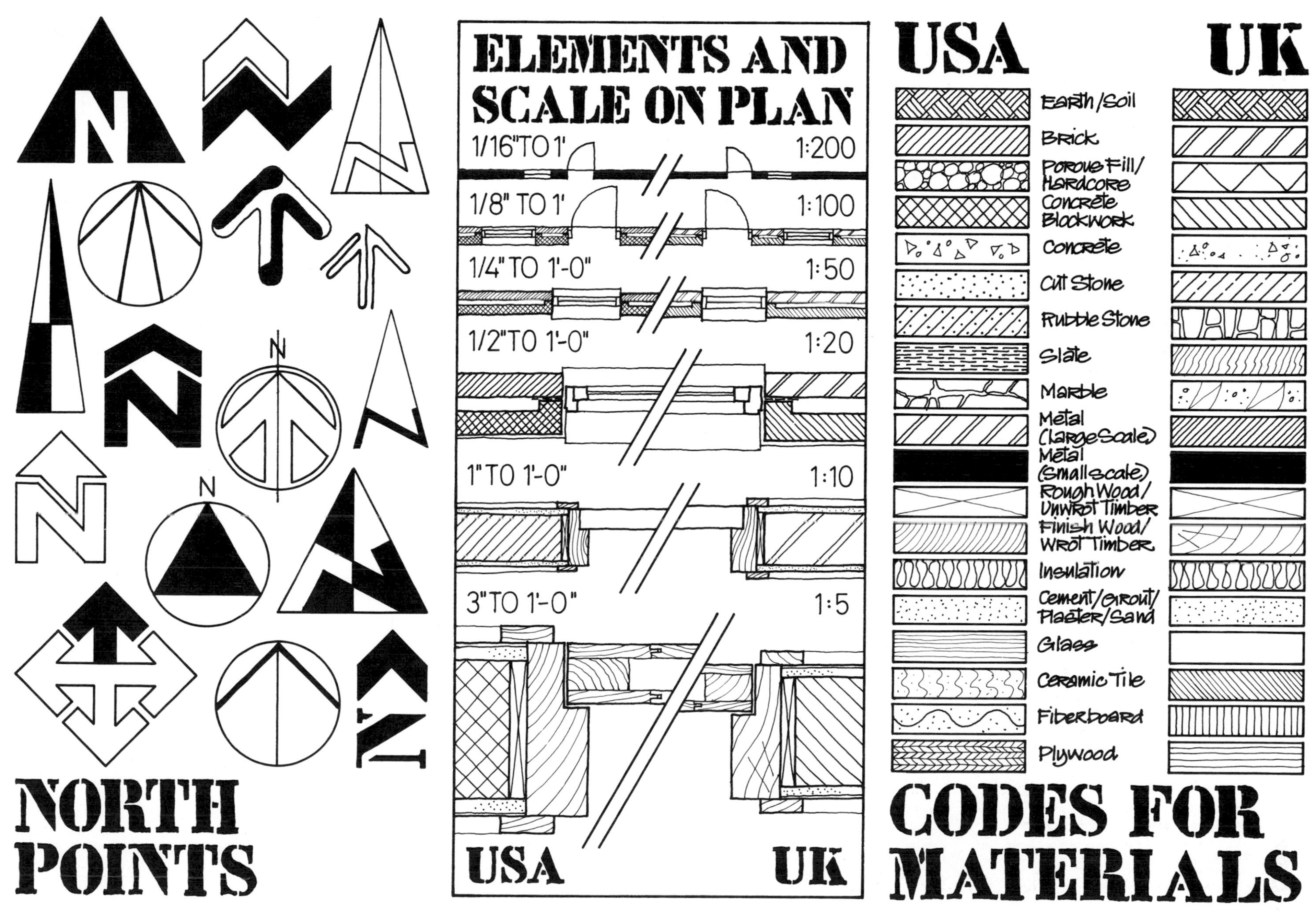

Template and Dry-Transfer Symbols

1 Manufacturers of templates and dry-transfer materials provide a vast array of aids for the rapid application of architectural symbols which are intended as an orthographic kit of parts in the creation of both production and design drawings.

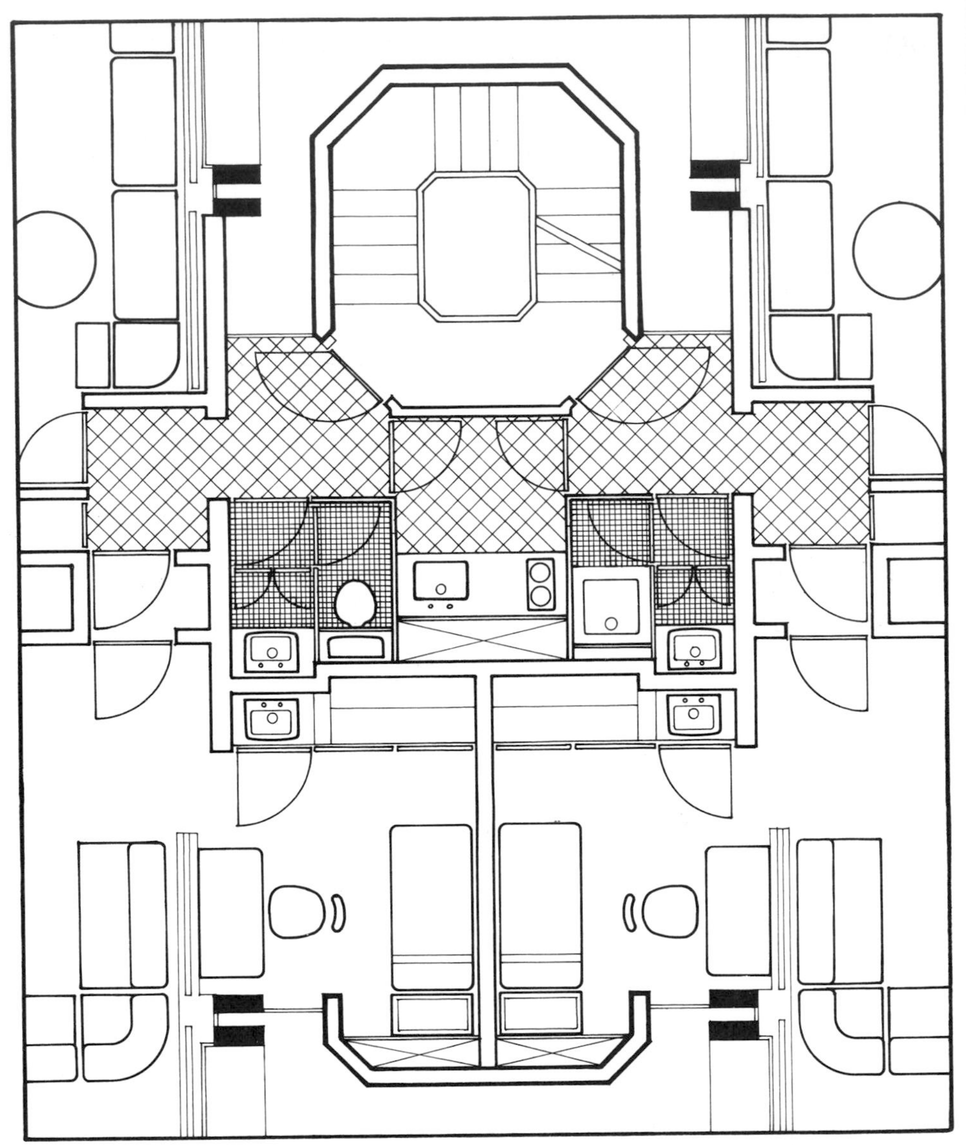

2 However, to totally invest in instant graphics is not only expensive but can short-circuit the drawing experience. Although these aids can be a useful expedient to the designer in a hurry, their exclusive use can encourage a superficial, universal stylism that denies the user a chance of developing a personal vision in design.

Developing Personal Codes

1 Plan. The tree is often the most dominant and repeated element in site and landscape plan drawings. This is usually indicated in abstract form within a circle--some designers using a double circle to instill a sense of depth.

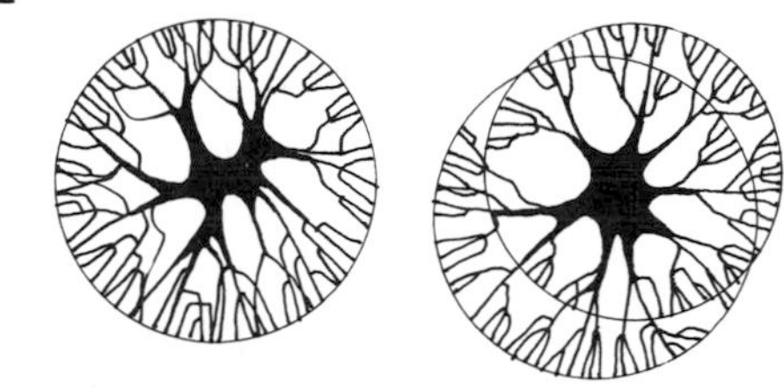

Rubber stamps for printing various sizes and species of tree are on the market, but you can make your own by carving personalized symbols on the face of an eraser--different faces, possibly, carrying different sizes of image. These can then be dipped in ink and tested on a scrap of paper before being used to produce quickly the densest of forests.

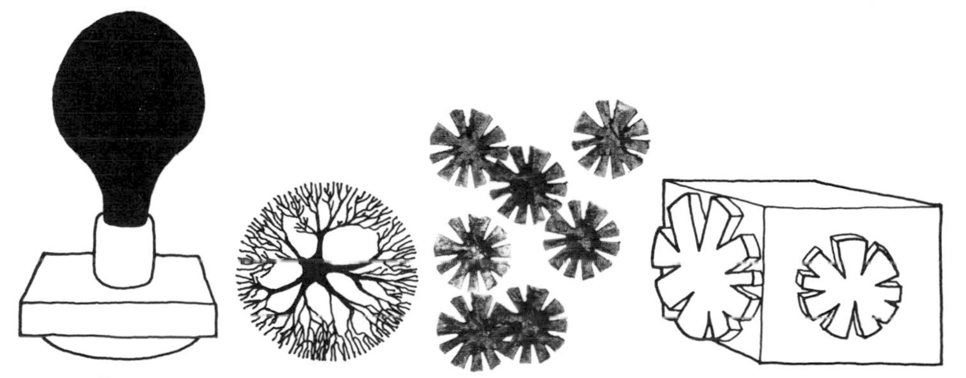

For a more pleasing print texture, symbols can be cut into the end-grain of timber or the sliced face of a potato--the latter, however, only lasting the duration of one drawing.

2 The only real method of developing a personal drawing technique for elevational representation is through a direct observation of the appearance of objects and their surfaces. It is to this end that the sketchbook and scrapbook (see page 30) play such a vital role in graphic communication.

This is an experimental elevation drawing based on a sketchbook study of the way various surfaces appear to behave in reality. It is from such studies that a more personal form of abstraction is developed.

Measuring Depth in Single-Point Perspective

The ability to quickly draw perspectives is important to the designer, but their construction can be daunting to the beginner. Perspective, however, is simply a means to an end and should be approached as such. When visualizing spaces which exist only in the mind's eye, the following method is fast and easily applied to different kinds of graphics.

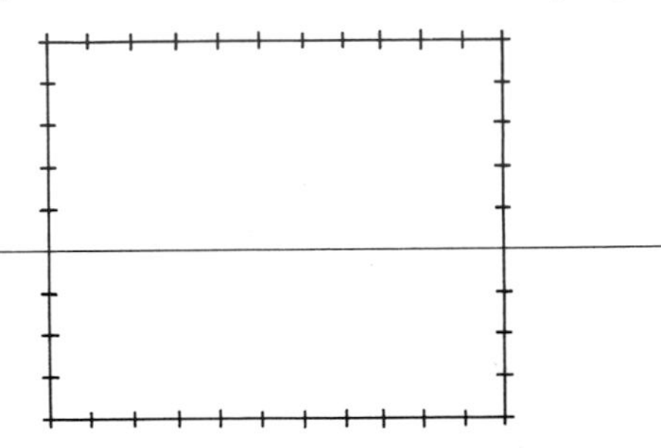

1 Select a scale and draw a "picture frame" on the drawing board. Mark off increments of equal measure around its edge. Next, draw in the eye level (horizon line)--this is assumed to be 5 feet (1.5 m) above the base line.

2 The vanishing point controls the direction of view. Position this on the horizon line to promote the best view--off center, if possible, to achieve a more dynamic drawing. Then, project radiating lines from the vanishing point through each of the base-line increments.

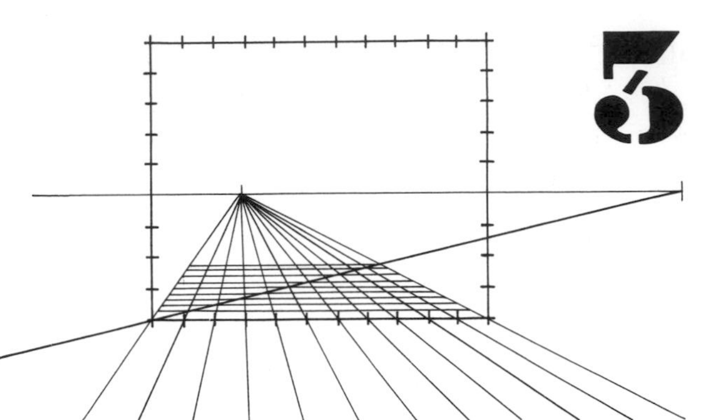

3 Locate a diagonal point outside the picture frame on the horizon line--its distance from the vanishing point representing that of the viewer from the picture-frame plane, i.e., the nearer its position to the vanishing point the more acute the foreshortening. Next, project a line from the diagonal point to the farther, lower corner of the frame. Where this crosses the radiating lines it establishes the equal units of measure as diminishing in depth.

4 The units of equal measure can also be projected in front of the picture frame by taking a line from the diagonal point through the nearer, lower corner of the frame.

5 After connecting the upper corners of the frame to the vanishing point together with the radiating lines on the remaining three sides of the space, the horizontal depth measurements can be extended around the framework to complete the grid. This can now act as an underlay guide from which the size and location of the components of an interior or exterior perspective can be scaled.

6 Perspective drawings worked from construction to final rendering on one drawing surface have to cope with the removal of initial and redundant construction lines. For this reason they often retain a constructed quality, appearing wooden and devoid of any atmosphere.

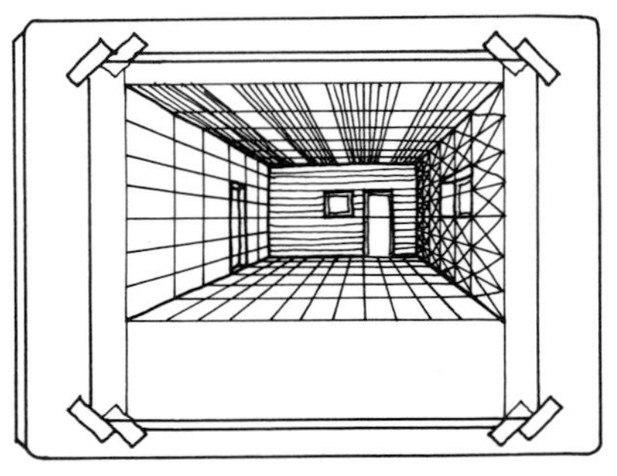

On the other hand, the underlay process separates the construction from the rendering stage, thus allowing a concentration on the introduction of tone, texture, color, and light and shadow, etc.

Basic Applications of Single-Point Perspective

1 Single point grids can be quickly constructed for use as underlays for building sections--an application guiding their rapid conversion into the three dimensions of a sectional perspective. However, in smaller buildings where more than one interior cell is involved, select a realistic location for the vanishing point. As a general rule, it can be positioned within the ground-level space.

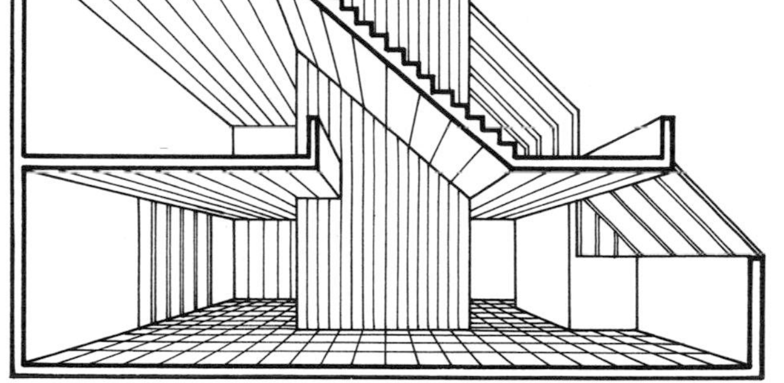

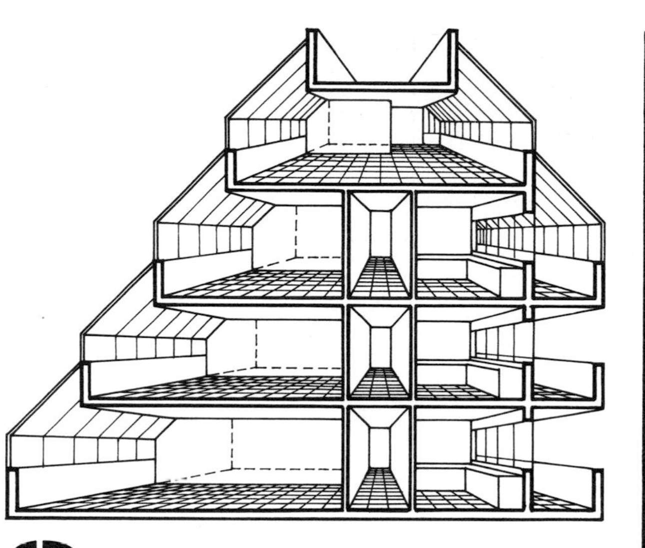

2 In larger-scale buildings containing multi-levels, each layer of space could respond to its own vanishing point.

3 Single point perspective coordinates can also be applied to bird's-eye views of interiors which are simple elaborations of a plan.

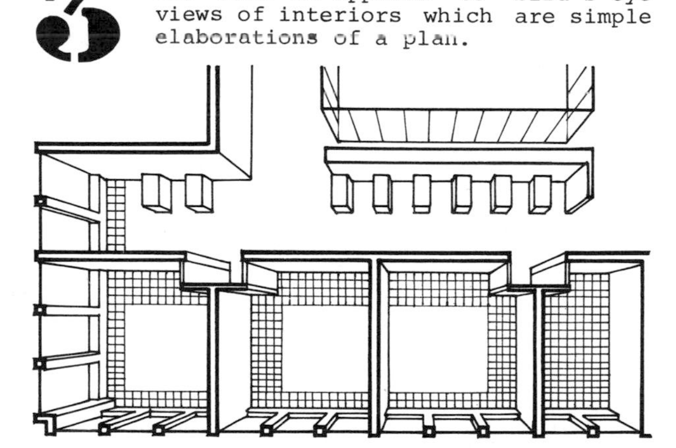

Selection of vanishing-point position is critical in order to obtain the best aerial view. In these drawings the plan coincides with the picture frame and, after projecting dimensioned increments in front of the plan, required heights can be established.

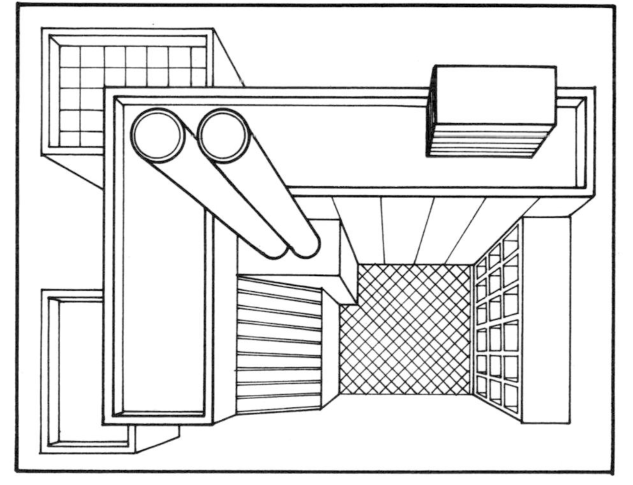

4 Similarly, plan views of individual or groups of buildings can be effectively transformed into bird's-eye views of their external appearance.

5 The use of sequences of one-point perspectives creates the opportunity of "walking" through the space of an idea.

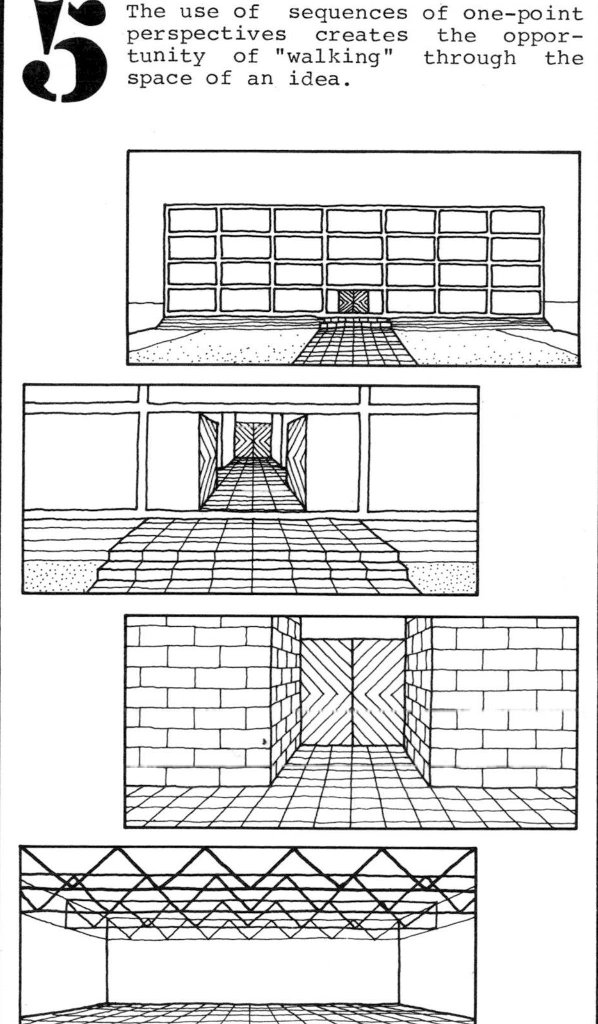

For the designer they function as a kind of cine camera which records an environment previously experienced in the mind's eye--the dynamics between one graphic "frame" and another providing a most informative and visually exciting method of communication.

Perspective Aids and Shortcuts

1

The central, single viewpoint is ideal for looking into interiors and along "tunnels" of exterior space. But the ability to freely move about the space of ideas and make drawings of them from a variety of standpoints necessitates an understanding of two- and three-point perspective.

The only genuine basis for understanding the more sophisticated perspective coordinates is from a first-hand experience via freehand sketching and objective drawing. However, one method first devised by Albrecht Dürer around 1514 is still used as an aid by beginners. This requires the making of a cardboard frame containing a regular grid of black thread.

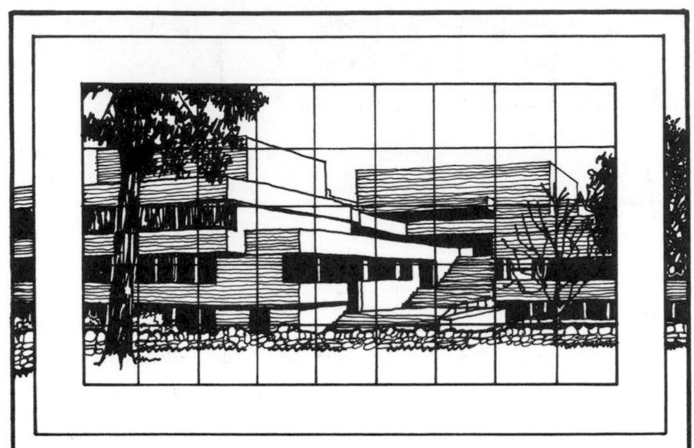

2

In use, the frame acts as a compositional viewfinder while the grid guides the transfer of converging lines. It is set up approximately 12 inches (300 mm) from the eyes and perspective coordinates transferred into a predrawn same scale or rescaled grid on the drawing surface.

A commercial version of this apparatus is on the market. It comprises an acrylic frame surrounding a rigid graphed film covered with sheet acetate. Views seen through the film are recorded in chinagraph pencil on the acetate before transfer--using carbon paper--to the drawing surface. Rescaled drawings are transferred using the grid method or a pantograph (see pages 80 and 81).

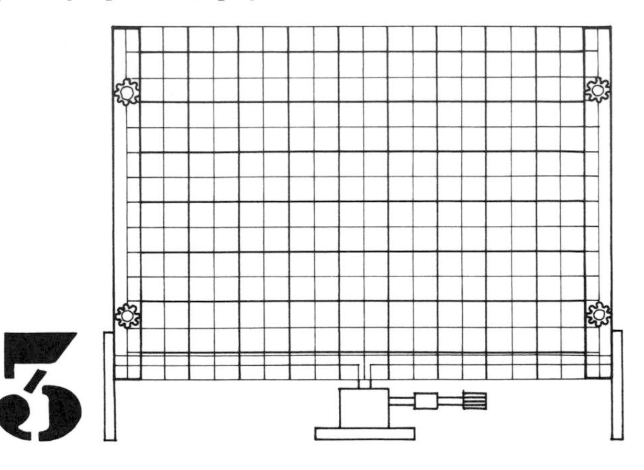

3

As a means of short-circuiting perspective construction, a variety of printed, ready-to-use underlays are marketed which include variations of one-, two-, and three-point perspective. These are placed under transparent material for evolving the coordinates of a new idea.

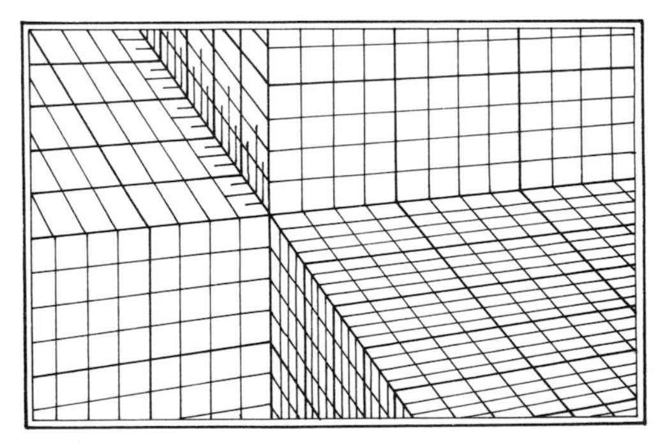

An alternative used by some designers is to originate on overlays placed over photographic illustrations which describe spaces similar to those in the mind's eye.

5

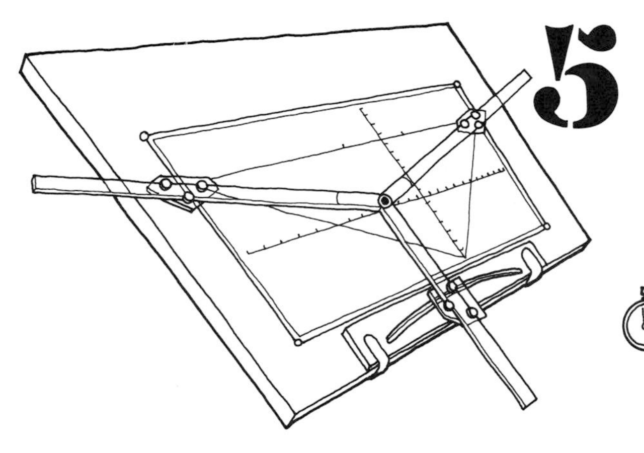

There are several proprietary perspective drawing machines. One is a three-armed instrument that is clipped to a drawing board. When set up, lines drawn along either of its adjustable lateral arms remain in correct perspective. Also, wherever the upright arm is positioned along its radius, correct vertical convergence is established.

6

Another uses a circular drawing board. The rotation of the board in combination with a spacer mechanism allows all forms of perspective and orthographic projections to be programmed and drawn.

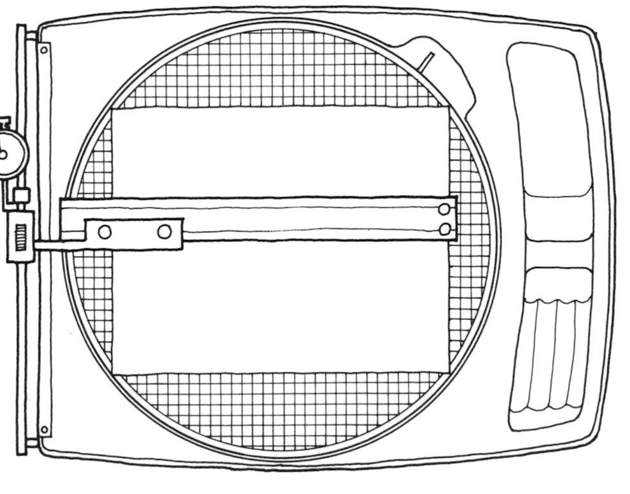

4 REPROGRAPHIC AND SIMULATION TECHNIQUES

Same-Size Tracing and Pantograph Rescaling

1

To transfer a same-size image, overlay a sheet of tracing paper on the original and fix with drafting tape. Carefully draw the image with a sharp, hard graphite lead.

The cleanest form of direct tracing is made via the light table. Transfer, however, depends upon the degree of translucency of both original and recipient materials. Do-it-yourself light tables are easily assembled from a sheet of thick glass placed over an empty drawer containing a small fluorescent light or a battery lamp. Any glare can be reduced by overlaying the glass with a sheet of heavy-duty tracing paper. Light tables are also useful for "at a glance" checking of large numbers of transparencies.

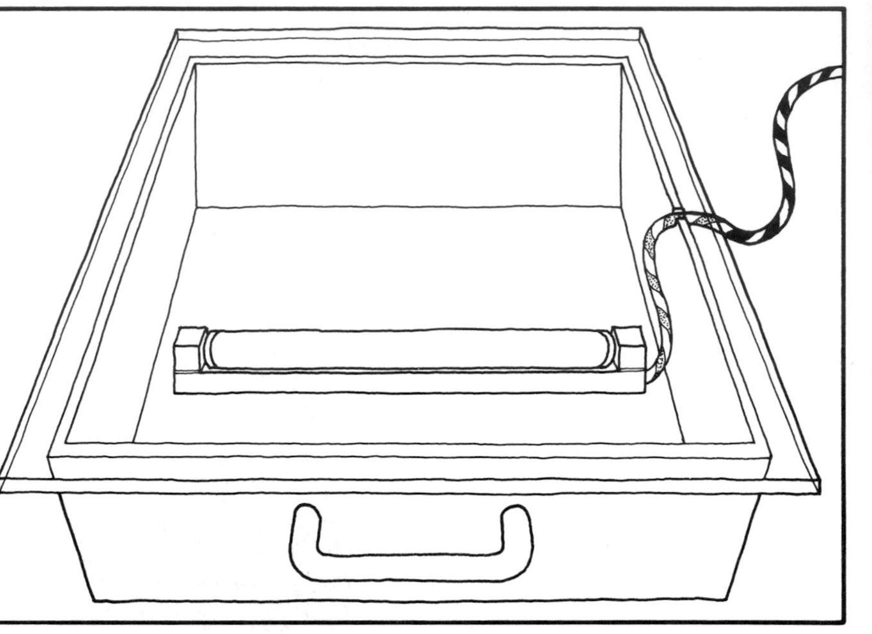

2

After completion, reverse traced image and redraw or shade with a soft graphite lead. The traced image can now be fixed faceup on a clean sheet of drawing paper and, via a third redrawing, accurately transferred.

For direct tracing, non-smear graphite and white-, yellow-, blue-, and red-coated sheets are available. Use them like carbon paper to transfer designs to most surfaces.

The pantograph is a demountable rescaling instrument comprised of four calibrated bars made either from metal, plastic, or wood. The bars can be readjusted along the calibrations for--on more sophisticated models--up to forty different ratios of enlargement and reduction.

For a reduction, the tracing pin (right) is hand-guided around the contours of the original image, while the drawing point (center) remains free to trace the rescaled image. For an enlargement, tracing pin and drawing point positions are dismantled and reversed.

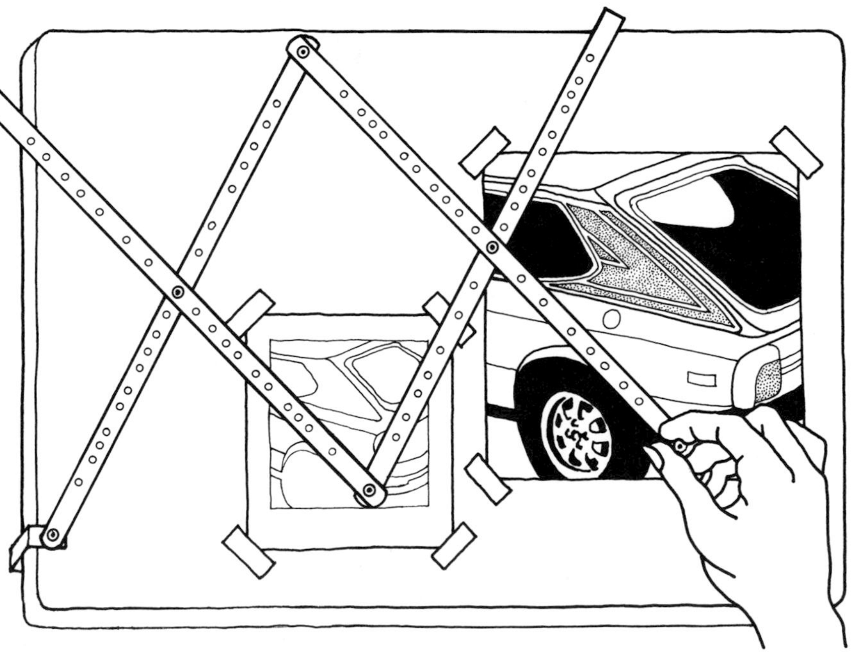

Enlarging and Reducing: Manual

A simple way of rescaling a drawing or a photograph accurately is to superimpose the image with a grid. This can be drawn directly onto the image or overlaid using tracing paper or film.

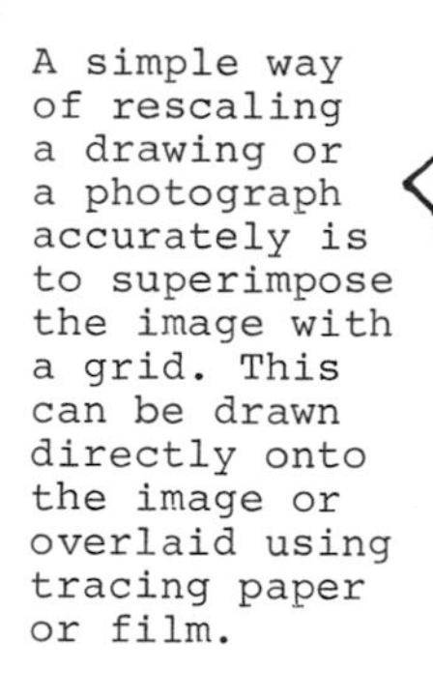

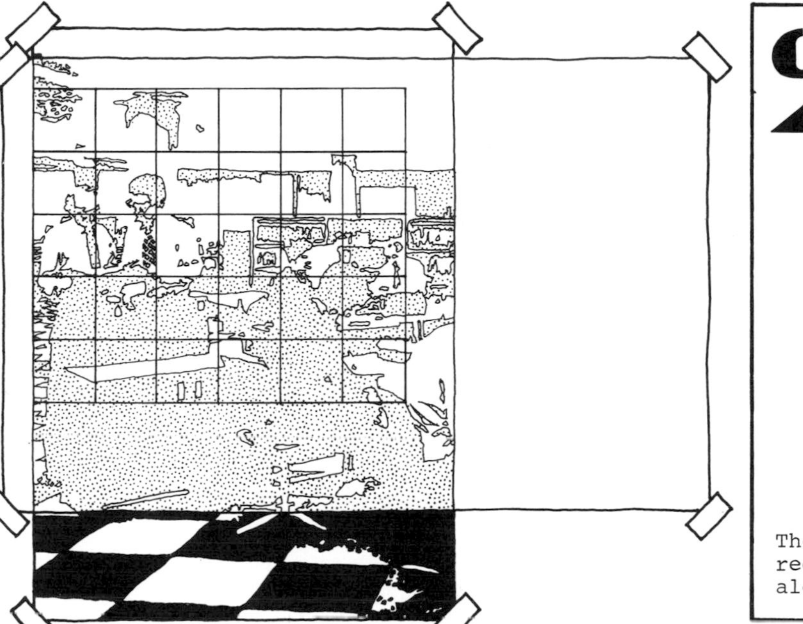

The grid should then be lightly duplicated in pencil to the scale required on the drawing board. Geometric drawings are best fixed alongside the original so that angles can be easily transferred.

Outlines, tones, or colors can now be confidently transferred one square at a time onto the artwork.

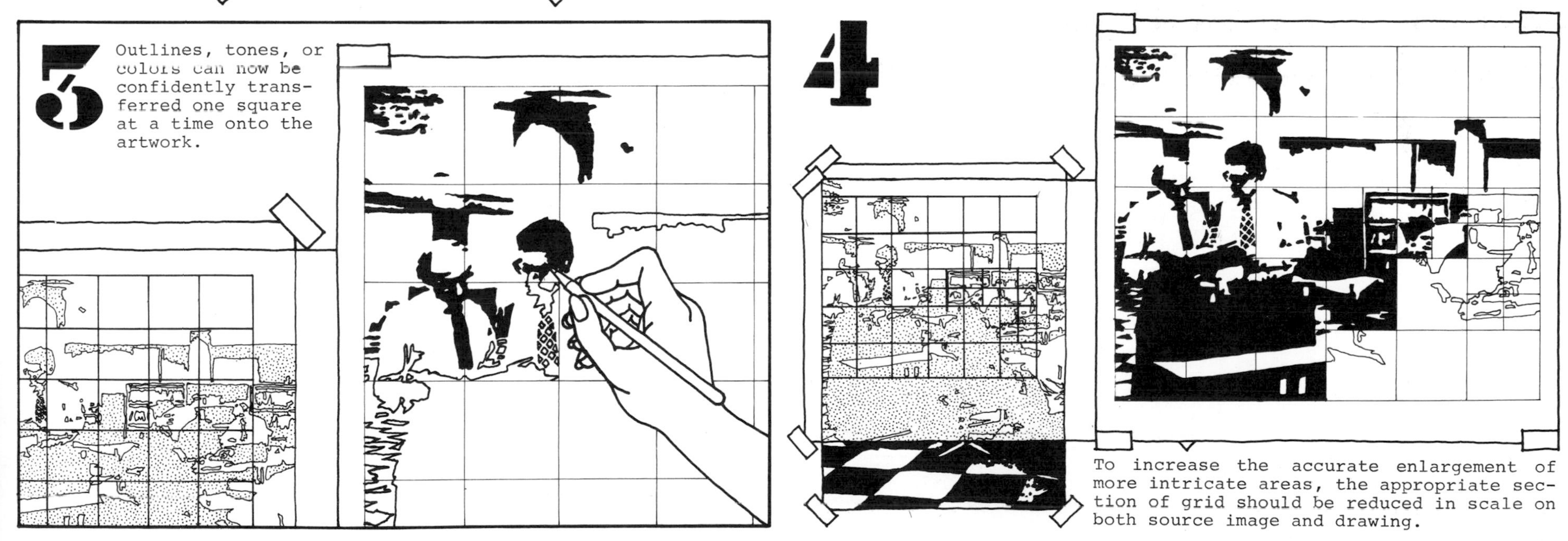

To increase the accurate enlargement of more intricate areas, the appropriate section of grid should be reduced in scale on both source image and drawing.

Enlarging and Reducing: Mechanical

1

Opaque projectors (Episcopes) are useful when enlarging artwork, drawings, or photographs for viewing or copying. Originals which exceed the retractable shelf size can be projected in sections.

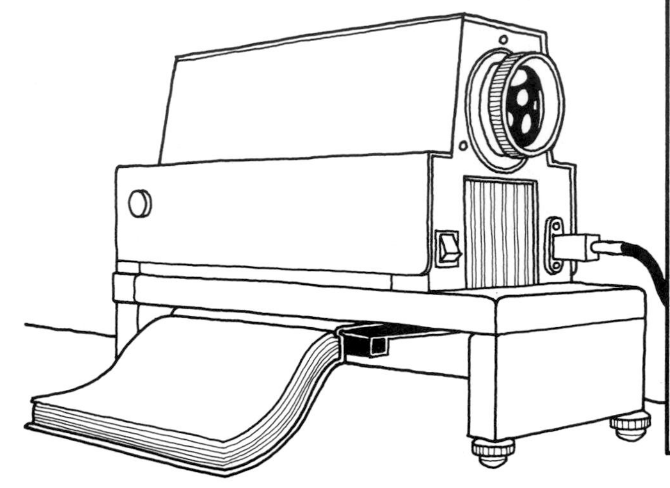

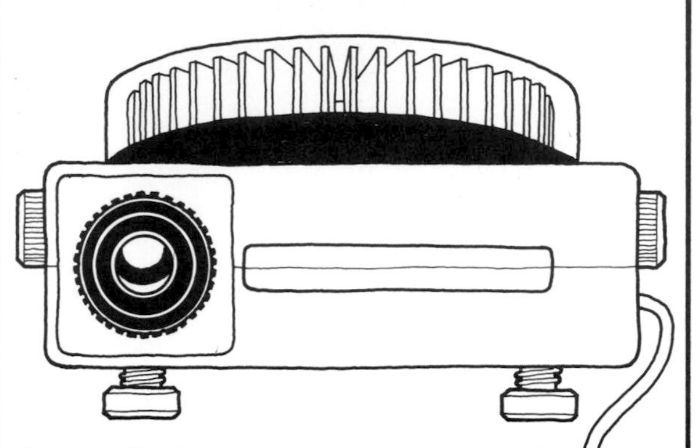

Slide Projectors are capable of throwing extremely large and detailed transparent images for graphic reproduction. Their enlargement potential is limited only by the amount of information contained on the slide and, when having taken a special transparency, the duration of processing.

2

Overhead Projectors accept images on acetate and film. Although essentially a presentation device, photo-negatives can be enlarged over short distances and ideas--worked in special water-based markers--originated directly on the stage, and immediately viewed at a larger scale.

4

The more sophisticated photocopying machines offer a 1/2 times and sometimes a 1/4 times reduction from opaque and transparent originals which fit within the dimensions of their platens. This is ideal for filing and reports, but regulate the tone control for optimum-quality halftone prints.

Indirect Projectors are sophisticated light tables. All kinds of graphic originals--even three-dimensional objects--can be placed on the copyboard for enlargement or reduction. Images are projected via a lens to the tracing table and transferred by the designer onto translucent material.

5

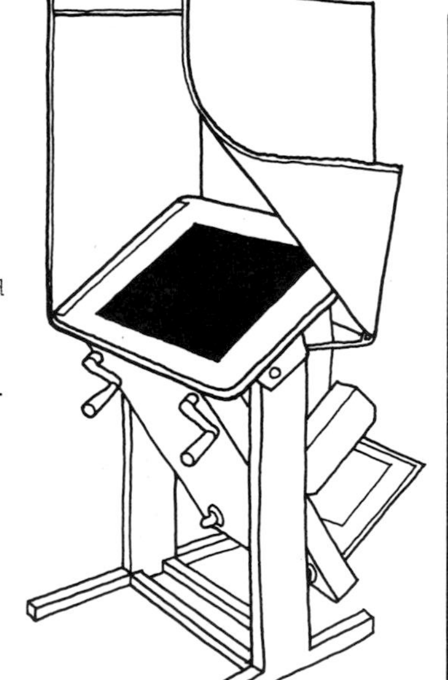

The Direct Projector is the ultimate rescaling machine. The master is placed on the copyboard and its image projected through a lens-and-mirror system for direct copying onto any drawing surface. Copyboard and drawing table sizes vary, but most permit a 4 times enlargement and a 1/4 times reduction.

6

Enlarging Visuals on Opaque Projectors (Episcopes)

Drawings or prints can be easily enlarged via the opaque projector method. Projected images can be traced in line on translucent material for diazo reproduction or worked directly in color on drawing paper.

Sequences of convincing drawings can be quickly delineated from projected photographs. If required, additional images from magazines, such as figures, foliage, and automobiles, can then be carefully projected into position and integrated into large visuals.

Using two carefully coordinated photographs--one of a design model, and one of its site--it is possible to first delineate the outline of the model, then to project and copy the setting before returning to the slide of the model to complete the drawing. The resultant integration of "existing" and "proposed" creates large and impressive presentation drawings.

Letterforms projected from dry-transfer sheets, typeface catalogues, magazines, or small-scale paste-ups can be enlarged for entitling large drawings or in the fast production of large posters.

The Photocopying Process

1

The smaller-sized reproduction capability of photocopy machines makes them an excellent means of producing instant reports and brochures. They also allow for paste-up and photomontage origination; for alterations, additions, and deletions to be made to drawings and text; and for reduction and enlargement. Originals larger than the platen size can be reproduced in sections.

2

3

The direct-transfer process uses print paper which is itself coated with a zinc-oxide photoconductor. The image is developed in the machine, using either a dry or liquid method. Output by direct photocopiers is limited to opaque material.

4

Input on most indirect photocopiers can include computer printouts, text and typescript, photographs, illustrations, and artwork in line, solid, halftone, or color--and even three-dimensional objects. Depending upon the machine, output can be same size or rescaled, single or double-sided, on plain or colored paper--or transposed into transparencies for overhead projection, overlays and offset or diazo masters.

There are two basic kinds of electrostatic photocopiers--indirect and direct transfer. In indirect transfer (xerography), the image of the original is formed in powder on a photoconductive surface in the machine before transfer to the print material--this is known as the "dry process." Another form of indirect-transfer copying using liquid developer is known as the "liquid-dry" process.

5

The advent of color xerography must be of interest to designers. Artwork can be color-processed by photocopier and reproduced in full color on bond paper or converted into color transparencies for overhead projection presentations. Color contact prints or enlargements up to 8 1/4" x 11 3/4" (A4) can be produced on opaque or transparent materials from 35-mm positive color slides.

The Diazo Print Process

Diazo (dyeline or whiteprinting) is a fast process of same-size printing from large original drawings worked in opaque mediums on translucent papers and film. The chemically treated print papers offer a basic range of image colors on finishes such as textured, matte, and glossy on various weights of paper.

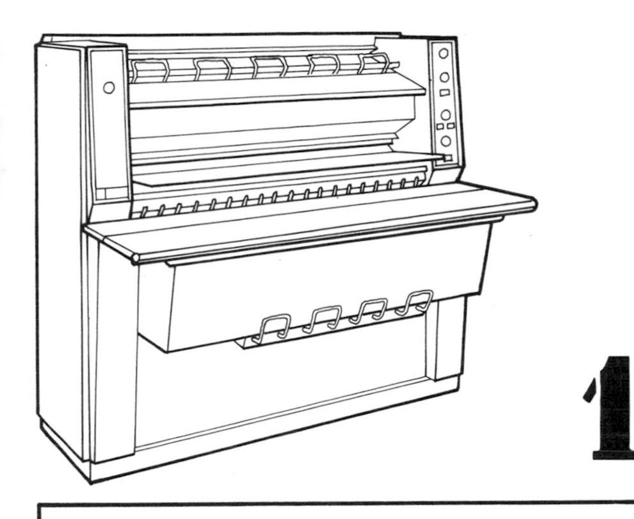

1

Originals are placed faceup over the side of the print paper with the light-sensitive coating, and fed into the machine for the first printing phase. This involves the exposure of the print paper as it rotates around a glass cylinder emitting a high-intensity ultraviolet light.

The second operation depends upon which diazo process is used. In the ammonia process--after automatic or manual separation from the original--the exposed print is developed in ammonia vapors; in the semi-dry process, the print passes through rollers carrying a developing solution.

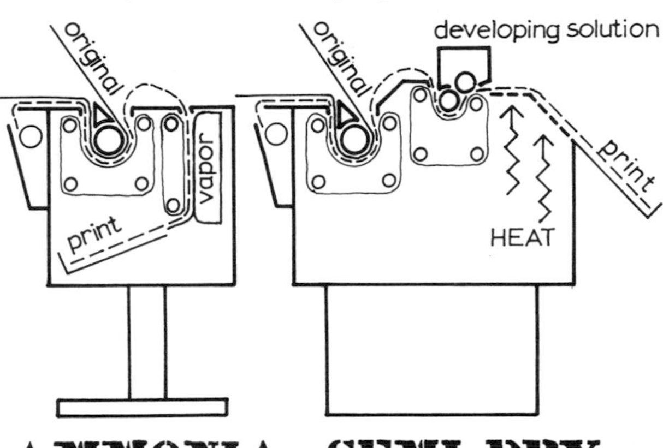

The ammonia process reproduces superior-quality prints--potential for color being inherent in the print paper, i.e., black-, blue-, sepia-, or red-line. The semi-dry process developers offer black, blue, red, and yellow color images--the print paper finish being more receptive to subsequent color washes. In the latter process, exposed glossy prints may be retrieved from the machine and various developers applied by hand to create multicolored images.

4

Levels of contrast between printed image and background are regulated by the exposure setting on the machine. The faster the setting, the less time the coating is exposed to the light, and, therefore, less coating will be burned off--producing a darker print. Experimental prints should be made with originals carrying tonal variations.

5

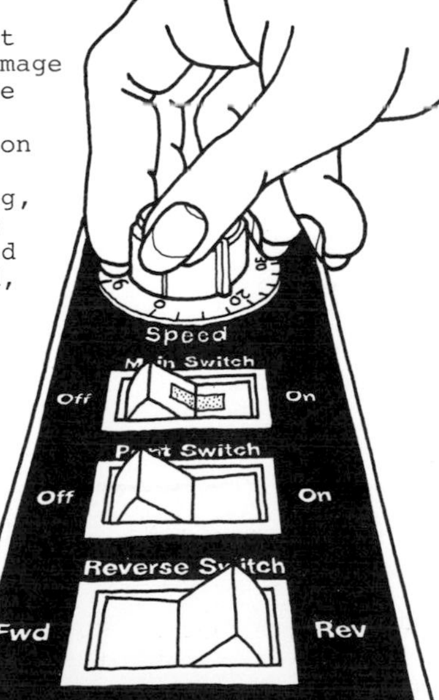

The original drawing is referred to as a "negative." For making extended print runs, amended drawings, and copies of negatives for the addition of different types of information, the negative can be transposed onto coated tracing paper, sepia paper, or polyester film--the latter being more durable. This print is known as an "intermediate" or "copy negative." To make an intermediate, place the negative face-down onto the coated surface of the recipient material and feed into the machine.

How to Enlarge a Slide into a Diazo Print

1 Pin a sheet of unexposed print paper to a wall in a darkroom or darkened studio (with the semi-dry diazo process use "normal" print paper; with the ammonia diazo process use black-line, blue-line, etc.).

2 Aim a projector fitted with a quartz halogen lamp at the print paper. Insert required slide, switch on, and focus the image.

3 An image size projected from a distance of 4 feet will take approximately thirty to forty minutes to expose. For larger images, the Inverse Square Law operates, i.e., doubling the image size requiring four times the exposure time. However, the progress of the exposure can be monitored by quickly switching the light in the room on and off.

4 When the exposure process is completed, protect the light-sensitive print surface until developing by diazo in the normal way. The developed print is useful in several ways, e.g., for coloring, and for integration with drawings, photomontage, collage, posters, and so on.

How to Diazo Print Photographic Images

1 Place a sheet of clear acetate film or thin, smooth, semi-opaque tracing paper into the feeder tray of an indirect-transfer photocopier designed to process translucent materials. The sheet size must be compatible with that acceptable to the machine.

2 Next, position the required photographic image or photomontage facedown on the glass platen and proceed with the photocopying operation.

3 The resultant print can now be used as a "negative" for reproduction by diazo printing (smaller format images photocopied on acetate can also be used as transparencies for overhead projection or as overlay pages in reports).

4 Prior to the diazo stage, an accompanying title or support caption can be applied directly to the film or tracing paper using inked or dry-transfer lettering.

5 Diazo reproduction of photocopied "negatives" proves highly economical for long runs of posters, handouts, and flyers, etc.

Two Experimental Diazo Prints

LINE WEIGHTS : PENCIL, INK, MARKERS

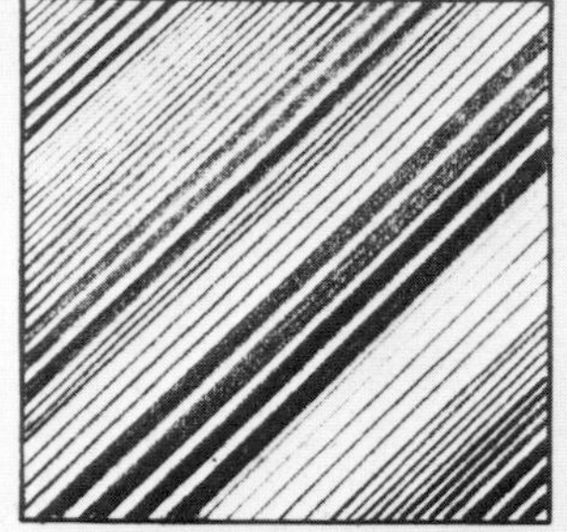

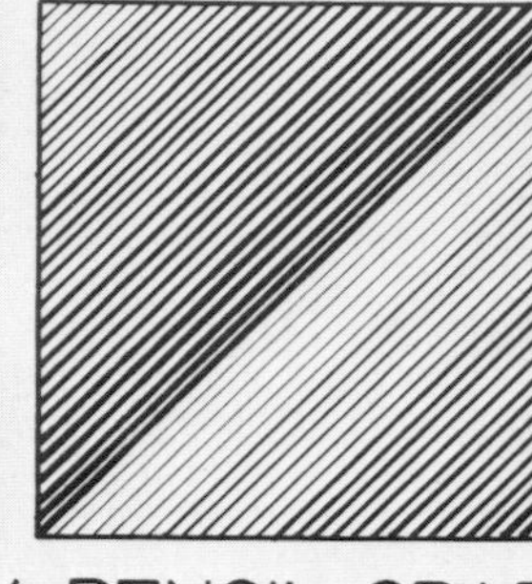

TEXTURES : INK, PENCIL, GRAPHITE DUST

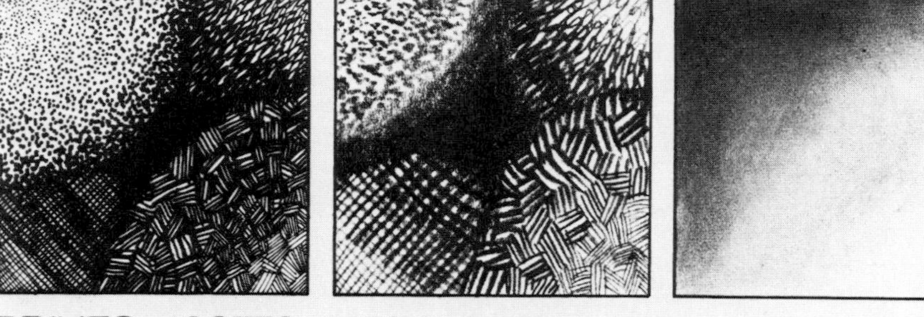

PRINTS : COTTON WOOL, TISSUE PAPER, POTATO

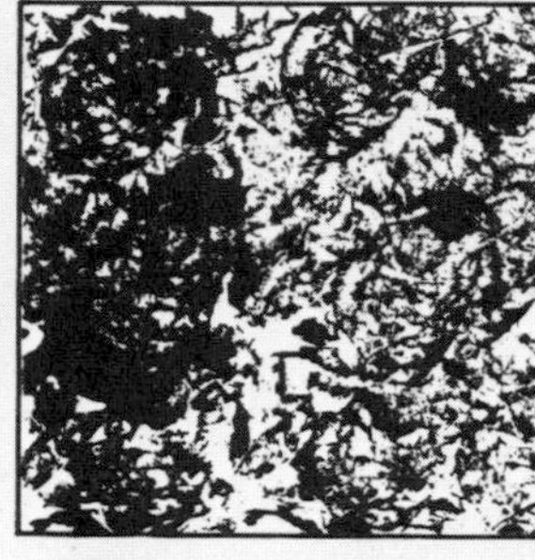

1 In order to discover the potential range of diazo effects, it is worth compiling an annotated reference "dictionary" of line weights, tonal values, and textures. Various inks, graphites, and methods of application on tracing paper and film should be explored.

2 Colored pencils, water-based markers, and aerosols used on diazo negatives are also potentials for creating tonal value and textures on the ultimate print. Experiment with colored lines, tonal gradations, and solids and after printing, mark and code the more useful pencils and pens for future diazo use.

Hints for Diazo Prints

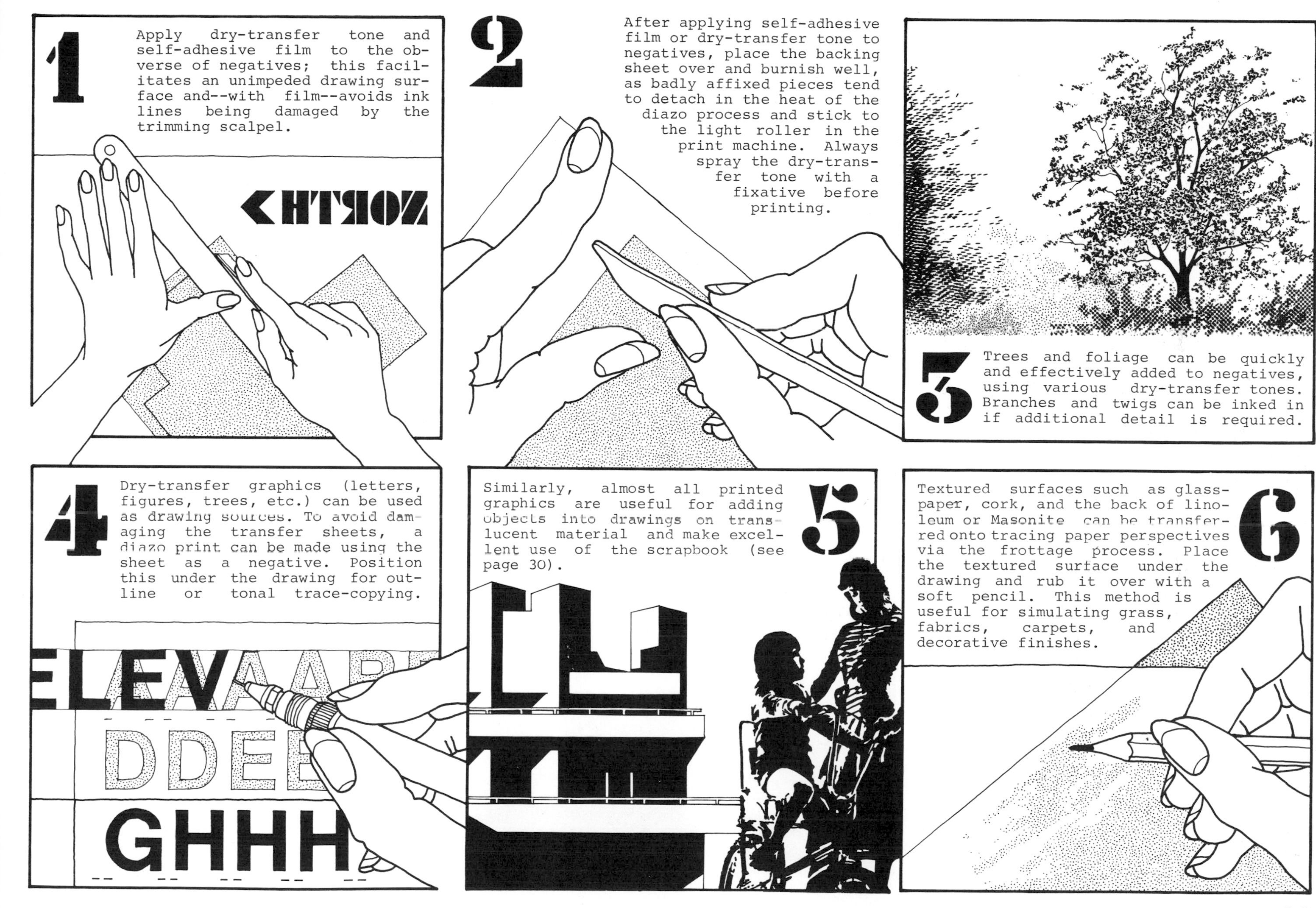

1 Apply dry-transfer tone and self-adhesive film to the obverse of negatives; this facilitates an unimpeded drawing surface and--with film--avoids ink lines being damaged by the trimming scalpel.

2 After applying self-adhesive film or dry-transfer tone to negatives, place the backing sheet over and burnish well, as badly affixed pieces tend to detach in the heat of the diazo process and stick to the light roller in the print machine. Always spray the dry-transfer tone with a fixative before printing.

3 Trees and foliage can be quickly and effectively added to negatives, using various dry-transfer tones. Branches and twigs can be inked in if additional detail is required.

4 Dry-transfer graphics (letters, figures, trees, etc.) can be used as drawing sources. To avoid damaging the transfer sheets, a diazo print can be made using the sheet as a negative. Position this under the drawing for outline or tonal trace-copying.

5 Similarly, almost all printed graphics are useful for adding objects into drawings on translucent material and make excellent use of the scrapbook (see page 30).

6 Textured surfaces such as glasspaper, cork, and the back of linoleum or Masonite can be transferred onto tracing paper perspectives via the frottage process. Place the textured surface under the drawing and rub it over with a soft pencil. This method is useful for simulating grass, fabrics, carpets, and decorative finishes.

Hints for Diazo Prints

1 Elevation drawings appear complete when a sky is added. After masking around the sky area on the obverse of the drawing, graphite dust--collected from a pointer--can be applied using a pad of soft tissue paper.

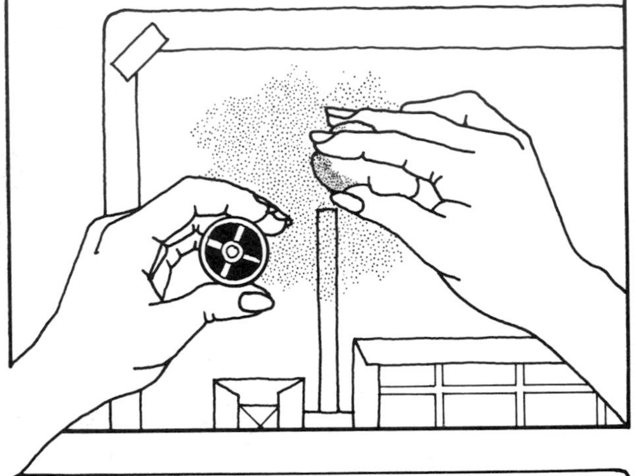

2 Cloud formations can then be indicated with a soft putty-type eraser; darker areas can be added into the drawing, using a soft pencil such as a 6B.

3 The completed image should then be stabilized with a spray fixative before printing.

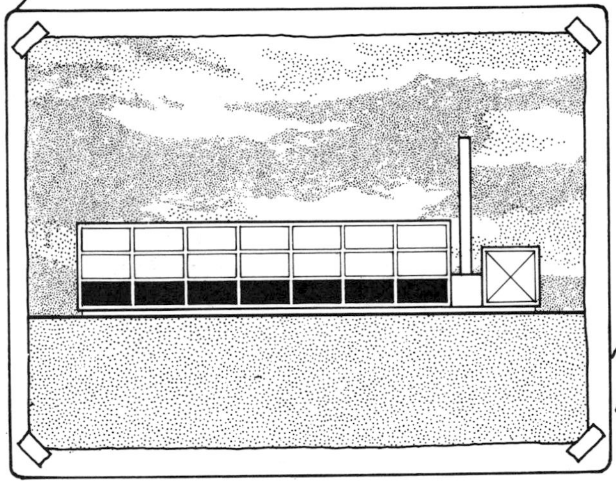

1 To establish sections and elevations on the sheet, the baseline can be effectively extended by using light aerosol spray (in red or green) on the face of the sheet.

2 Titles can be integrated by trace-cutting the required lettering in frisket overlaid on a typeface alphabet--then positioned onto the sheet.

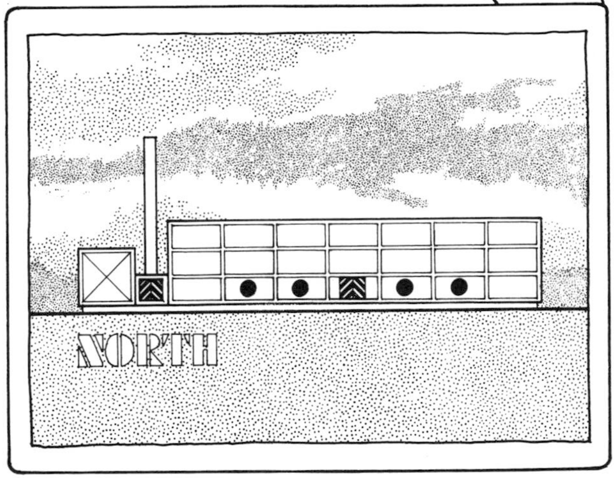

3 After the spray operation and prior to printing, the frisket is removed to reveal the title against its tonal background.

Hints for Diazo Prints

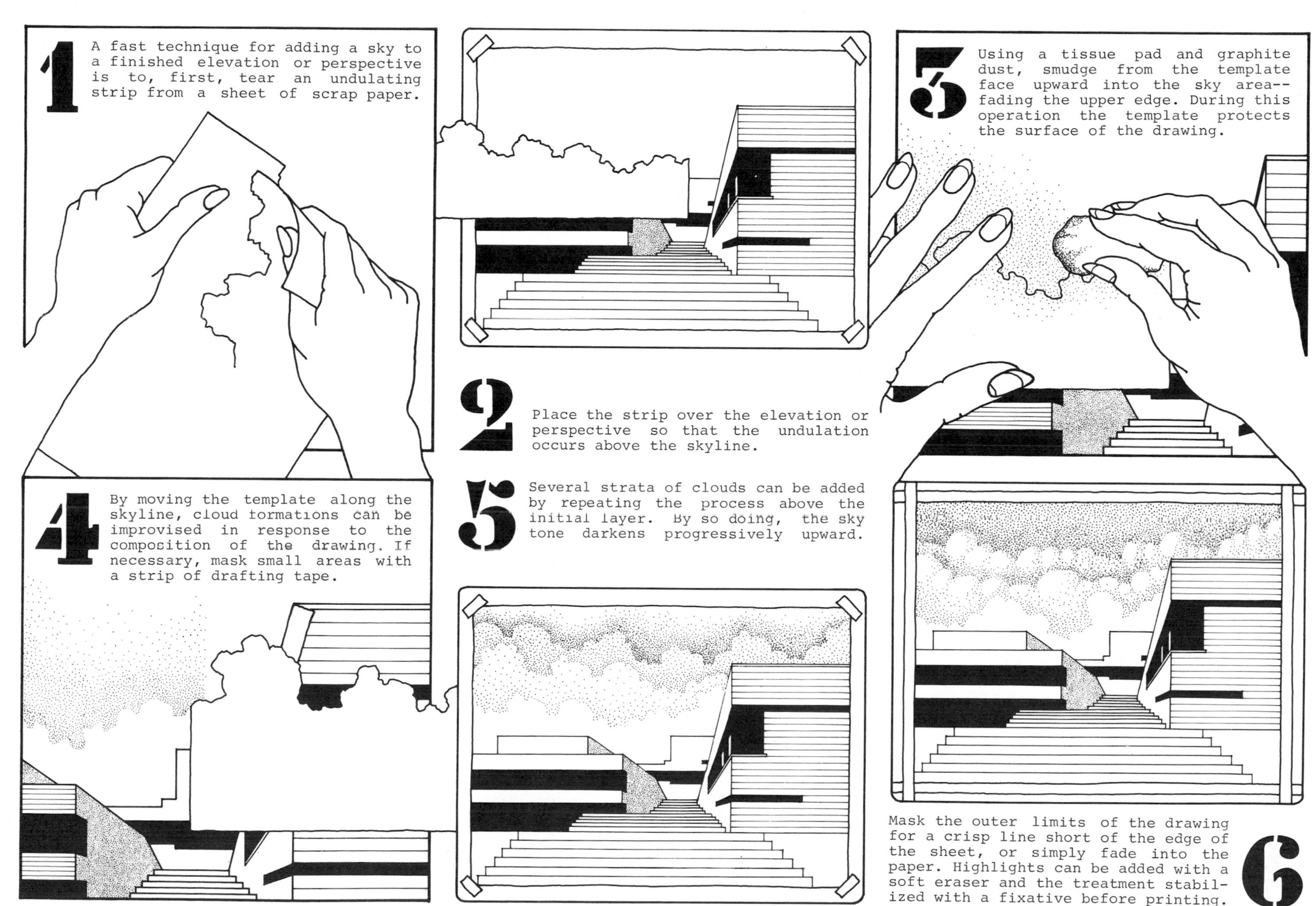

The Camera as a Design Tool

1

The camera is a primary design aid. It is essential to the analytical recording of environment, as a support to drawing techniques, the documenting of completed projects, and--in conjunction with a slide projector--the transforming, rescaling, and presenting of pictures from artwork and models.

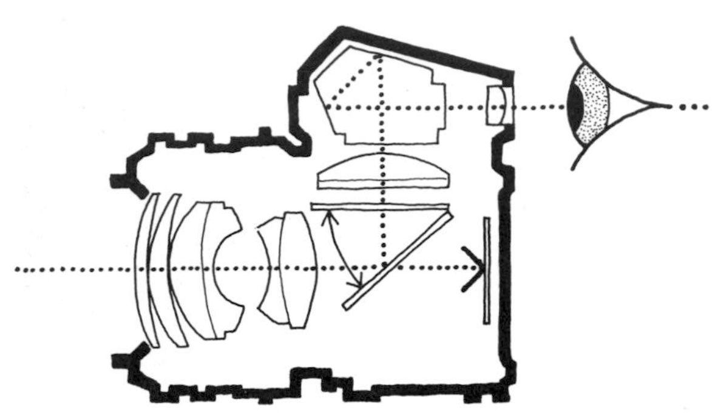

The most practical camera for all these design functions is the single-lens reflex, as it allows a virtually identical viewfinder preview of the ultimate image.

Photographic prints can be used as underlays, and projected slides used as overlays, in the production of directly traced, same-size analytical drawings of space, i.e., design drawings which extract and focus upon a particularly relevant aspect of an image.

N.B.: The camera should never be used to substitute a drawing experience for, being "one-eyed," its discriminatory powers are severely limited when compared with the dynamics of human vision.

2

The single-lens reflex camera is adequate for all kinds of daytime studio and fieldwork without the need for auxiliary lighting. When buying new or second-hand, make sure that the camera body will accept interchangeable lenses.

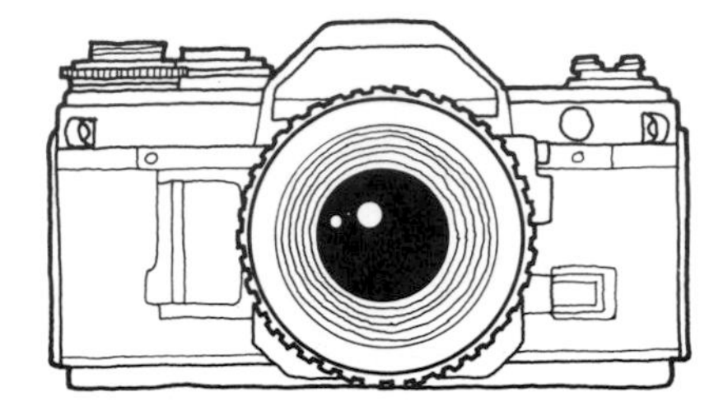

A recommended general-purpose lens for most outdoor and indoor design photography is an f/2.8, 50-mm Macro lens. Additional recommended specialized lenses are 28-mm wide-angle lens for interiors, eye-level views, models, and photography in tight spaces; 135 telephoto lens for the long-distance avoidance of warped perspective on details and large elevations.

Beyond the photographic creation of still pictures, the designer should also experience the fourth dimension when image-making--for it is movement which is central to our understanding of space. Video tape recording (VTR) not only necessitates a dynamic perception in its use, but also provides instantaneous playback together with the potential of linking the designer to a mass audience.

3

The Polaroid camera is a useful design tool. Its instant, fixed-size monochrome or color prints are appropriate for on-the-spot graphic references which can, if required, be enlarged by opaque projector for tracing.

6

Its use, however, requires some preplanning and, in order to save time and tape, intentions should be clearly determined prior to filming.

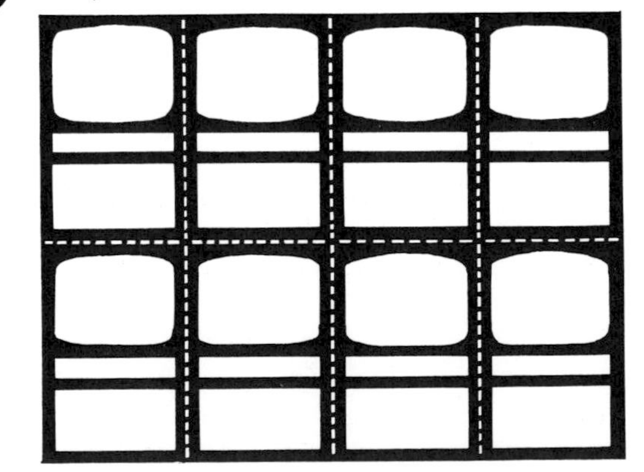

TV storyboards are marketed for the planning and communicating of ideas for video sequences. These are in booklet form containing pages of perforated 3"x4" frames--accompanied by spaces for titles and audio notes.

Analytical Photo-Sketch Techniques

1 Using a squared-up photograph as a source, several techniques based upon a range of perceptual attitudes can become the basis for future freehand drawing techniques.

2 In this drawing, only the massing has been isolated through a delineation of skyline and base line.

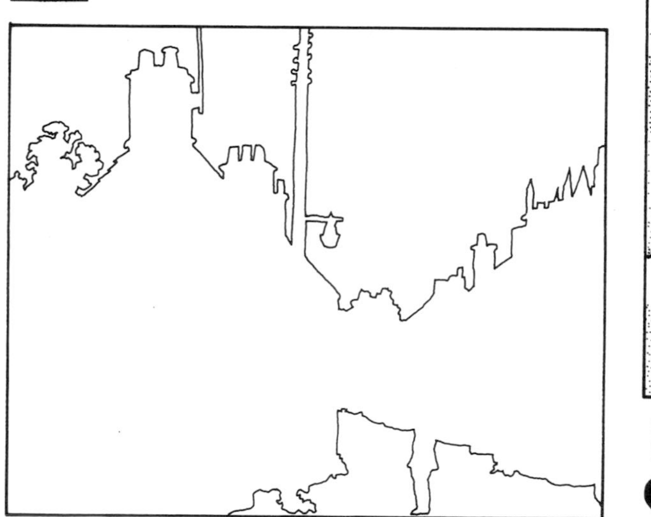

3 Another method is the translation of the tonal range in the photograph into a system of four tones--plus white paper--in the drawing.

4 A drawing concentrating purely on the configuration and the surface quality of materials and substances.

5 This is a drawing of space; a delineated study of the shape of sections of space between objects--rather than outlines of form.

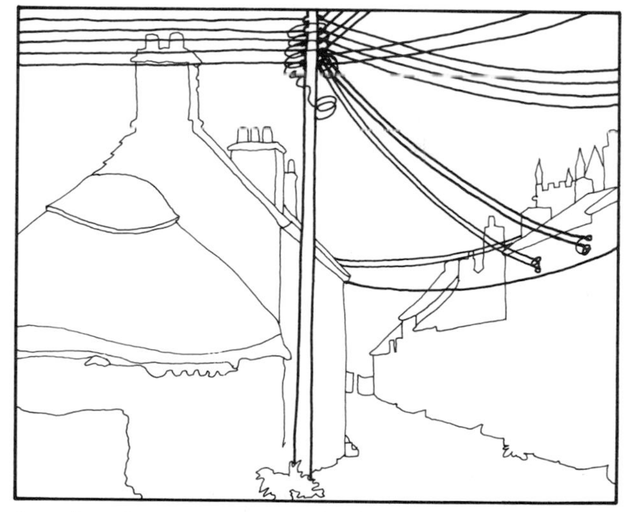

6 Drawing is a means of visually analyzing and recording aspects of our visual experience; each drawing should, therefore, make a point and communicate it clearly.

Camera in Design: Site Appraisal

1 Existing sites can be systematically documented with the camera. First, photograph the long-distance implications of the site from vantage points such as tall buildings or hillsides.

Conversely, the on-site shots should record spatial links from inside out: routes and shuttered, filtered, sneak, and panoramic views into surrounding space.

2 Next, shoot all access routes and visual links--sneak glimpses, views, etc.--from around the immediate site periphery looking in.

4 On-site photographs should also document the mass and details of the impinging forms: materials, openings, textures, colors, etc.

5 Make annotated sketches which describe your impressions of the quality of each of the subjects of the above photographs.

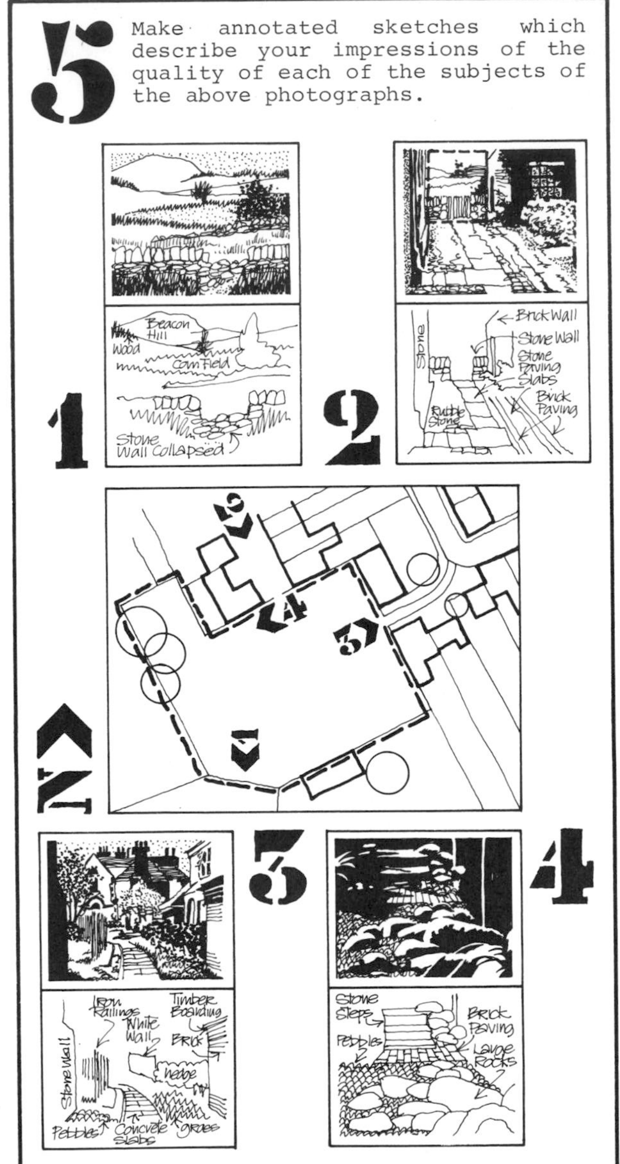

Photographs should be coordinated with a key plan showing direction and the position of each shot--this aids orientation during future reference in design.

Functions of Models in Design

1 Conceptual models are three-dimensional diagrams fabricated from responsive materials--flexible in substance or module--which symbolize the components and relationships of a new design idea.

2

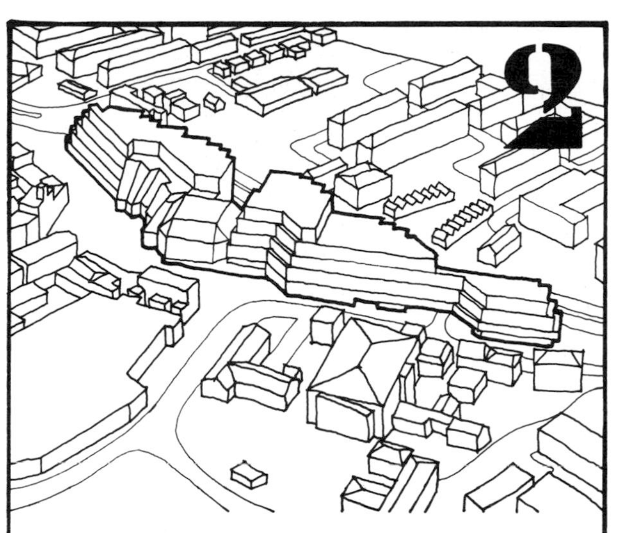

Block models carve the external mass of a developing idea, often exploring the implications of an intended built form in relation to its site and surrounding mass.

3 Skeletal models examine the functional determinants in isolation from surrounding features. They can act as physical working drawings studying structure, assembly, or service systems.

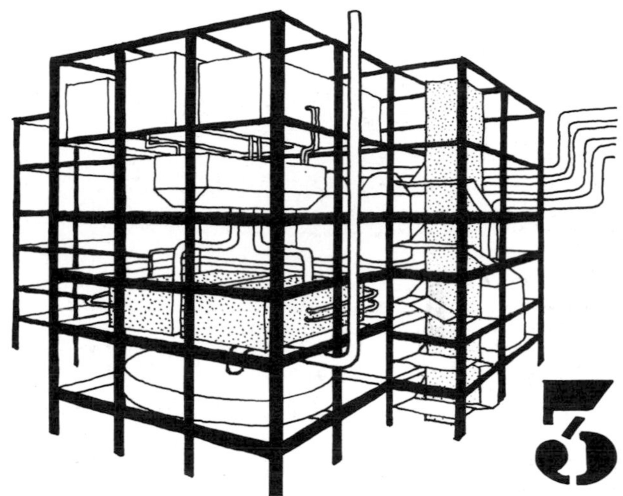

4

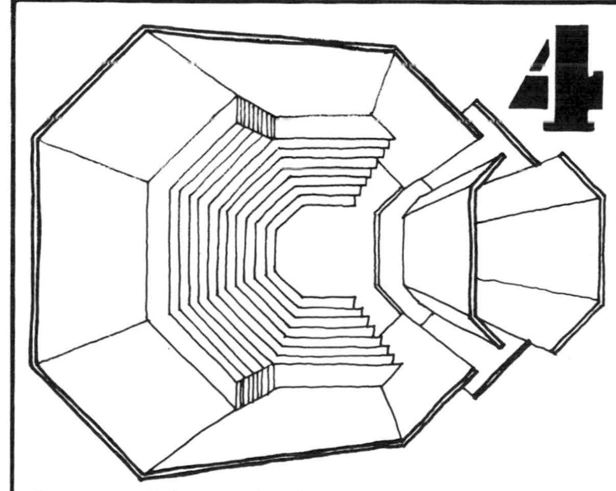

Space models articulate plane and surface in exterior or interior, individual, or sequential space. Sophisticated versions can simulate both natural and artificial illumination.

5 Presentation models represent the total composition of a design solution and communicate its finality. Being built for promotion rather than decision-making, they are less flexible.

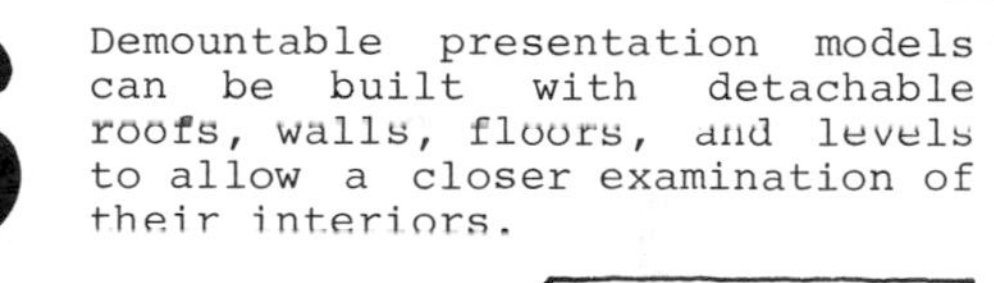

6 Demountable presentation models can be built with detachable roofs, walls, floors, and levels to allow a closer examination of their interiors.

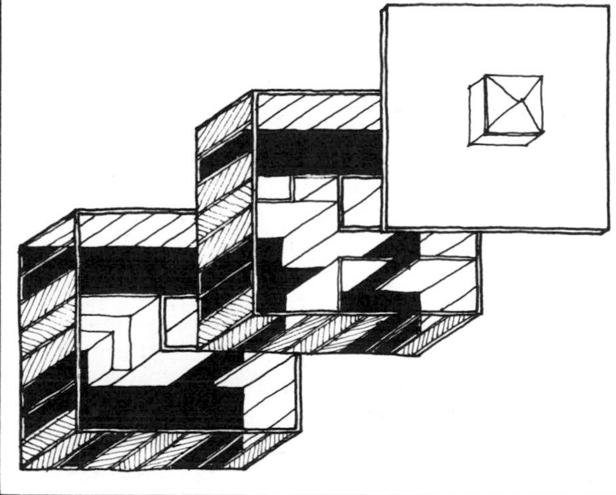

Basic Modelmaking Materials and Finishes

Modelmaking Adhesives

1 General-purpose spirit and petroleum-based contact adhesives are applied to both surfaces and left to dry between--depending upon which proprietary glue is used--ten seconds and fifteen minutes. The surfaces bond immediately when pressed together. They are used for plastic laminating and wood veneering, plastic foam (not Styrofoam), Masonite, metal, to wood and many other materials. Remove excess glue with carbon tetrachloride or acetone (nail polish remover).

2 Balsa cement is a cellulose-based, quick-drying, clear adhesive formulated especially for balsa wood modeling. It is also useful for general modeling in wood, card, metal, sheet acetate, and glass. Dried-on glue can be removed with acetone, or cut away with a sharp blade.

3 Polystyrene (plastic) cement is for use only with hard plastic materials such as solid polystyrene (not to be used with Styrofoam). Fast-drying and clear, it is removed with acetone or carbon tetrachloride.

4 Polyvinyl acetate (PVA) glues are marketed in washable and non-washable forms. Washable PVAs do not bond strongly. They set in twenty to thirty minutes and are suitable for gluing cardboard, foam plastics, and most materials. Solid materials such as wood should be pinned or clamped together during the drying process. Normal PVAs cannot be cleaned out of fabric when dry.

5 Epoxy resin impact adhesives are two component glues: one tube contains resin, the other hardener. Mixed together, they give a powerful bond to most--and between different--materials, including metal, wood, china, glass, and rubber. Drying time can be accelerated through the admixture of additional hardener. Epoxy resin glues are impervious to solvents; excess glue should be wiped off or cleaned with paint remover before setting.

6 Special custom glues include polyvinyl chloride (PVC) for PVC material and polythene; proprietary non-dissolving pastes for Styrofoam; special adhesive cements for bonding; and acetone solvents for fuse-welding, acrylic sheets, and celluloid.

Basic Cutting Tools for Modelmaking

Industrial razor blades, scalpels with replaceable blades, craft knives with retractable and replenishable snap-off blades, and circle cutters or swivel blade knives for cutting thin sheets of paper, card, balsa wood, Styrofoam, acetate, etc.

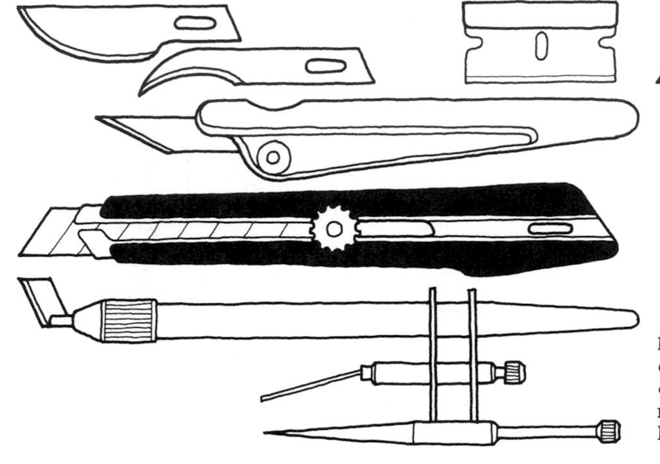

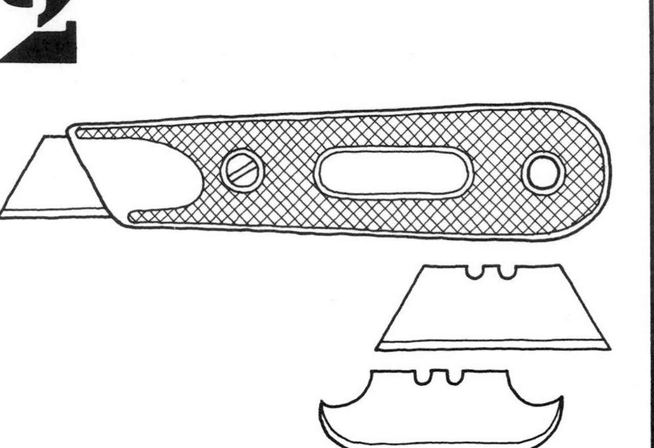

Heavy-duty plasterboard knife with assorted double-pointed and interchangeable blades for general cutting--especially thicker sheet material such as matting boards, cork, cardboard, balsa wood, etc.

For accuracy, cut slowly using a sharp blade or cutting edge; for safety, cut against a firmly held 1/8-inch-thick metal straightedge--always cutting away from fingers. Work on a rigid baseboard such as plywood, blockboard, or plate glass. For lighter cutting work, there is a proprietary "self-healing" cutting mat with graphed sections.

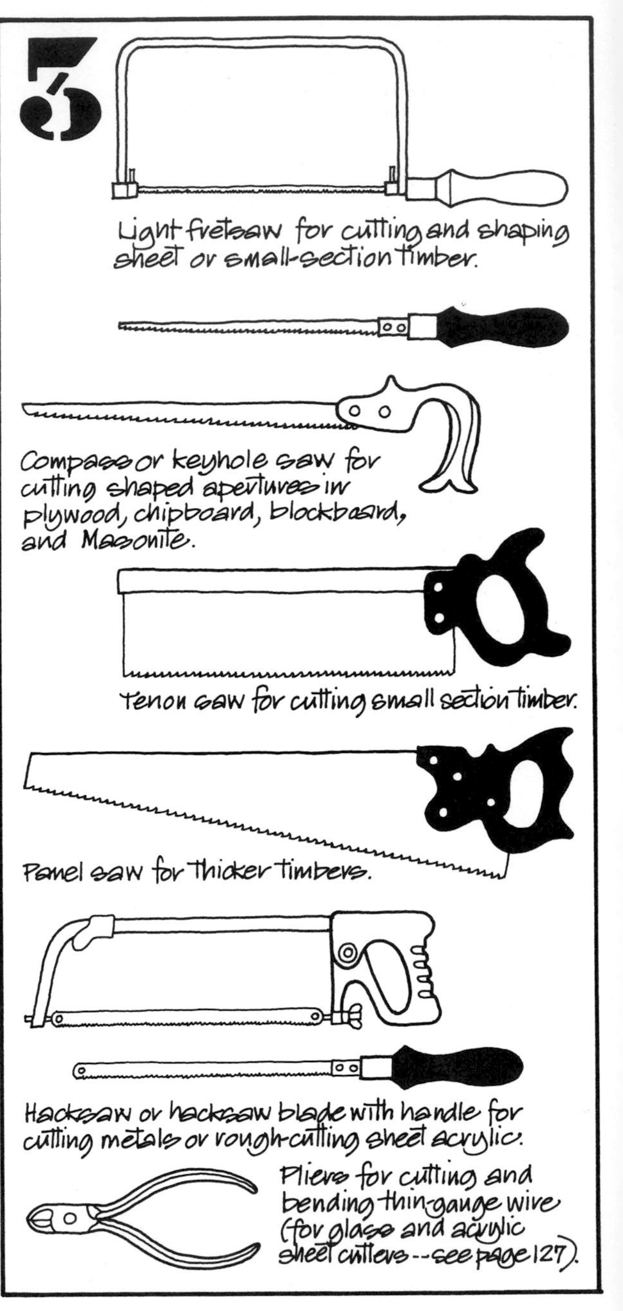

Light fretsaw for cutting and shaping sheet or small-section timber.

Compass or keyhole saw for cutting shaped apertures in plywood, chipboard, blockboard, and Masonite.

Tenon saw for cutting small section timber.

Panel saw for thicker timbers.

Hacksaw or hacksaw blade with handle for cutting metals or rough-cutting sheet acrylic.

Pliers for cutting and bending thin-gauge wire (for glass and acrylic sheet cutters--see page 127).

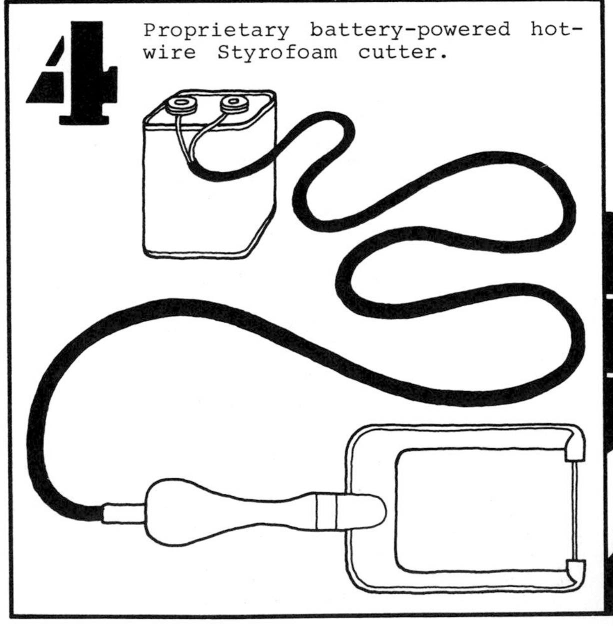

Proprietary battery-powered hot-wire Styrofoam cutter.

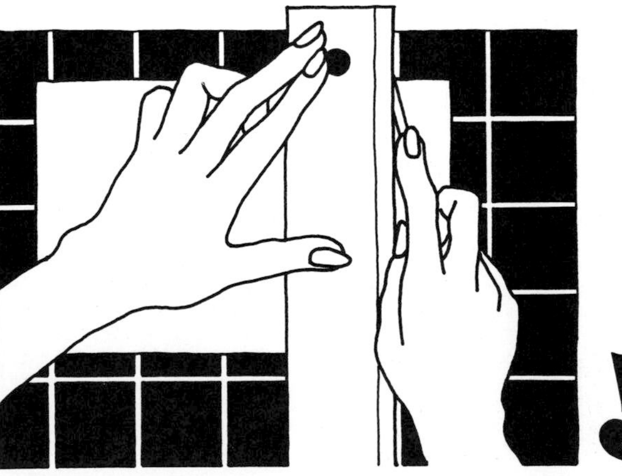

How to Make a Styrofoam Hot-Wire Cutter

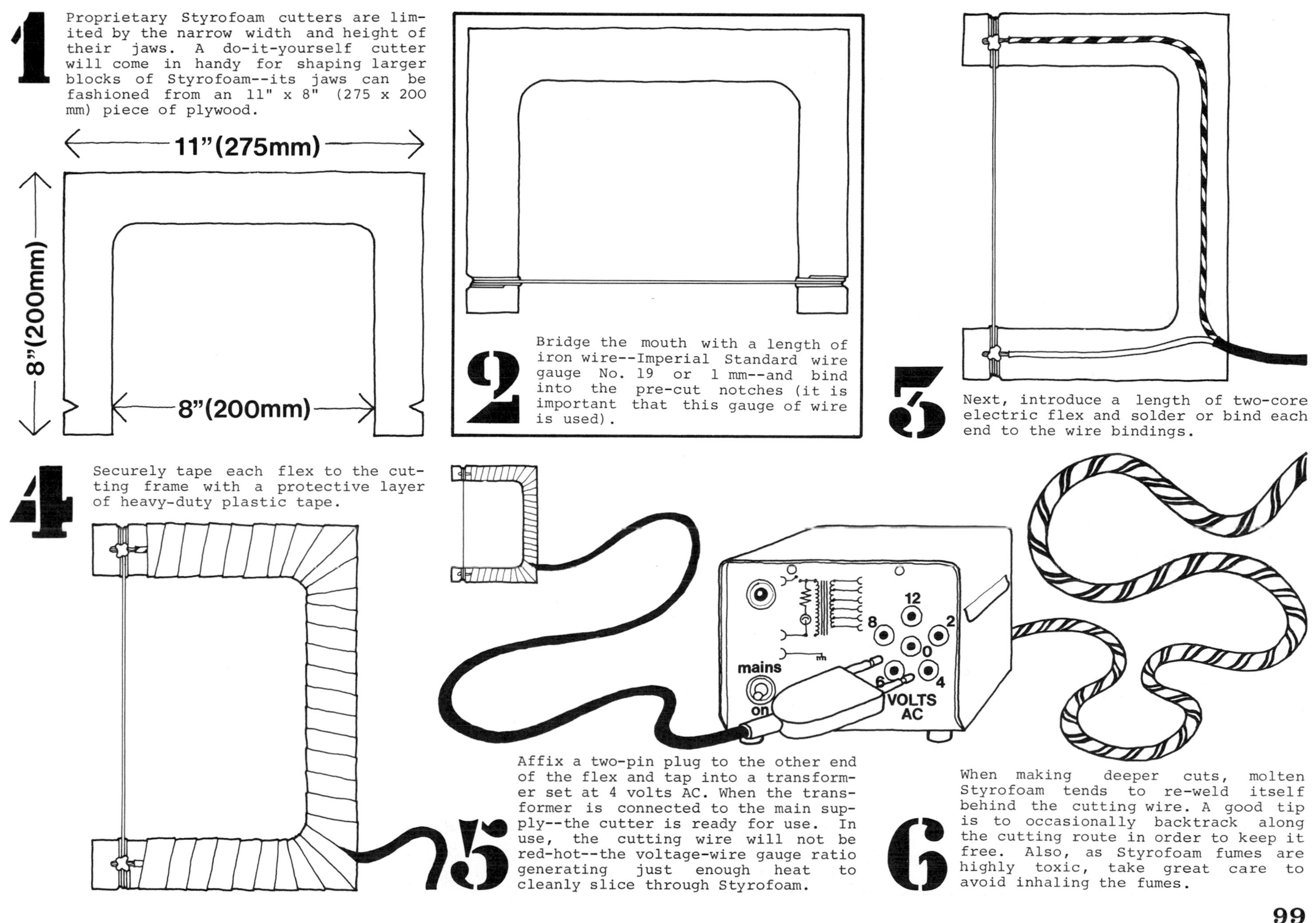

1 Proprietary Styrofoam cutters are limited by the narrow width and height of their jaws. A do-it-yourself cutter will come in handy for shaping larger blocks of Styrofoam--its jaws can be fashioned from an 11" x 8" (275 x 200 mm) piece of plywood.

2 Bridge the mouth with a length of iron wire--Imperial Standard wire gauge No. 19 or 1 mm--and bind into the pre-cut notches (it is important that this gauge of wire is used).

3 Next, introduce a length of two-core electric flex and solder or bind each end to the wire bindings.

4 Securely tape each flex to the cutting frame with a protective layer of heavy-duty plastic tape.

5 Affix a two-pin plug to the other end of the flex and tap into a transformer set at 4 volts AC. When the transformer is connected to the main supply--the cutter is ready for use. In use, the cutting wire will not be red-hot--the voltage-wire gauge ratio generating just enough heat to cleanly slice through Styrofoam.

6 When making deeper cuts, molten Styrofoam tends to re-weld itself behind the cutting wire. A good tip is to occasionally backtrack along the cutting route in order to keep it free. Also, as Styrofoam fumes are highly toxic, take great care to avoid inhaling the fumes.

How to Make a Site Model

Build site models on a rigid base such as chipboard or blockboard. Contours can be assembled from glued layers of colored card, Styrofoam, cork, or Masonite.

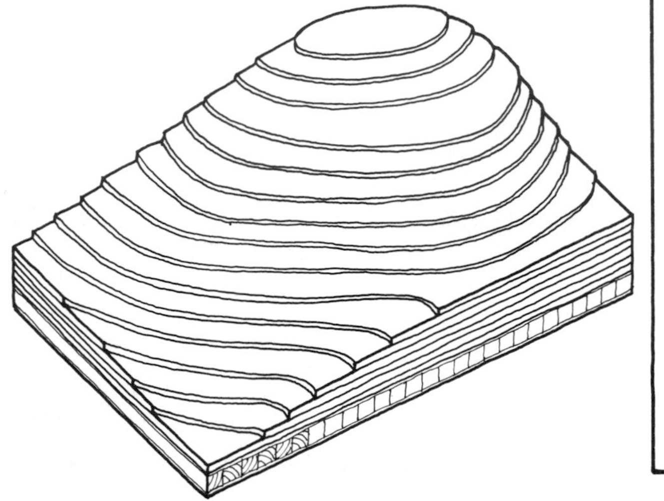

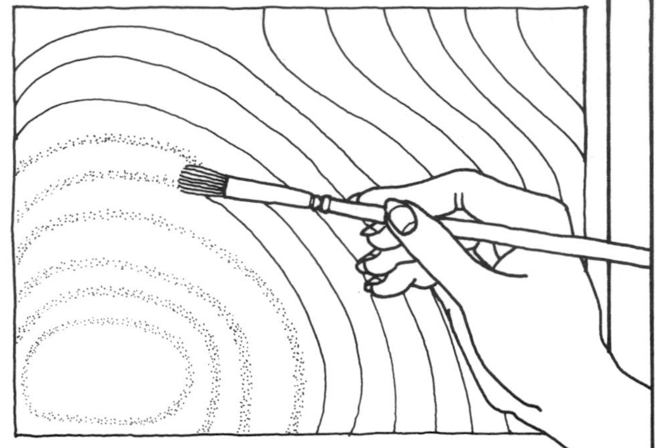

2

If required, contours can be softened with a thin coat of emulsion paint or smoothed off with plaster of paris or a water-based crack-filler medium.

3

For realism, finished surfaces can be painted or sprayed, or coated with glue to receive "powdered grass." Colored particles can be mixed from tempera, sawdust, wallpaper paste, and water (mix, allow to dry, then apply).

4

Trees and foliage can be represented by steel wool, sponge, table tennis balls, paper, twigs, wood shavings, eggshells, or dyed lichen. They can be supported on matches, nails, toothpicks, or pins.

5

Surrounding buildings can be represented by blocks of wood or Styrofoam, Plasticine, cardboard, or even lumps of sugar or toast.

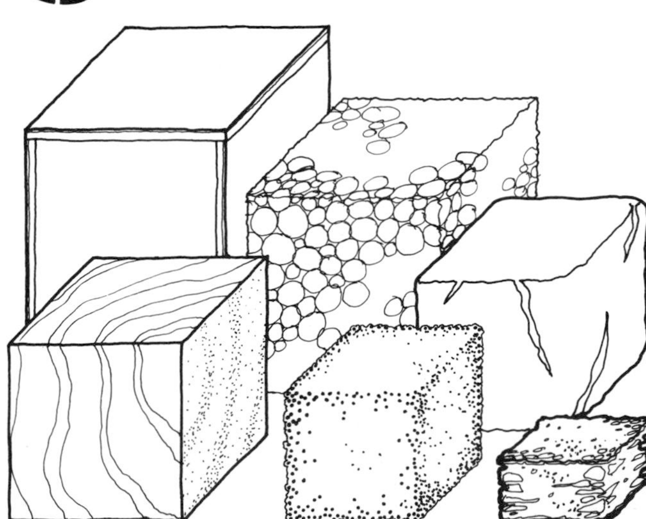

6

Aluminum foil, mirror glass, or sheets of acetate, acrylic, or dry-transfer color film can represent water; cars and figures can be carved--in a simplified form--from balsa wood. Remember that it is always cheaper to invent.

Tips When Making Presentation Models

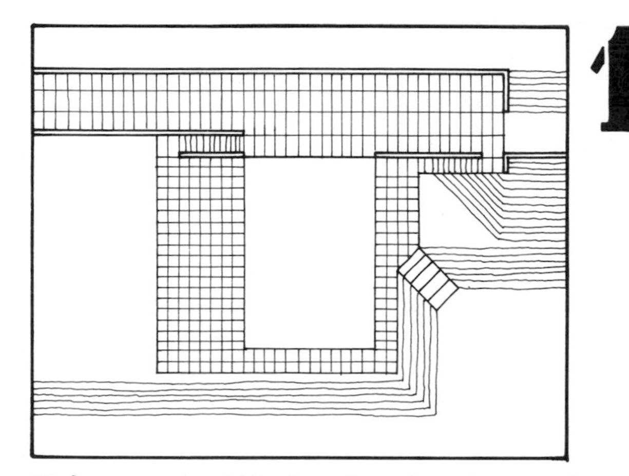

1

Work on a solid baseboard such as plywood blockboard, chipboard, or fiberboard. Indicate groundplan and topographical details of surrounding layout: landscape, paths, streets, etc. Any contours can be laminated using sheet cork, Styrofoam, card, or balsa wood; the base model can then be painted, color-sprayed, or left in a natural finish.

2

Transfer dimensions from orthographic drawings to the required scale on selected model-making material (card-mounted diazo-printed orthographics can be cut out and assembled into fast, effective models).

3

Decide upon a finish: plain, scored, painted, or laminated. To avoid warping, such treatments--including the cutting of apertures--should be worked on the flat prior to assembly.

4

Cut out the basic components of the model --always cutting with the surface finish uppermost. Corners can be butt jointed or mitered for a more professional finish.

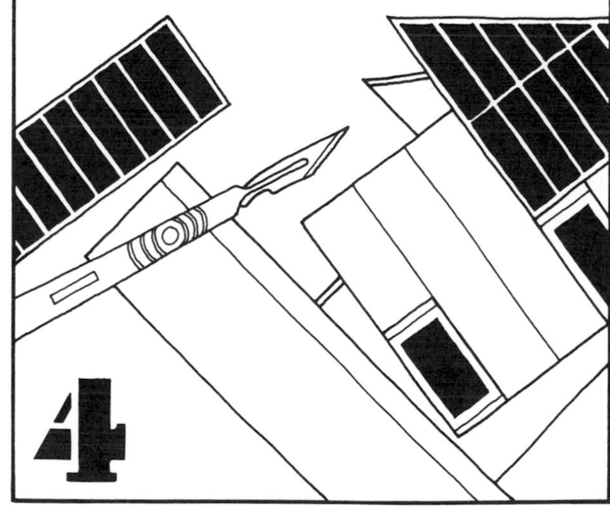

5

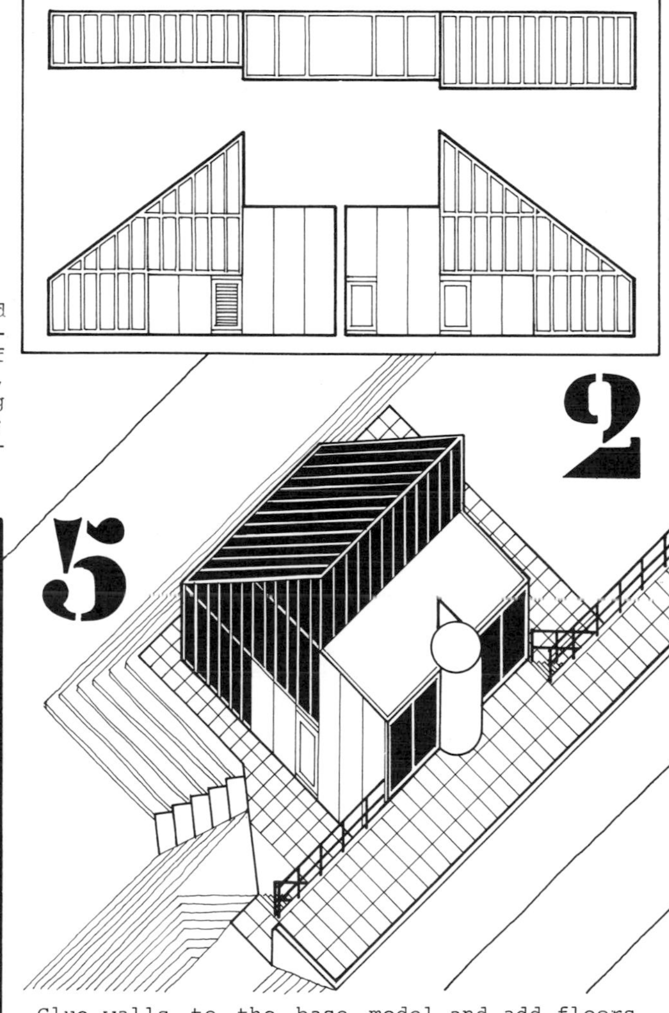

Glue walls to the base model and add floors and roof. Any further appendages such as garden walls, canopies, balconies, etc., can then be added. After the gluing stage, carefully rub joints with fine-grade glasspaper or remove blobs of hardened glue with scalpel.

6

Finally, introduce surrounding base treatments such as trees, shrubbery, people, etc.

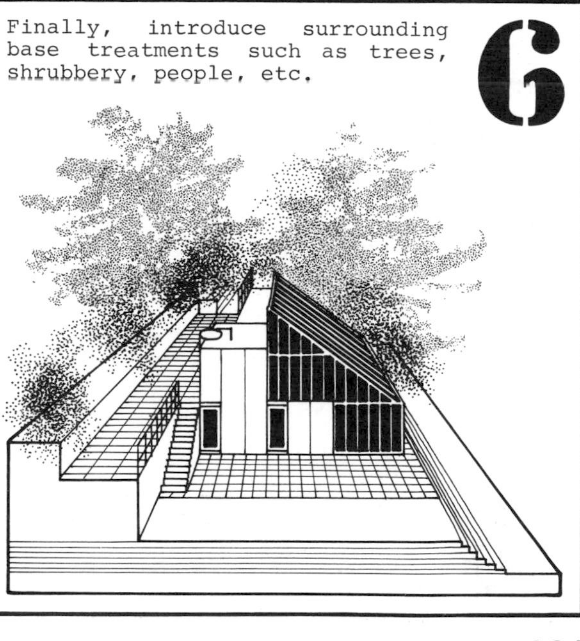

Models as Graphic Aids

1 All types of models become useful devices from which to make perspective sketches either exploring or presenting exterior and interior space.

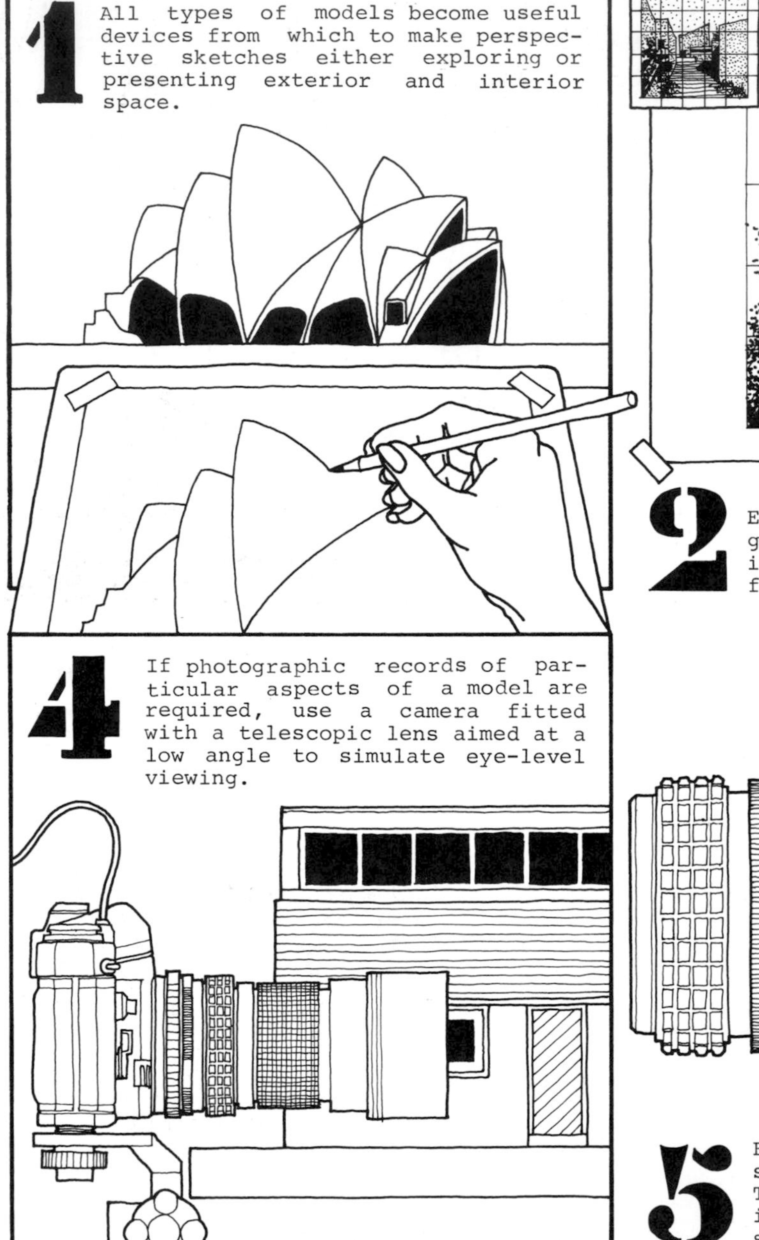

2 Exteriors of models can be photographed using a Polaroid camera--the instant print being used as a source for a drawing.

3 Models can be carefully photographed for a convincing photomontage--the cut-out print being superimposed via heat-mounting into a larger photograph of the actual site.

4 If photographic records of particular aspects of a model are required, use a camera fitted with a telescopic lens aimed at a low angle to simulate eye-level viewing.

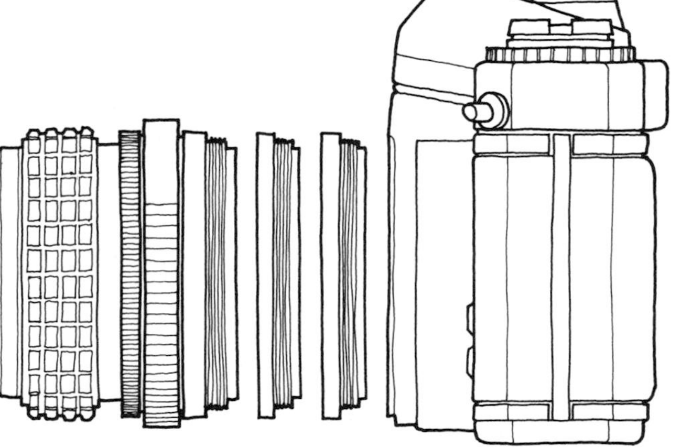

5 For more detailed photographs, insert spacer rings between lens and camera. This is effective for focusing on isolated features, as the rest of the shot will be out of focus.

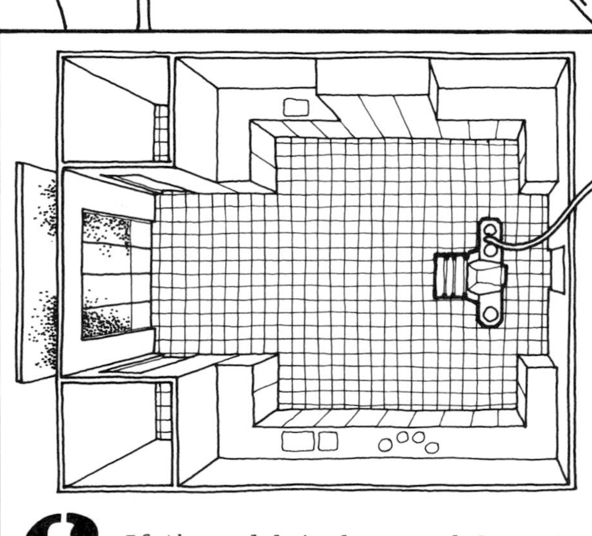

6 If the model is large and demountable, you can place the camera inside. When taking interior shots use a wide-angle lens.

Using a Modelscope

1

One of the pitfalls of small-scale models is a fascination with miniaturism resulting from the richness of visual information provided by the smallness of models. This is known as the "Gulliver" gap, that is, the disparity in size between the designer and his model. For example, if a pencil is closely examined, it is possible to see more than halfway around its stem; in models this effect is duplicated when viewing columns which, if perceived at full size, would not provide such a rich array of visual information.

Similarly, the visual richness of all model elements would correspondingly reduce when their forms are reproduced at full size.

Modelscopes bridge the "Gulliver" gap, for they allow penetration and the visual assessment--at eye level--of the spaces inside and around models.

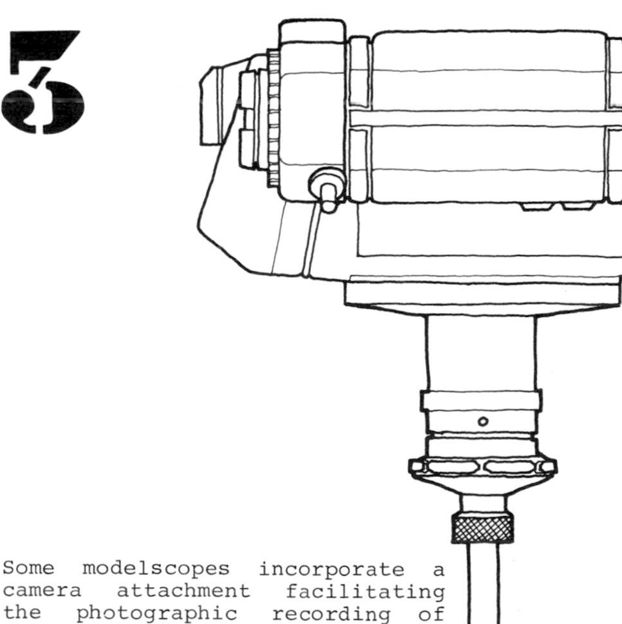

Some modelscopes incorporate a camera attachment facilitating the photographic recording of interior and exterior space.

Modelscope lenses provide narrow fields of vision and require plenty of illumination. Generally, photographs tend to be of poor quality with some distortion around the edges.

In order to simulate a larger field of vision, it is advisable to take triple exposures, which give a viewing angle of 100 degrees.

Courtesy: Abbott Modelscopes

Increasing the "Reality" Illusion

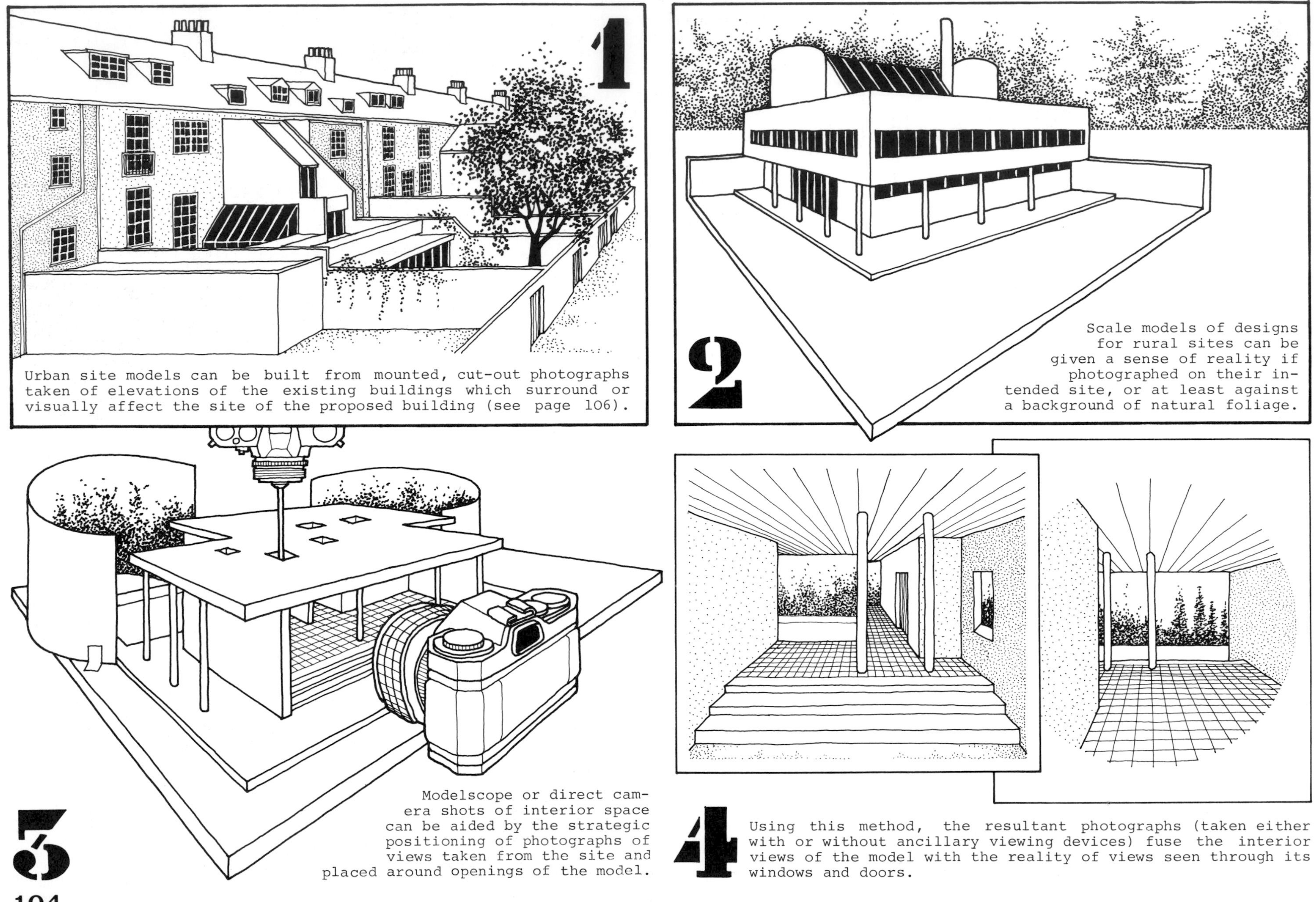

1. Urban site models can be built from mounted, cut-out photographs taken of elevations of the existing buildings which surround or visually affect the site of the proposed building (see page 106).

2. Scale models of designs for rural sites can be given a sense of reality if photographed on their intended site, or at least against a background of natural foliage.

3. Modelscope or direct camera shots of interior space can be aided by the strategic positioning of photographs of views taken from the site and placed around openings of the model.

4. Using this method, the resultant photographs (taken either with or without ancillary viewing devices) fuse the interior views of the model with the reality of views seen through its windows and doors.

Video-Aided Design

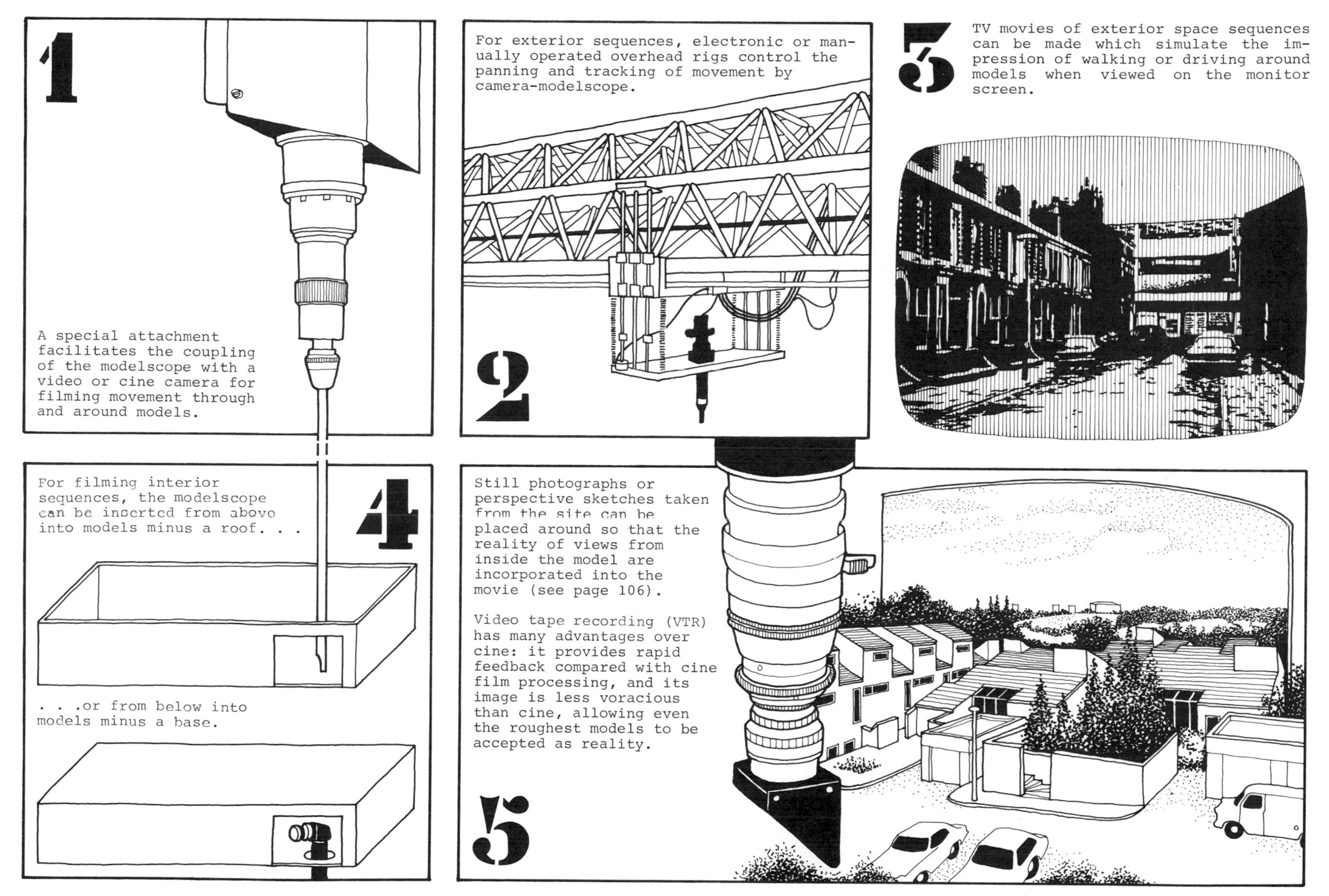

Hints When Making Models for Video

1

When making video films from site models, combinations of photographs, drawings, and three-dimensionally modeled objects can produce scaled "stage sets" which are assimilated by the camera-modelscope lens into an acceptable viewing reality on the monitor screen. However, there are some tricks which enhance the final illusion.

2

When photographing elevations of existing buildings for use in laminating cardboard models, use a camera fitted with a perspective correcting lens. This eradicates image distortion in the prints and allows the accurate mating of composite prints on longer elevations.

3

Unphotographed areas such as recesses and exposed butt joints on print laminated models--especially those using white card--read as "unreal" when viewed on the monitor. Such exposed details can be blended in using a pencil. Also, unphotographed roof planes which will be seen by the camera can be made from black or gray card.

4

Immaculate surfaces and flat, open spaces also read as unreal on filmed sequences. This starkness can be overcome by a moderate sprinkling of "powdered grass" on roads, sidewalks, open sites, and, especially, around the base of trees.

5

A good sky is simulated by surrounding the site model with a screen of white card. Against this, photographs or perspective drawings of views along roads leading off the parameter of the base can be located to create an excellent illusion of the spaces beyond the scope of the model.

6

Scale models of people appear static and unreal in filmed sequences. However, some movement can be simulated within models. For example, using black thread, one can pull a model automobile across the advancing path of the modelscope lens. Also, model trees might be agitated to add a further touch of filmed realism.

5 PRESENTATION AND EXHIBITION

Hand Lettering as a Design Component

1

Badly formed and spaced lettering is not only frustrating to decipher but it also betrays a lack of discipline in the communicant.
When hand-lettering drawings, aim for clarity of communication rather than the development of a self-conscious style -- many designers sacrifice legibility by falling into the stylism trap.

WHEN PRINTING UPPERCASE IN PENCIL, PEN, OR MARKER, FORM EACH LETTER USING DELIBERATE, SEPARATE STROKES. AS A GENERAL RULE, AIM FOR COMPACT LETTER FORMATIONS WITH JUST MORE THAN ONE LETTER WIDTH BETWEEN WORDS AND, TO AVOID "KNITTING," AT LEAST HALF THE LETTER HEIGHT BETWEEN LINES.

2

Lowercase printing can simply be a refined version of a personal handwriting style.

Beginners should construct lettering between two horizontal guidelines on drawing paper...

... or employ a graphed underlay when lettering on translucent material.

Apply minimal pressure when using special lettering nibs-- never press down on the nib.

If lettering with a flat nib, hold the pen at an angle of 45 degrees to the line of writing-- brand-new nibs require some adjustment to your writing action, so do not be too upset by initial mistakes.

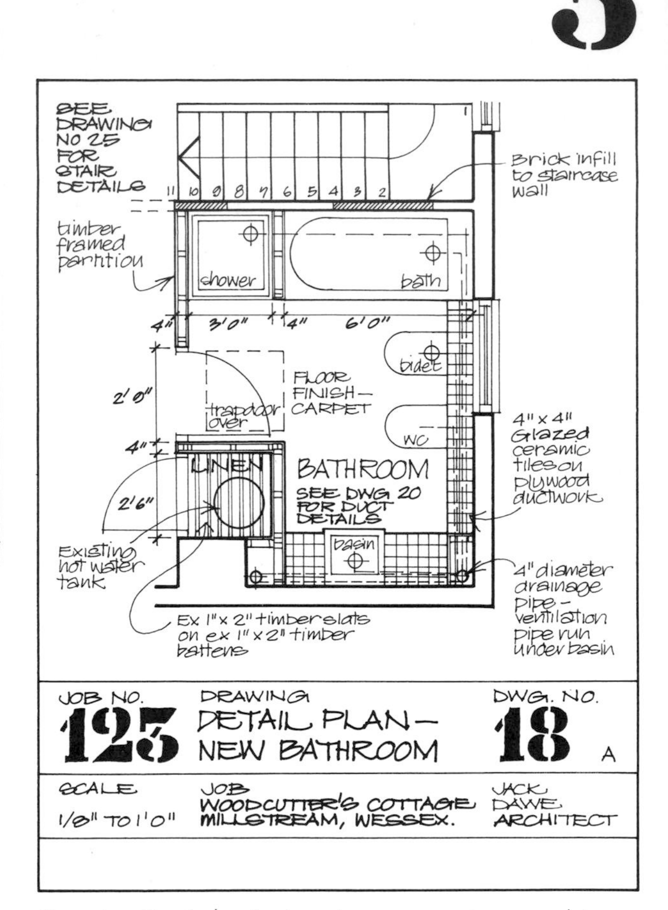

Complex technical drawings require a hierarchy of letter sizes---each layer of written information functioning in different ways and being read at different distances from the drawing. For example, main titles should be read in conjunction with the whole sheet; subtitles (type of drawing, name, scale, etc.) should be legible without interference with drawing; labels (functions of various spatial zones, etc.) should be clearly perceived as part of their drawn zones; and captions (references, details, construction information, etc.) should be clearly related or annotated with their drawn counterparts.

Stencil and Letter-Guide Lettering

1 Stenciling templates made from oil board, metal, and plastic offer a wide range of letter sizes in both upright and oblique styles. Clear templates are best, as they allow an unimpeded view of the lettering operation in progress--enabling spacing to be calculated simultaneously.

2 Several proprietary lettering guides are coordinated with the technical pen nib sizes--being color-coded for ease of identification during the use of various guides on one drawing. Guides are also available for use with ball-point pens and fine-lead clutch pencils.

3 Profiles of templates are usually designed to be suspended above the drawing surface to prevent smudging. If this is not the case, several strips of drafting tape stuck onto the contact surface will suffice. For accurate alignment of words or lines of text, stencils should be rested on a T square or a set square during lettering.

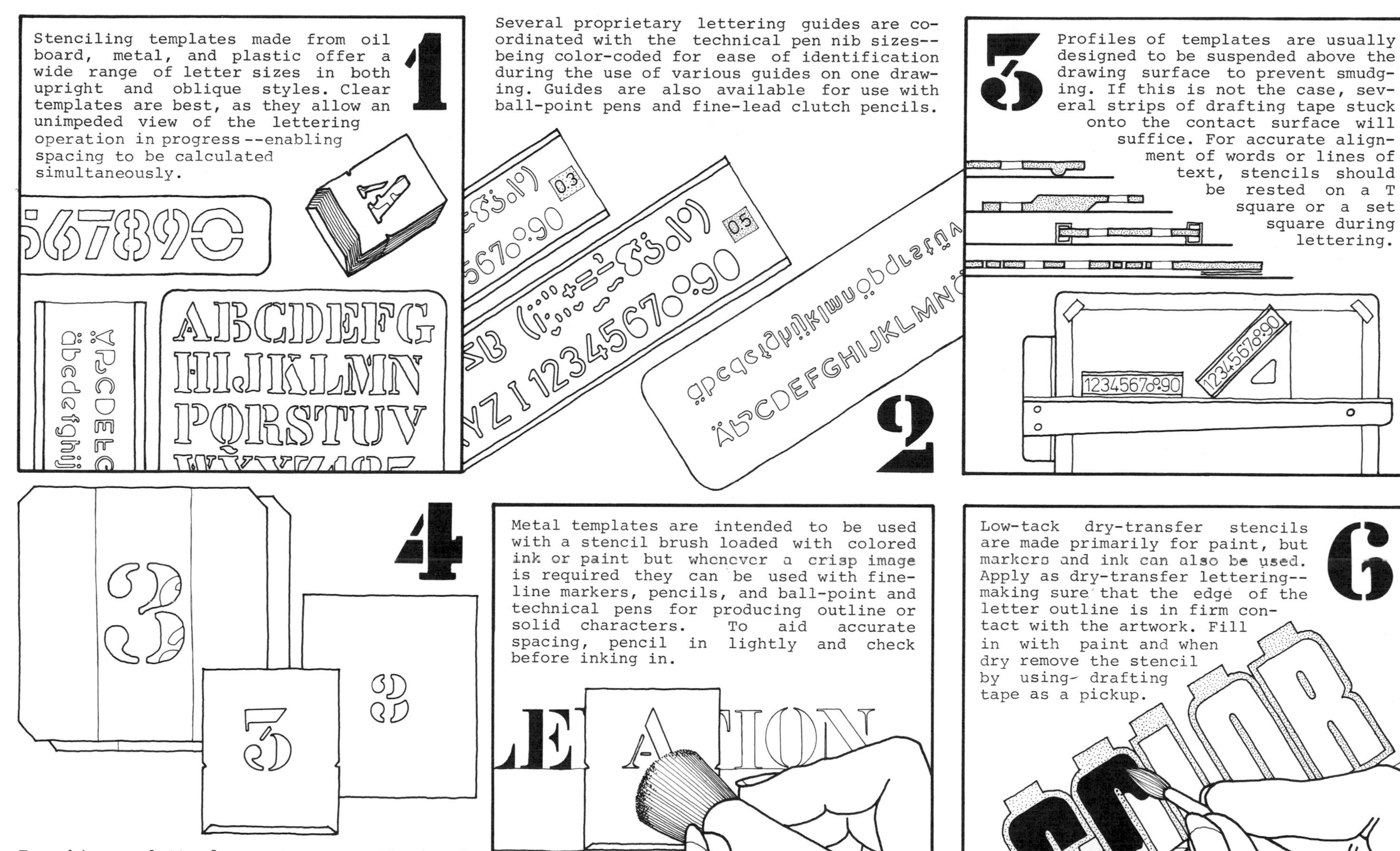

4 For bigger letterforms, box stencils (used by warehousemen for labeling containers) are relatively inexpensive and provide an economical range of functional styles. Their individual metal letters and numerals are ideal for titles, report covers, posters, and exhibitions.

5 Metal templates are intended to be used with a stencil brush loaded with colored ink or paint but whenever a crisp image is required they can be used with fine-line markers, pencils, and ball-point and technical pens for producing outline or solid characters. To aid accurate spacing, pencil in lightly and check before inking in.

6 Low-tack dry-transfer stencils are made primarily for paint, but markers and ink can also be used. Apply as dry-transfer lettering--making sure that the edge of the letter outline is in firm contact with the artwork. Fill in with paint and when dry remove the stencil by using drafting tape as a pickup.

Mechanical Methods of Applying Lettering

1

Dry-transfer lettering is available in black, white, and basic colors and produced in a rich array of typefaces and sizes--ranging from small, tape-dispensed characters to sheets of alphabets and large individual letters. Although expensive, proprietary instant lettering offers the designer a highly professional finish. A good tip is to make a diazo print or photocopy directly from each newly purchased sheet. The prints can then be used as underlays for tracing (see page 89).

2

When mass-producing large-scale text or main titles, e.g., for posters or exhibition panels, set up instant lettering on film or tracing paper and diazo the required number on glossy print paper. When using the semi-dry diazo process, key words can be colored by sponging on the appropiate developer (see page 85). The prints can be trimmed and, if required, heat-mounted on board.

3

Individual, large, self-adhesive vinyl letters are available in a limited range of typefaces and colors--usually black, white, and red--and are good for exhibition work. To apply, peel back upper section of backing paper and preplan the layout by aligning on a pre-drawn guideline or a strip of drafting tape. To fix letters, press exposed vinyl into position before removing lower section of backing paper. Complete the operation by gently rubbing over the entire letter.

second year

4

Infinity City
Hyperspace:
the ultimate
environment

Typewriter characters, particularly lowercase, are effective at large scale--the advent of the interchangeable "golfball" head increasing the choice of character and size on one machine. Text or main titles can be photographed and enlarged into opaque or translucent prints--the latter being useful as a diazo negative. Photographic or glossy diazo prints can then be heat-mounted on board to create professional-looking posters, large report covers, and exhibition panels.

5

Lettering can be typed directly onto small drawings on tracing paper--the maximum size depending on the width of carriage. Use yellow carbon paper behind the sheet to make the lettering dense enough for diazo reproduction. Alternatively, lettering can be typed onto a special low-tack transparent film which is cut into panels before being stuck into position on the drawings. This method is useful for adding written information into working drawings.

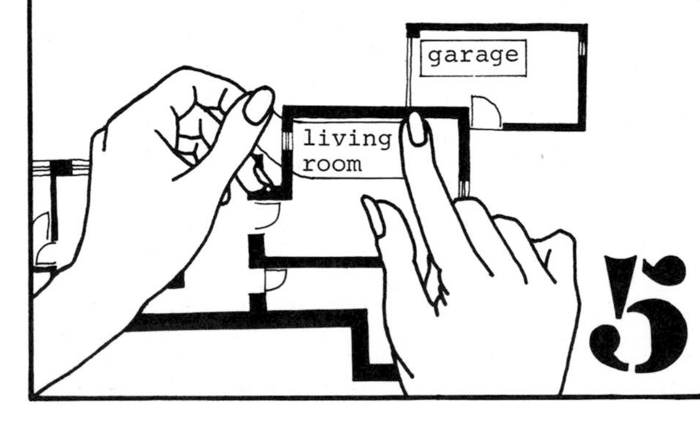

6

Typing machines have been developed for introducing lettering onto larger technical drawings. They can be attached to drafting machines, parallel-motion units, or used on the bench top. Typing machines print letters and symbols from a variety of keyboards and type sizes.

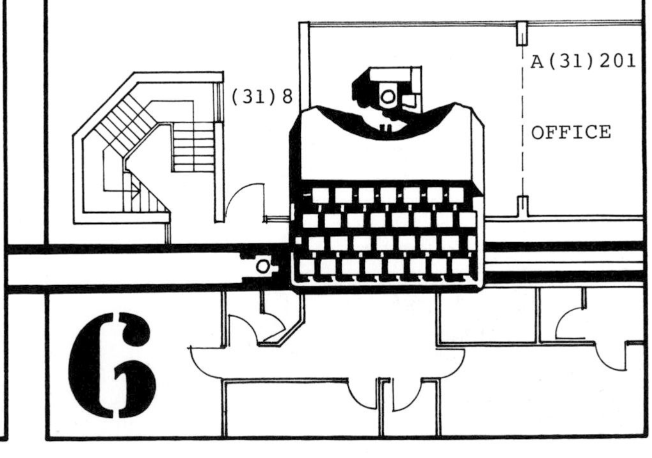

Hints for Applying Dry-Transfer Lettering

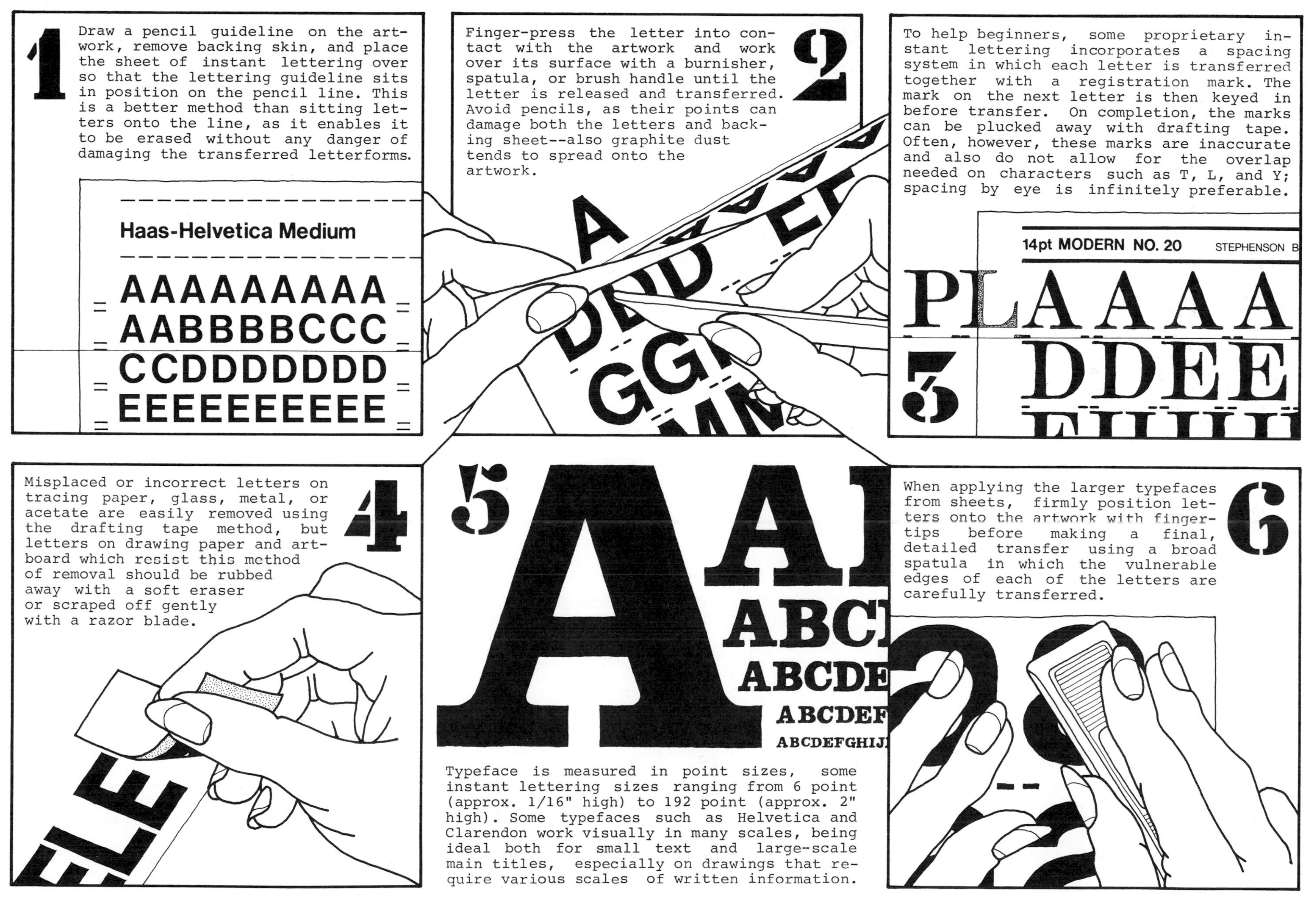

1 Draw a pencil guideline on the artwork, remove backing skin, and place the sheet of instant lettering over so that the lettering guideline sits in position on the pencil line. This is a better method than sitting letters onto the line, as it enables it to be erased without any danger of damaging the transferred letterforms.

2 Finger-press the letter into contact with the artwork and work over its surface with a burnisher, spatula, or brush handle until the letter is released and transferred. Avoid pencils, as their points can damage both the letters and backing sheet--also graphite dust tends to spread onto the artwork.

3 To help beginners, some proprietary instant lettering incorporates a spacing system in which each letter is transferred together with a registration mark. The mark on the next letter is then keyed in before transfer. On completion, the marks can be plucked away with drafting tape. Often, however, these marks are inaccurate and also do not allow for the overlap needed on characters such as T, L, and Y; spacing by eye is infinitely preferable.

4 Misplaced or incorrect letters on tracing paper, glass, metal, or acetate are easily removed using the drafting tape method, but letters on drawing paper and artboard which resist this method of removal should be rubbed away with a soft eraser or scraped off gently with a razor blade.

5 Typeface is measured in point sizes, some instant lettering sizes ranging from 6 point (approx. 1/16" high) to 192 point (approx. 2" high). Some typefaces such as Helvetica and Clarendon work visually in many scales, being ideal both for small text and large-scale main titles, especially on drawings that require various scales of written information.

6 When applying the larger typefaces from sheets, firmly position letters onto the artwork with fingertips before making a final, detailed transfer using a broad spatula in which the vulnerable edges of each of the letters are carefully transferred.

Dynamic Forms of Presentation Graphics

1 The exploded or expanded drawing is utilized by many kinds of designer, for it visually explains more complex assemblies, connections, and jointing between various materials.

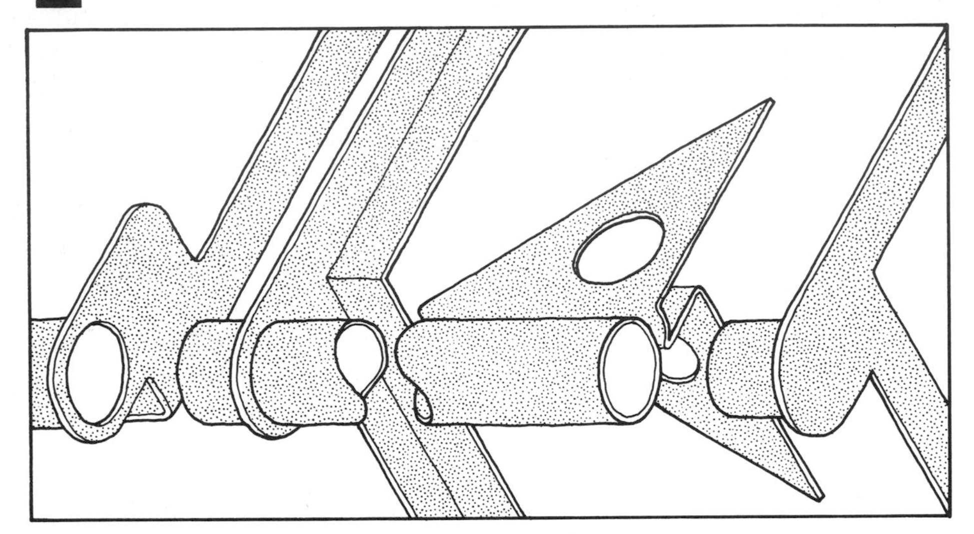

2 The X ray or cutaway drawing allows visual access to selected inner workings--often giving a simultaneous interior-exterior view of a hollow form. In a sense, plans and sections are cutaway graphics, and as with all such drawings, the "cut" should be positively indicated.

3 Comic strip formats dispense sequential information involving action in time and space. Similarly, narrative graphics can be fun to "read" and creatively employed to take an observer on a graphic tour of a spatial concept, e.g., around and through a design for a building.

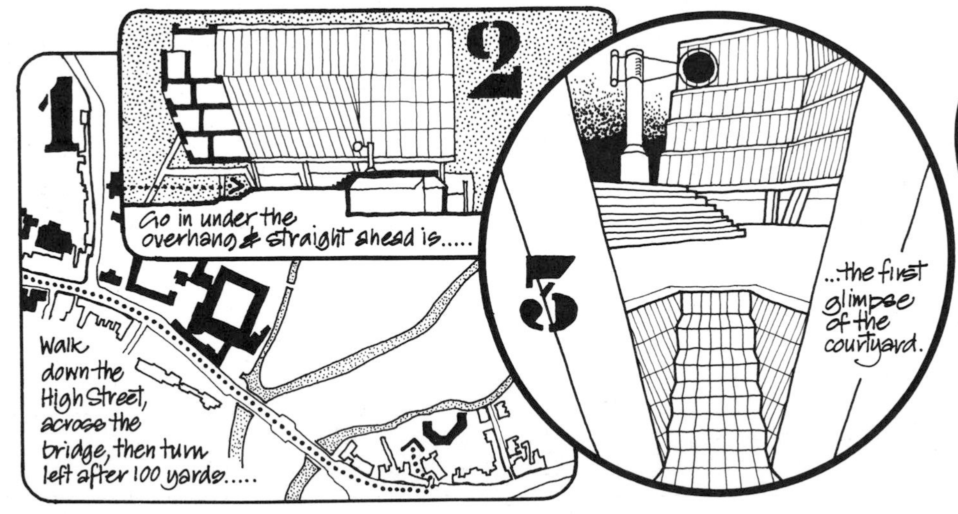

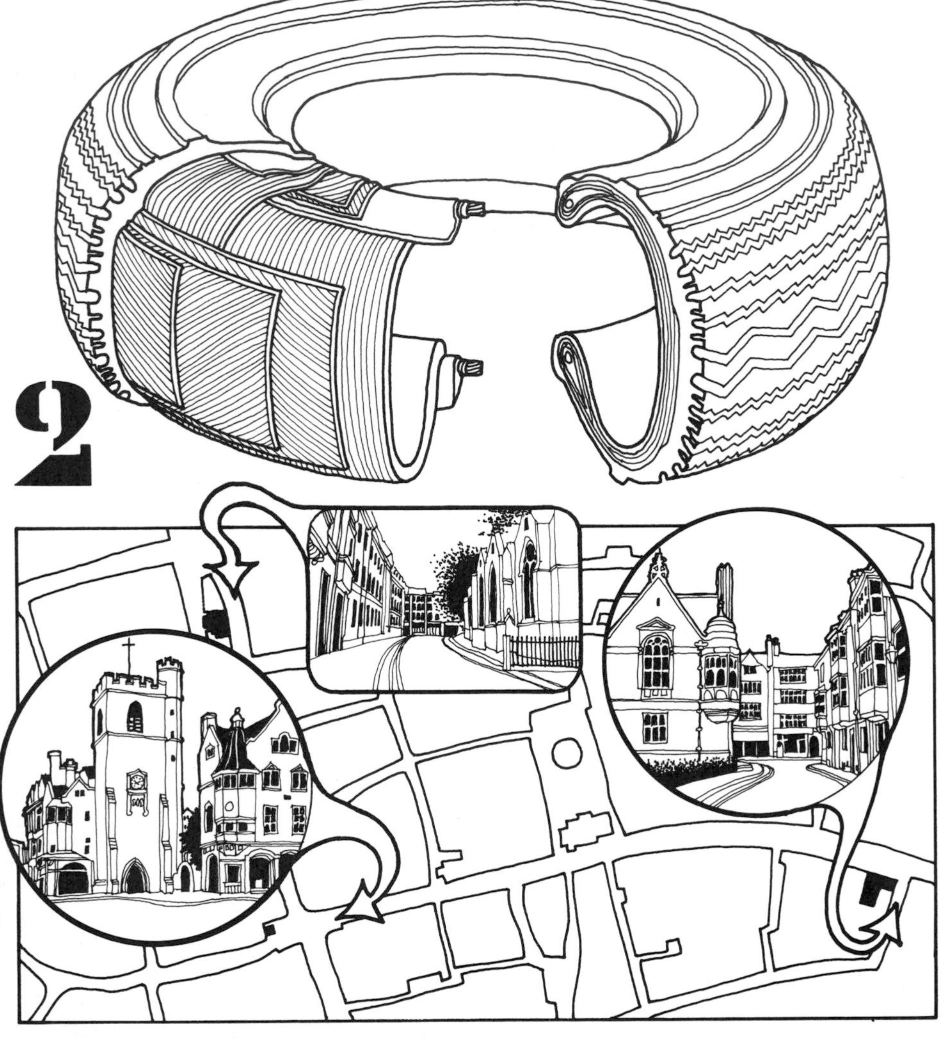

4 One method of presenting detailed information within broader formats such as site plans is to introduce framed, magnified graphics. These could be either annotated on-site drawings or photographs keyed into their background frame of reference.

How to Enliven Statistical Graphics

Statistical diagrams such as graphs, tables, bar charts, or histograms and matrices, etc., can be made more visually exciting and more readable through the addition of color and support imagery. A fast method is to integrate--via photomontage--relevant images from magazine photographs. This reportage technique can convert a potentially dull visual into an attractive and professional-looking graphic for wall displays and reports.

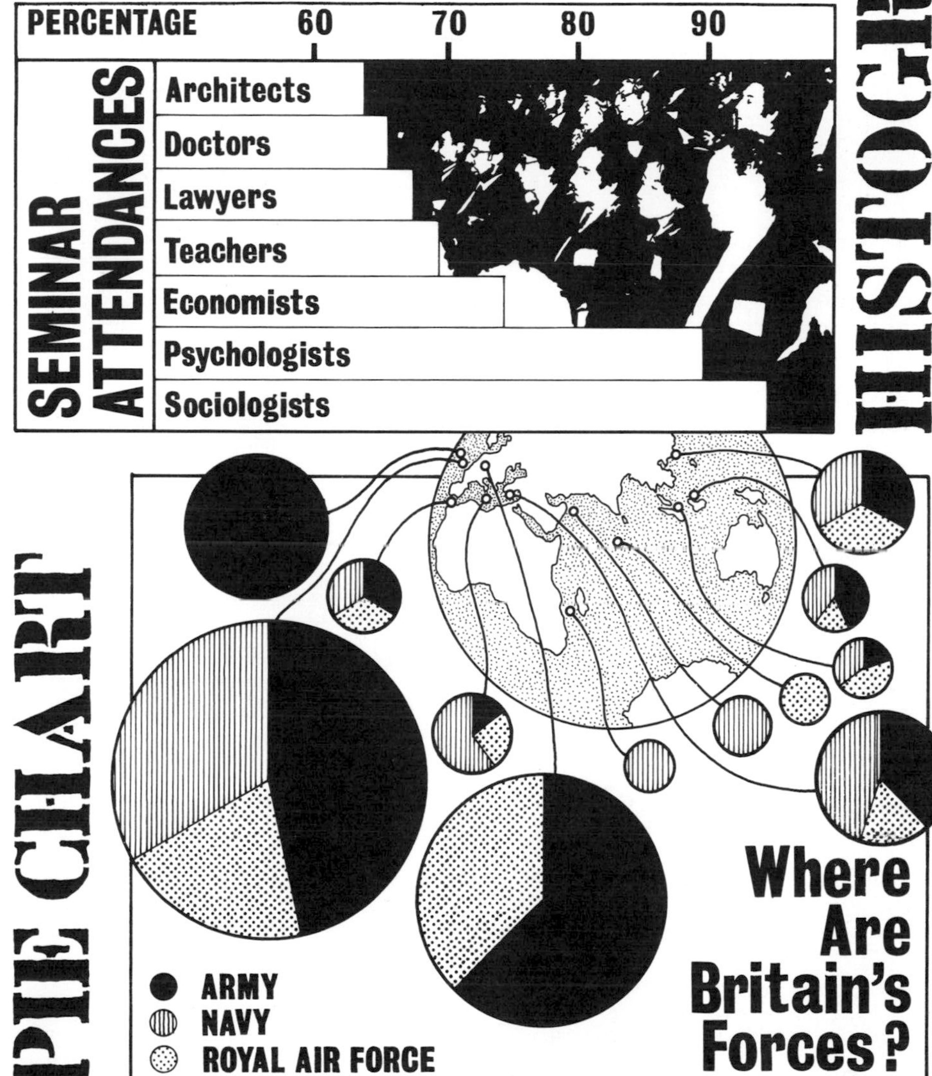

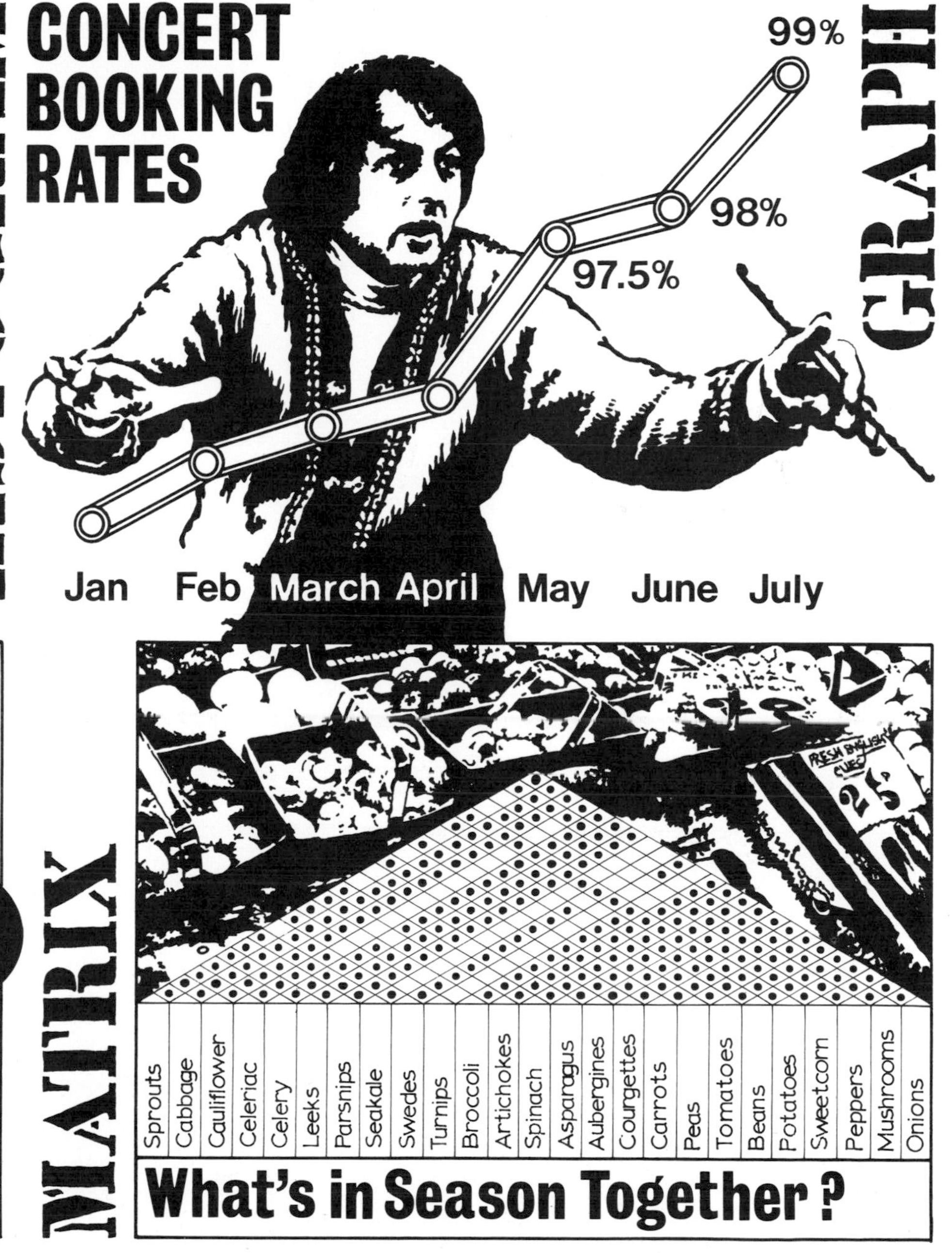

Optical Matting (Mounting) Layouts

1

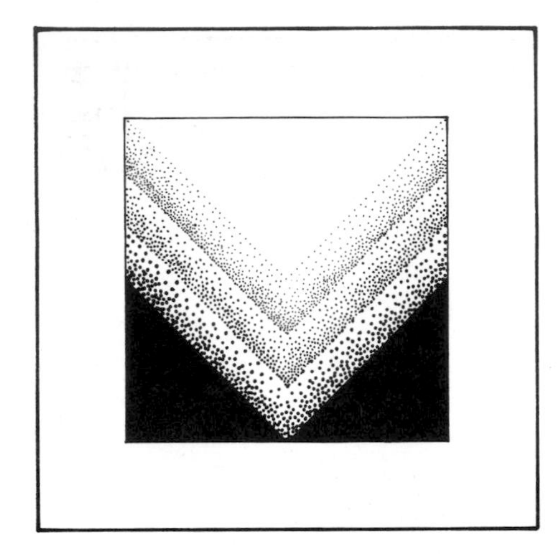

When artwork is mounted dead-center of mounts, an optical effect causes the image to appear lower than its actual physical location on the surround--a visual phenomenon in which the image appears to slip down the mount.

2

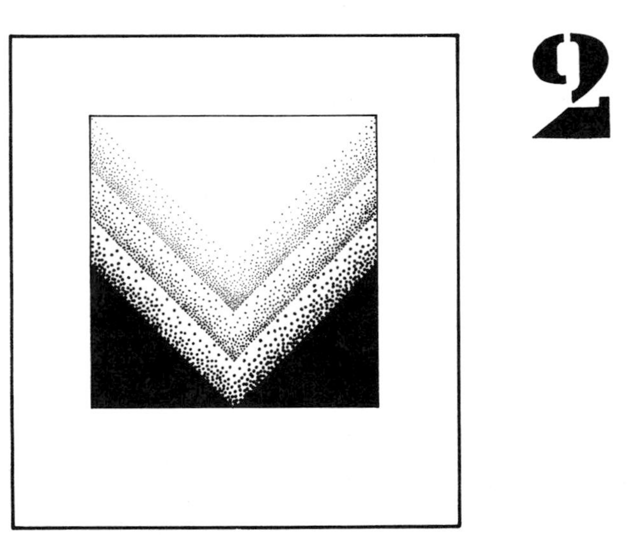

This figure-ground illusion can be corrected by mounting the artwork slightly higher than halfway on support sheet. An ideal mount proportion is equal frame width top and sides, with a slightly deeper width at the bottom.

3

On both portrait (vertical) and landscape (horizontal) formats, this compensatory image-frame relationship not only visually stabilizes the artwork, but allows for the introduction of lettering as an integral component of the layout.

The juxtapositioning of multiple and dissimilar sized images on one mount is a figure-ground design problem. Avoid the confusion of scrappy layouts by introducing a vertical and horizontal order in which the spaces between and around images are as considered as the relationship between the images themselves.

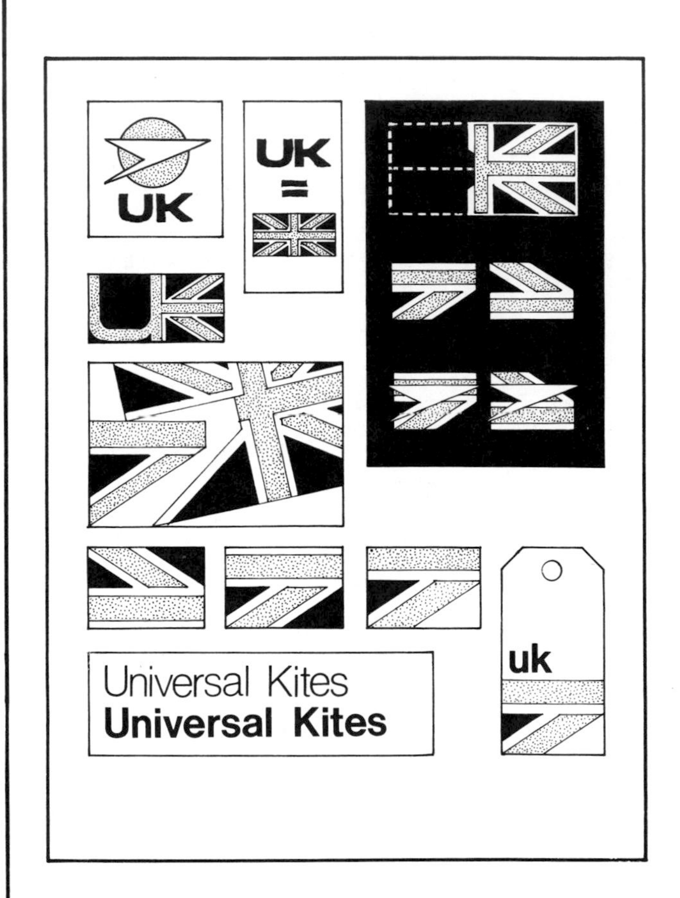

4

Cutters and Trimmers

1 Guillotine-type all-purpose paper cutter with gridded indicator board and guide-rule edge for accurate repeat cuts. There are several versions of this trimmer, from the small portable models to the larger, bench-integrated types. However, to avoid harm to fingers, they should only be used when fitted with a cutting guard.

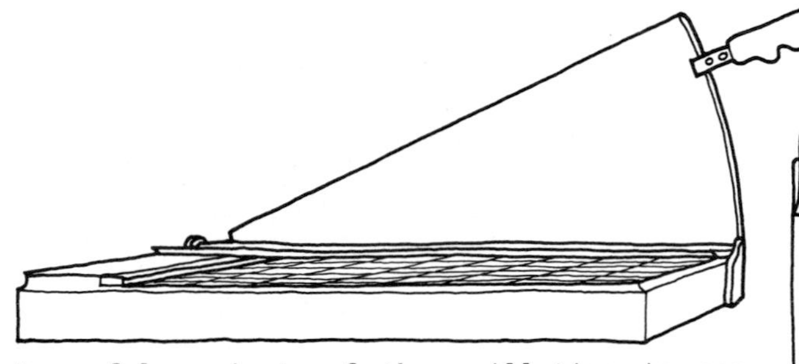

A useful variant of the guillotine is one which utilizes a clamp for securing materials such as linoleum and fiberboard which are acceptable to its heavy-duty blade. This version is fine for trimming small reports.

2 Trimmers using the sliding rotary-action cutting head come in a range of sizes. They are designed to cut papers, thin cards, foils, and film materials in absolute safety. Their baseboard indicators and guide-rule edge facilitate the accurate introduction of sheet material to the blade. Some carry markings visible in normal red or orange darkroom lighting--others incorporating a quick-feed attachment for dispensing rolls of material.

3 When drawn against a straightedge, this chrome-plated mat cutter can produce both straight or beveled windows in mounting card. Its blade adjustment sets both angle and depth of cut--making it also useful for scoring modelmaking boards prior to bending or curving.

4 The "T square" version of the guide-rail cutter made from light magnesium. Its cutting blade is drawn along the guide rail after being set for straight- or bevel-edge incisions.

There is also an 8-foot guide rail with integral sliding precision-head cutter designed to trim or cut a wide variety of materials such as paper, board, film, and fabrics. This device is placed over the material on a flat surface and the cutter drawn along its track.

5 The bench-top orbital cutter for the accurate removal of ovals or circles from papers or boards.

Cutting compass: bow compass with lengthening arm and cutting head.

How to Window-Mount Artwork

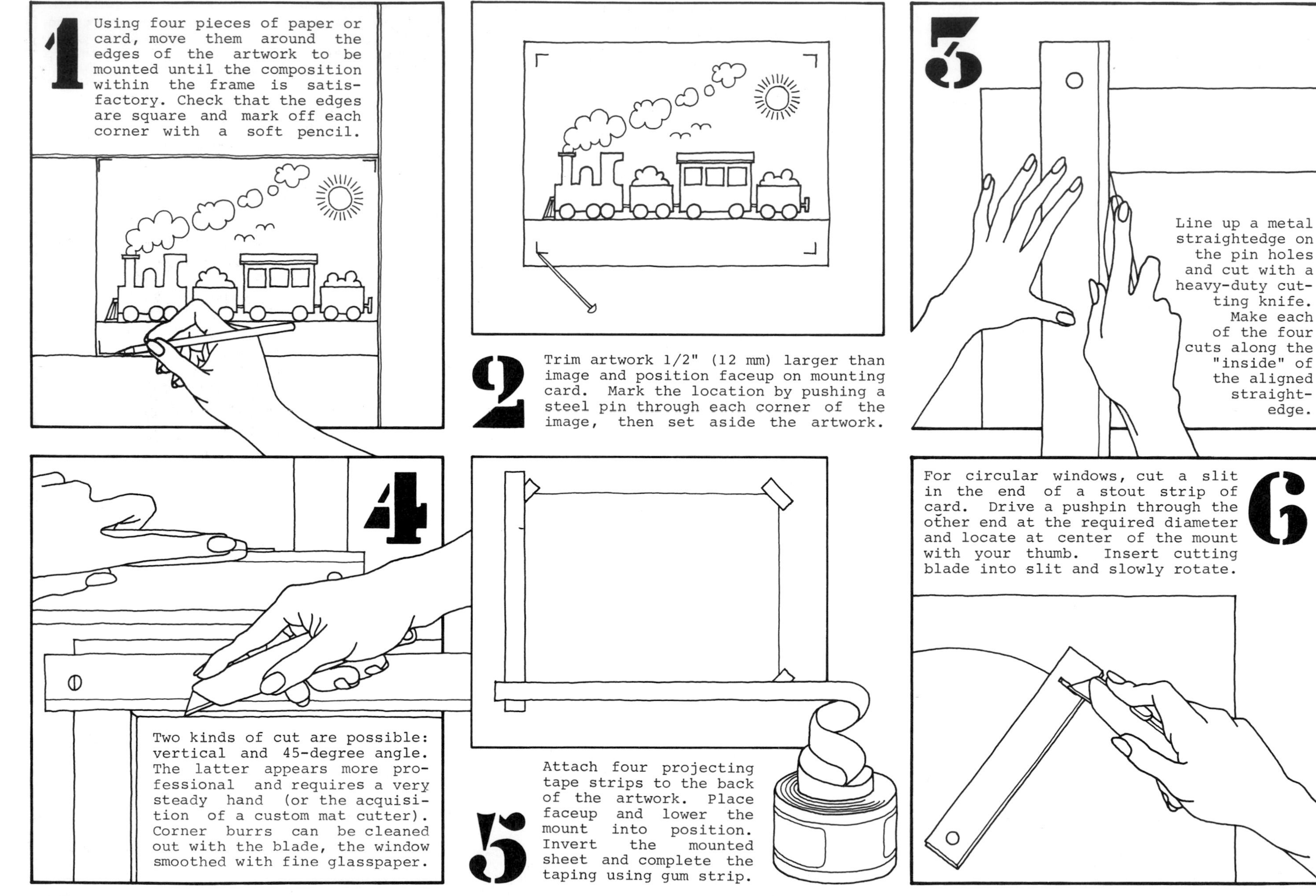

How to Heat-Mount Artwork

1 The heat-mounting process is ideal for laminating photos, paintings, and drawings to an artboard support. First, trim the artwork to about 1/4" (6 mm) larger than the required size. Then, cut a piece of heat-mounting tissue to a size slightly larger than the artwork. Place the artwork facedown onto a clean surface and cover it with the piece of mounting tissue.

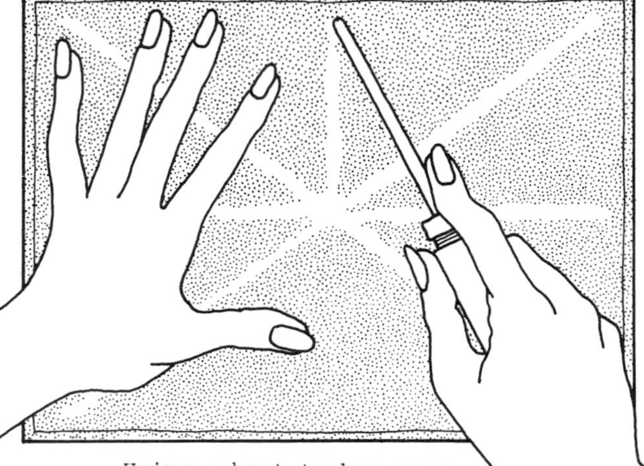

2 Using a heat tacker or a soldering iron, touch-tack the tissue to the back of the artwork, working from the center outward in a star shape to within 1/2" (12 mm) of edges and corners.

3 Now trim back both the artwork and the tissue to the required size, preferably using a paper trimmer or a guillotine.

4 Position image onto the mount and restrain with finger and thumb while inserting the heat tacker on each of the corners between the artwork and tissue--spot-tacking the image to the mount.

5 Protect the artwork and mount in a folded sheet of paper and insert faceup into the mounter with heat at operational level--apply pressure for fifteen seconds. On removal, the artwork is laminated to the mount.

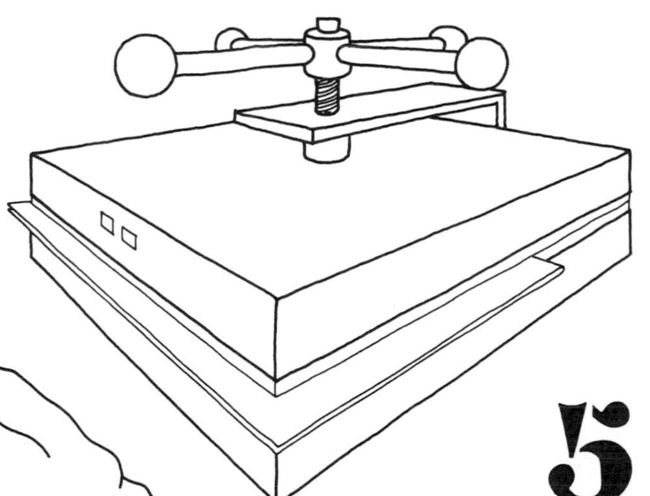

6 The heat-mounting process can be duplicated with a domestic iron at sizzle heat. To avoid air bubbles, iron outward, spiraling from the middle. Generally, the heat-mounting process is not suitable for photocopies and certain types of printing inks. If in any doubt, first check by testing a sample piece.

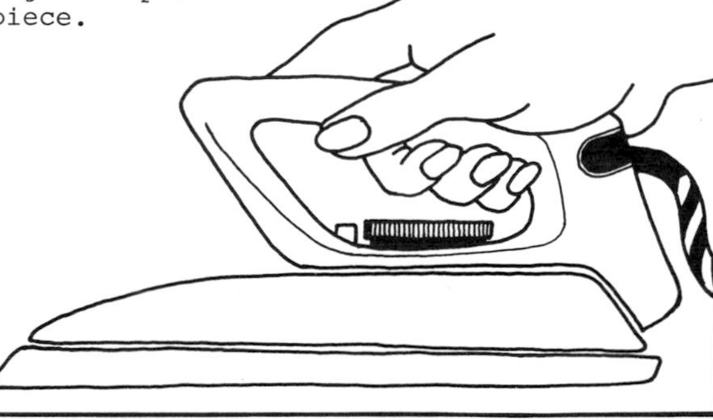

Display Mounting Materials

1

The nature of the exhibition surface usually dictates the method of hanging artwork. Pinning is ideal for softer pin-board surfaces--pins ranging from the traditional pushpin to a variety of map tacks and indicator chart pins with colored heads in metal and plastic. Some designers, however, find pinheads to be a distracting element in displays and prefer the more invisible types of fixing methods.

2

These include double-sided adhesive tapes, rings, and tabs, together with adhesive putty--although the latter, if used for extended periods, can discolor both drawing and wall surfaces. An unobtrusive fixing for harder surfaces is dressmaker's toughened steel pins. These can be gently tapped--even into plaster walls--and later retrieved with a pair of pliers.

3

Corners of drawings on paper subject to frequent pinning are liable to disintegrate. Many types of reinforcements can be applied: self-adhesive paper rings, discs, tabs, and eyelets for punched holes. A simple method is to affix tabs of drafting tape to the back of each of the corners.

4

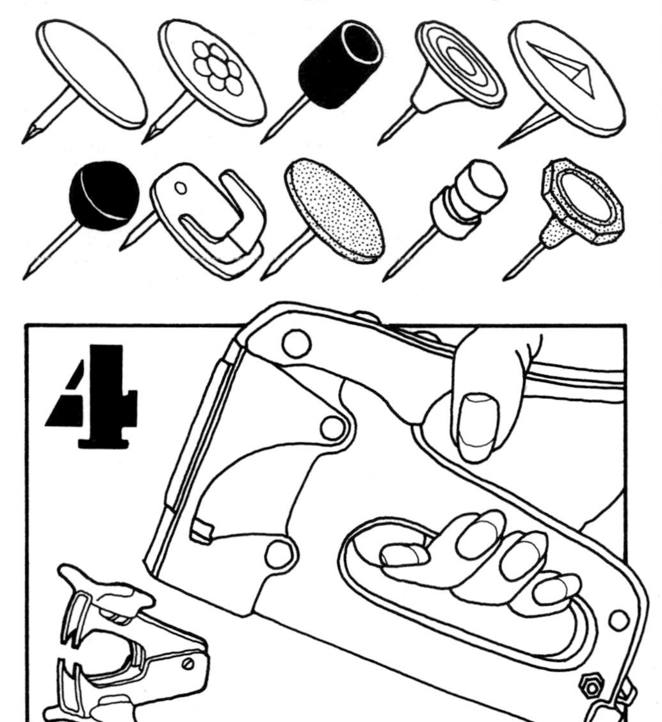

Stapling is the lightning display method, but it is not recommended for presentation drawings, as it can damage the work and the display surface. Staple guns should be used with discretion, and to save time and fingernails, the used staples removed with the special extractor.

5

An effective "look, no hands" method is to suspend artwork on stiff board, display panels, and especially three-dimensional objects with "invisible" nylon fishing line.

6

Paper backing sheets in monochrome or in color can be applied to obliterate inadequate exhibition surfaces. These function to unify, personalize, and identify the display of an individual or group. The color, as with matting boards, should not visually conflict with, or overpower the artwork itself.

Tips for Presenting Design Ideas

1

Display layout is yet another visual expression of a designer's creative ability--wall-mounted presentations often functioning to represent this ability in the designer's absence.

Drawings and models should therefore be exhibited to clearly express design intentions, and whenever possible reflect problem-solving techniques. Exhibition materials should also be mounted in relation to the eye level of a seated or a standing observer group.

Oral introductions are often important supplements to design presentations, and especially in critiques, it is worth preparing reference notes which aid the verbal description of key design aspects.

2

As a critique is intended to function as a teaching vehicle, include all the initial conceptual developments of design ideas--either wall-mounted or in the workbook. This disclosure allows insight into your design routes and aids constructive criticism.

3

To avoid irritating displays, always show plan drawings with their north points facing in the same direction. Similarly, aim for a uniformity and compatibility of sheet sizes, drawing scales, and lettered information.

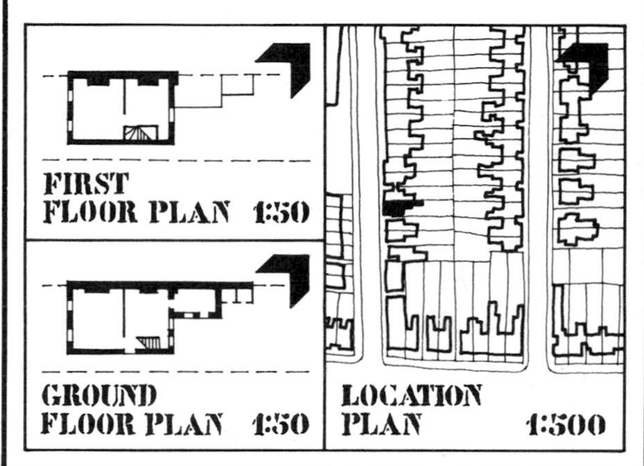

4

Scale models tend to become focal points in displays. They can be wall-mounted for aerial viewing or projected and suspended using string and pushpins for eye-level viewing.

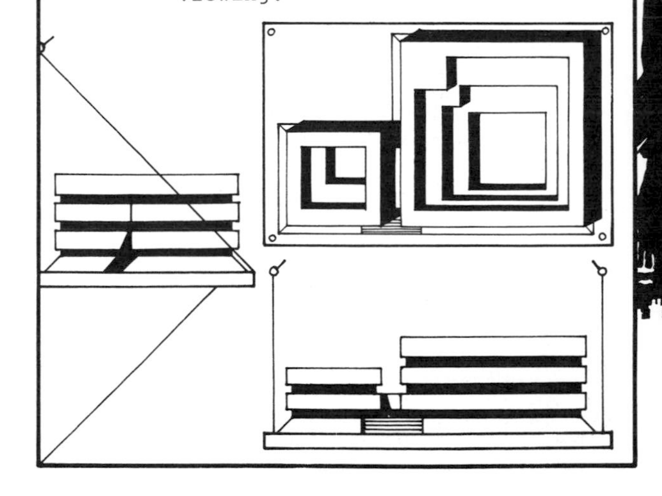

5

A fascination for models can, however, distract critics from drawings you wish to be seen. If this situation is anticipated, only disclose a presentation model at the appropriate moment in the presentation sequence.

6

A valuable method of experiencing and communicating construction details is to "build" them in relief form from balsa wood, card, or plasticated sheets, etc., on a board support. This technique clearly demonstrates an understanding of connections between materials.

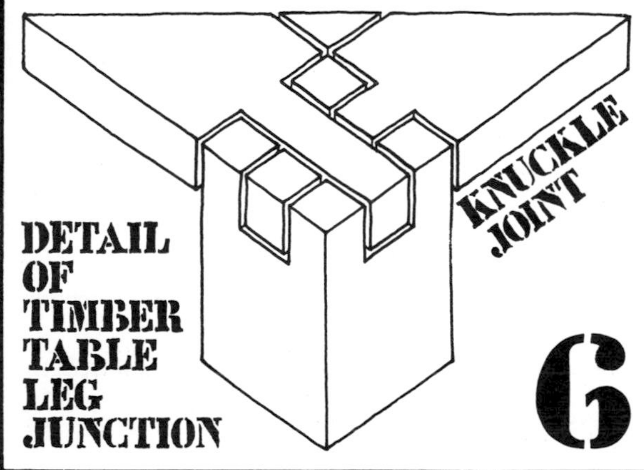

Slide Projector Presentation

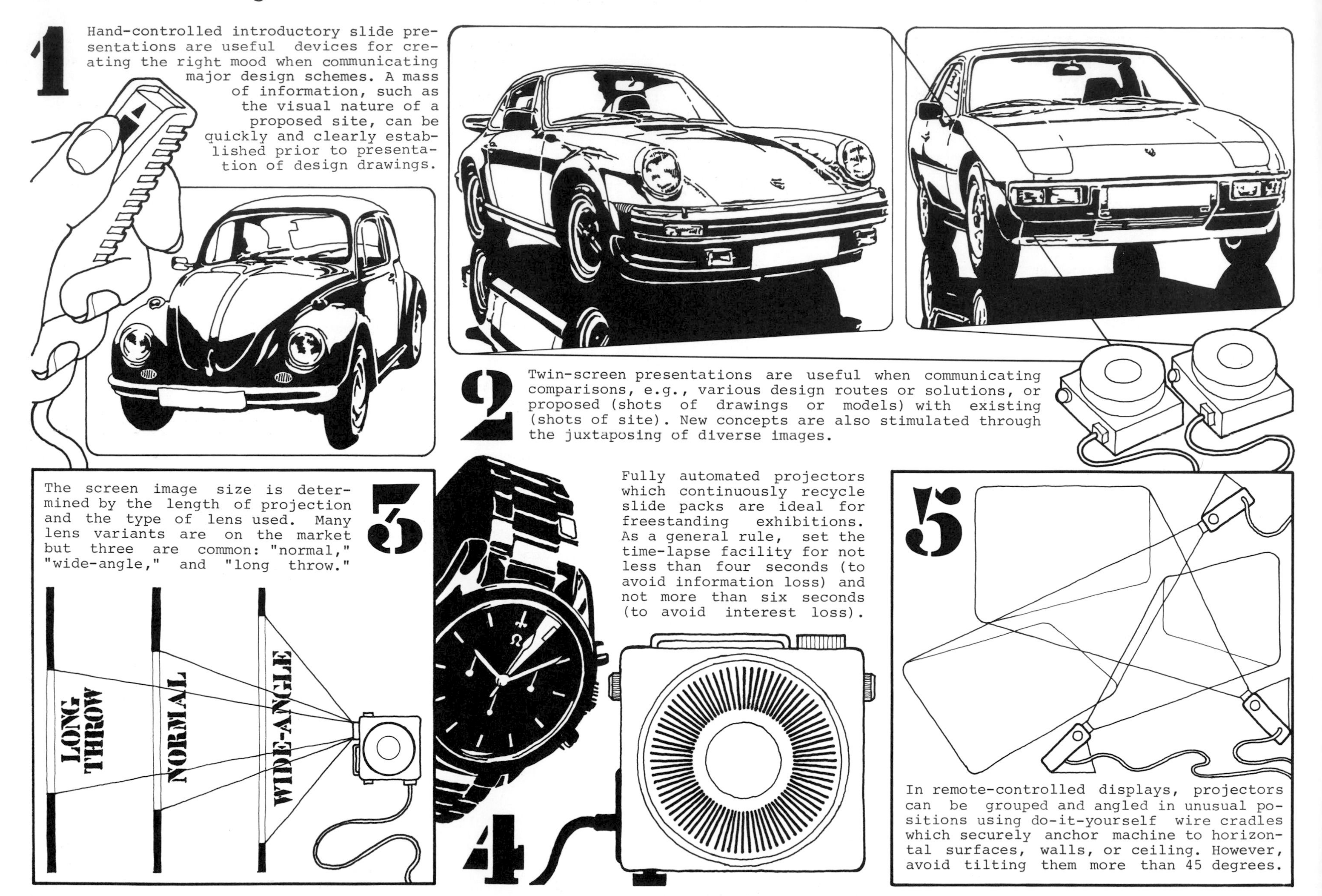

1 Hand-controlled introductory slide presentations are useful devices for creating the right mood when communicating major design schemes. A mass of information, such as the visual nature of a proposed site, can be quickly and clearly established prior to presentation of design drawings.

2 Twin-screen presentations are useful when communicating comparisons, e.g., various design routes or solutions, or proposed (shots of drawings or models) with existing (shots of site). New concepts are also stimulated through the juxtaposing of diverse images.

3 The screen image size is determined by the length of projection and the type of lens used. Many lens variants are on the market but three are common: "normal," "wide-angle," and "long throw."

4 Fully automated projectors which continuously recycle slide packs are ideal for freestanding exhibitions. As a general rule, set the time-lapse facility for not less than four seconds (to avoid information loss) and not more than six seconds (to avoid interest loss).

5 In remote-controlled displays, projectors can be grouped and angled in unusual positions using do-it-yourself wire cradles which securely anchor machine to horizontal surfaces, walls, or ceiling. However, avoid tilting them more than 45 degrees.

How to Make a Back Projection Booth

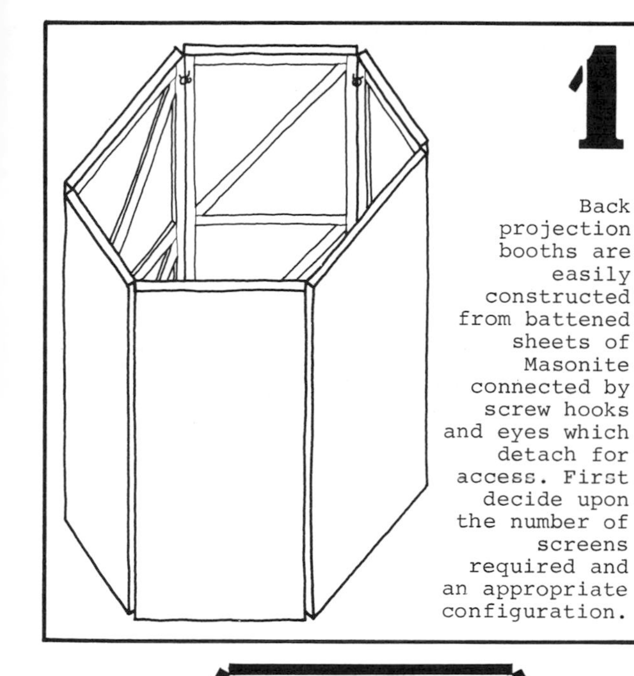

Back projection booths are easily constructed from battened sheets of Masonite connected by screw hooks and eyes which detach for access. First decide upon the number of screens required and an appropriate configuration.

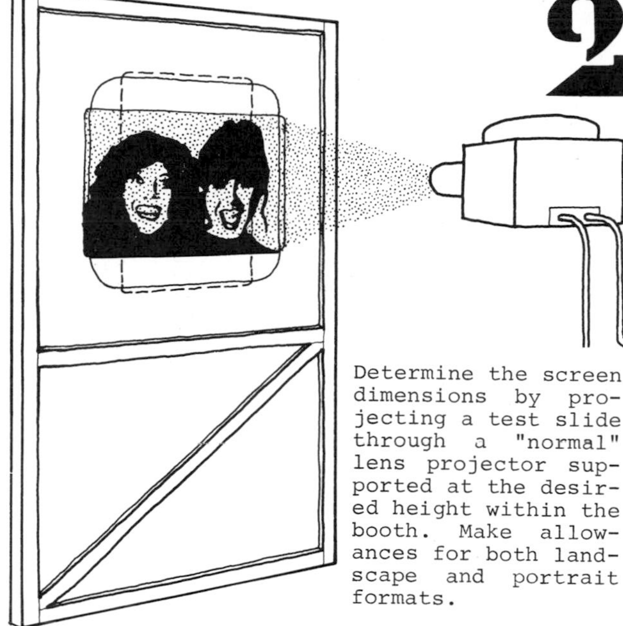

Determine the screen dimensions by projecting a test slide through a "normal" lens projector supported at the desired height within the booth. Make allowances for both landscape and portrait formats.

3

Mark off the image and cut out the screen aperture with a saw--smoothing off the cut with glasspaper. Heavy-duty tracing paper makes an excellent projection screen; this should be stretched across the inside of the aperture and affixed with gum-strip tape or staples.

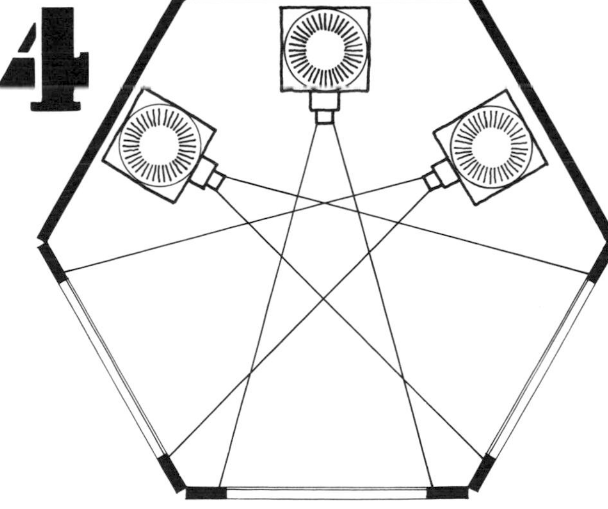

A whole series of remote-control projectors can be positioned within the booth for multi-image back projection. Although several beams pass through each other, their respective projected images remain unaffected.

In more confined booths, the beams can be bounced out of tight corners, using mirrors. However, as a mirrored projection corrects the pseudoscopic image of direct back projection, load the slides to compensate.

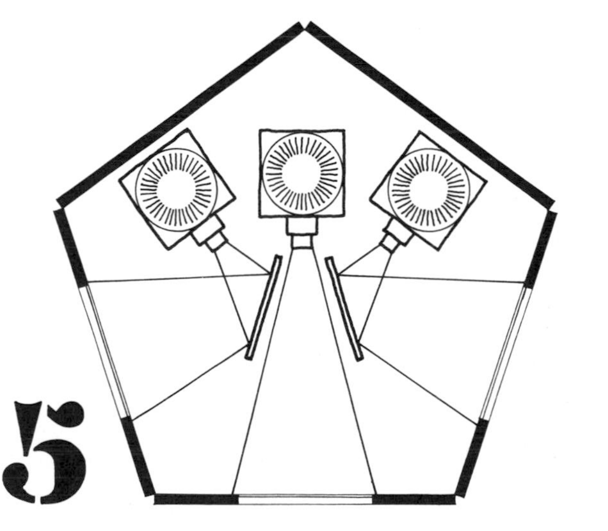

Avoid glare on the screens. If unavoidable, construct a cardboard cowl which casts a shadow across the screen. Deflect any direct light from entering the booth by making up a canopy from black polythene sheet or cardboard.

Two Basic Freestanding Exhibition Layouts

The layout potential of proprietary display screen systems is endless, but two basic configurations control movement and interest levels in different ways.

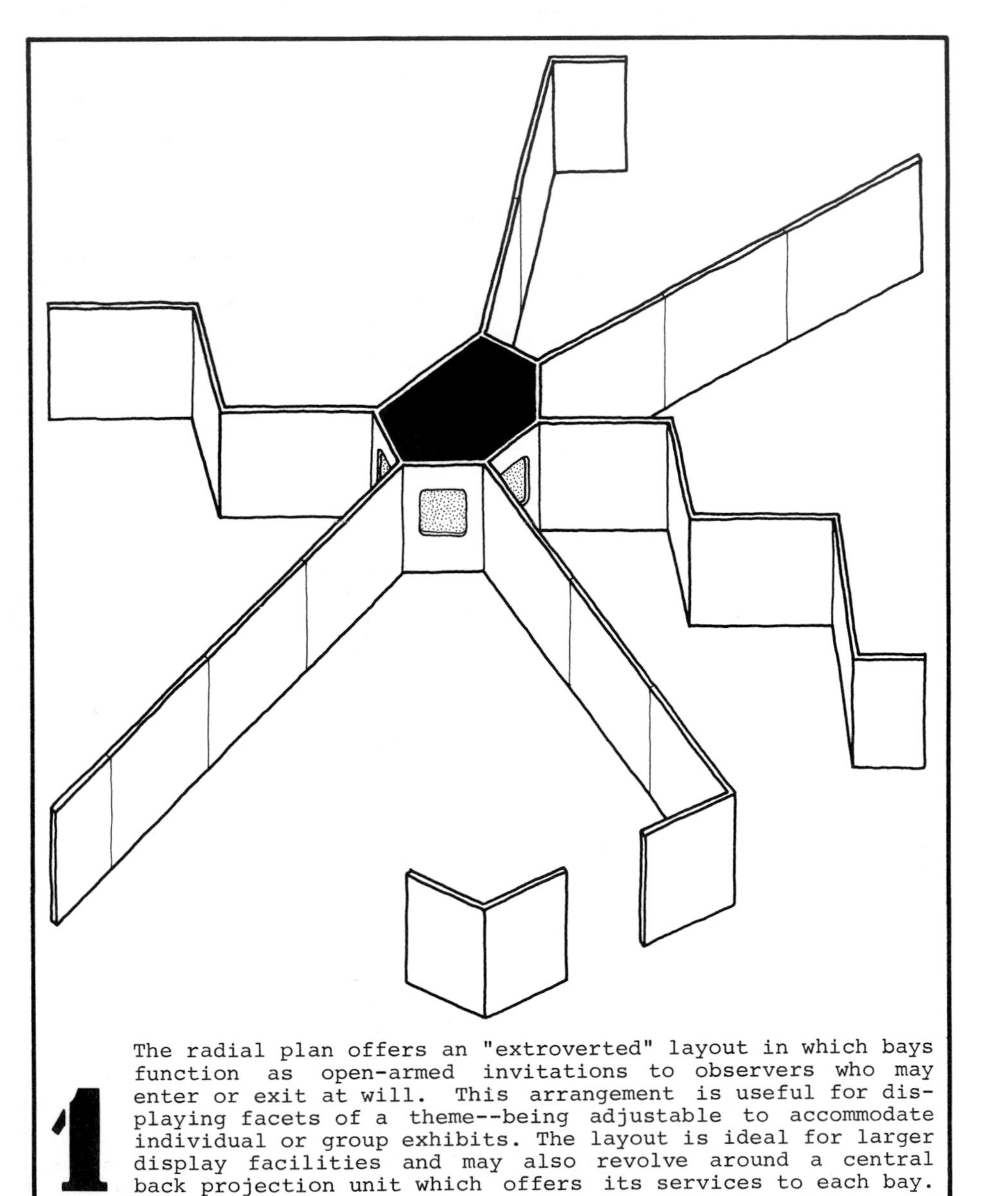

1 The radial plan offers an "extroverted" layout in which bays function as open-armed invitations to observers who may enter or exit at will. This arrangement is useful for displaying facets of a theme--being adjustable to accommodate individual or group exhibits. The layout is ideal for larger display facilities and may also revolve around a central back projection unit which offers its services to each bay.

2 In screening and detaching observers from their immediate environment, the enclosed or "introverted" layout is conducive to a deeper concentration on displays. Internal maze-like screen arrangements can respond to the nature of the exhibits and articulate a funneled exploration of its interior, utilizing, if necessary, the element of surprise. The dotted areas indicate potential back projection booth locations.

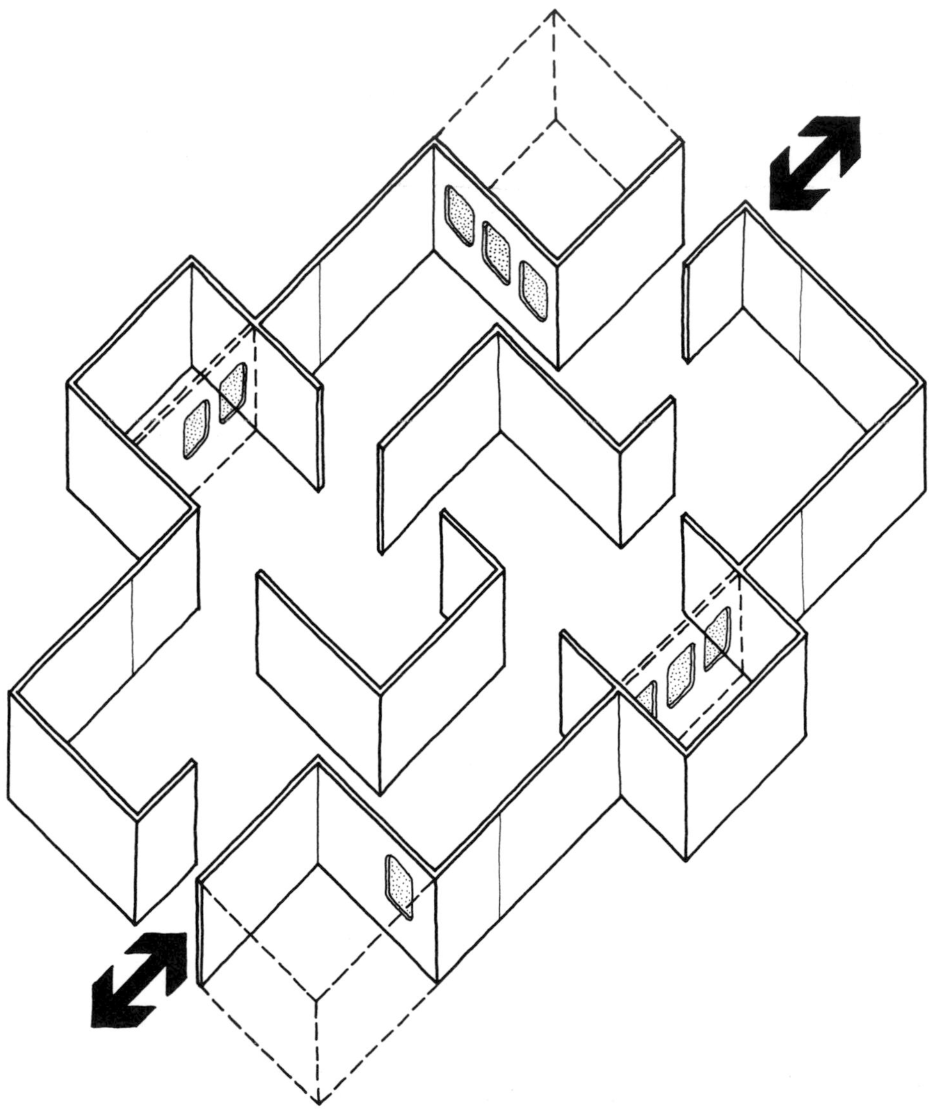

Tips When Mounting Freestanding Exhibitions

1

1 WHITE HOUSE PROJECT
ROSA VELT
KEN EDDY
NICK SUNN
P. NUTZ

A simple method of coordinating exhibitions is to run an information band of paper or thin card above and throughout the display. This could be color-coded to identify exhibition zones and receive dry-transfer or stenciled annotation.

BILL STICKERS

Three-dimensional lettering is highly effective if illuminated obliquely from above. Shadows can be cast from letters simply formed from strips of card glued end-on to a backing sheet or the display surface. Alternatively, block letters can be cut from cork, Styrofoam, or wood and pinned into position.

2 3

Do-it-yourself Masonite panels with apertures or screens can be introduced into proprietary display systems to receive TV monitors, cine, or multi-pack back projection. Colorless, frosted 1/8-inch (3 mm) thick translucent sheet acrylic makes an excellent back projection screen when cut to size, framed, and suspended--or built into screen displays.

4

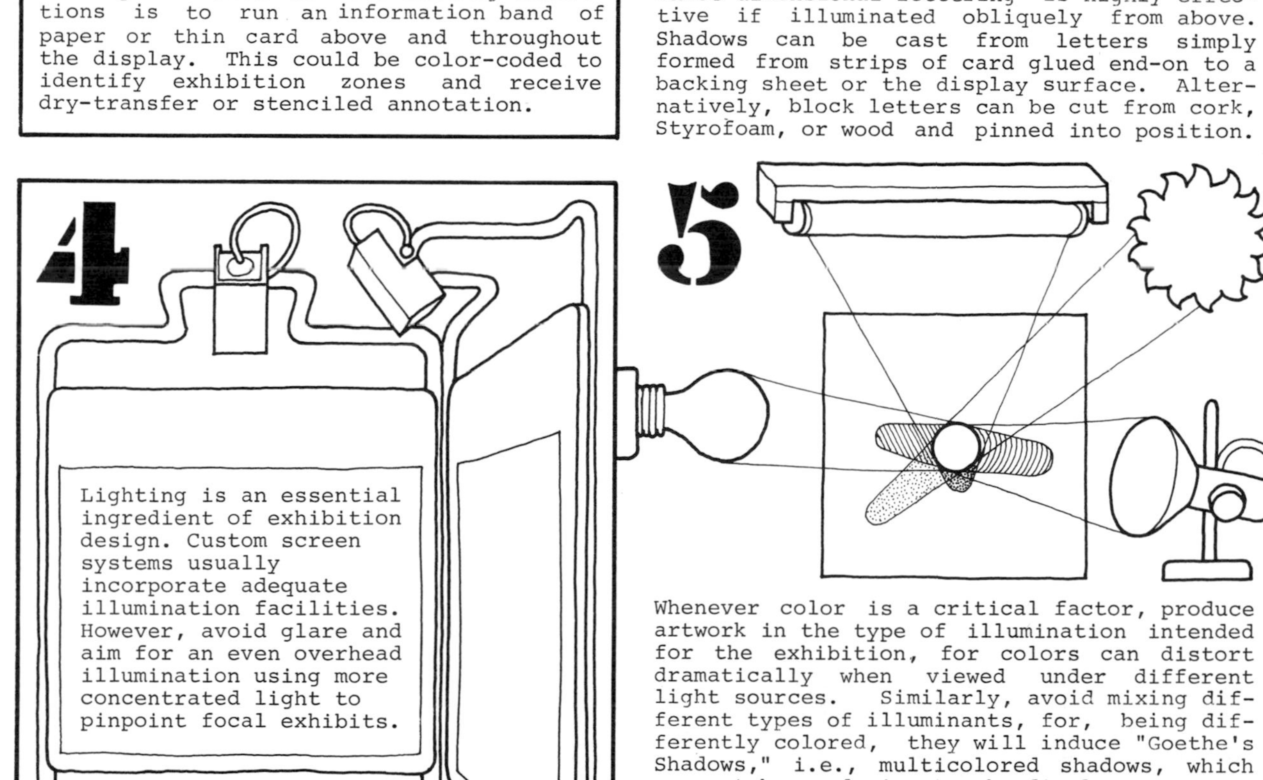

Lighting is an essential ingredient of exhibition design. Custom screen systems usually incorporate adequate illumination facilities. However, avoid glare and aim for an even overhead illumination using more concentrated light to pinpoint focal exhibits.

5

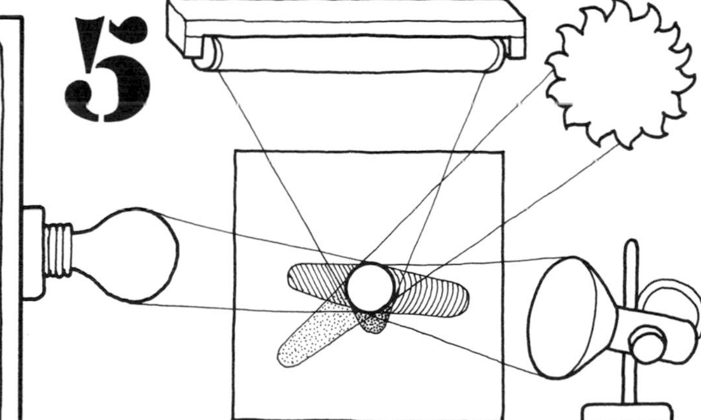

Whenever color is a critical factor, produce artwork in the type of illumination intended for the exhibition, for colors can distort dramatically when viewed under different light sources. Similarly, avoid mixing different types of illuminants, for, being differently colored, they will induce "Goethe's Shadows," i.e., multicolored shadows, which may not be conducive to the display.

6

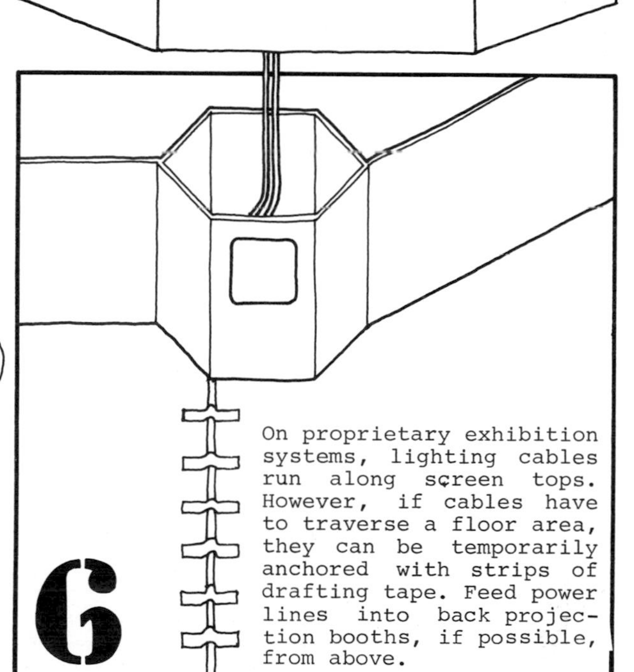

On proprietary exhibition systems, lighting cables run along screen tops. However, if cables have to traverse a floor area, they can be temporarily anchored with strips of drafting tape. Feed power lines into back projection booths, if possible, from above.

How to Compile a Report

1

Reports are miniature exhibitions which progressively unfold their contents of words and pictures in a page-by-page sequence. Specialist aspects of design solutions and even complete projects can be stored, proliferated, and communicated in this format--being portable and conducive to various methods of reproduction.

However, design schemes planned for transfer into report form should initially be worked in a size acceptable by the chosen reprographic process. Conversely, reports should be capable of disassembly for use in wall displays.

Although this format can exploit a range of exciting communication techniques, reports should essentially be informative, relevant to the problem, and both easy and enjoyable to read. Contents should follow an ordered structure to aid the logical disclosure of information and ideas.

A basic framework might include:

A TITLE PAGE
B ABSTRACT
C PREFACE
D INTRODUCTION
E AN ORGANIZATION OF PARAGRAPHS AND SECTIONS
F CONCLUSION
G BIBLIOGRAPHY
H INDEX

biguity. There are exceptions in the case of some drawings where the brain fails to settle for a single solution. The best example of the phenomenon of spontaneous depth reversal is the Necker Cube (see Fig. 6). Ambiguity in depth is only one kind of ambi-

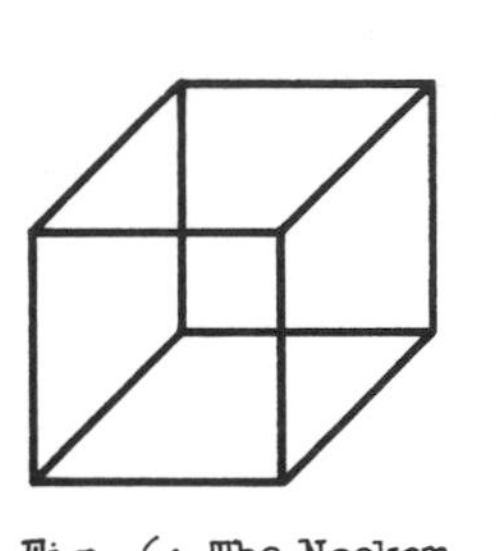

Fig. 6: The Necker Cube illustrates the phenomenom of spontaneous depth reversal.

2

Paste-ups of text and in-text illustrations can be duplicated in monochrome, or, depending upon photocopying facilities, in color. Illustrations should always be visually related and annotated with their textual references.

4

Photographs, drawings, and glossy diazo prints can be laminated on thin card for use as full-page illustrations. These might be overlaid with pages of clear acetate carrying inked, dry-transfer, or photocopied information (see page 84). For a sneak preview effect, windows cut into a preceding page can isolate a selected area of an illustration or frame captions or titles.

3

For ease of identification, title pages or even complete sections can be color-coded or shaped to include tabulated reference panels. Stencil-type letterforms can be cut into introductory pages and "colored" by the paper of the following page.

Overlay techniques can superimpose statistical data on pictorial images in tables, charts, and graphs; more complex material can be transmitted via a succession of transparent acetate pages worked in ink and dry-transfer color.

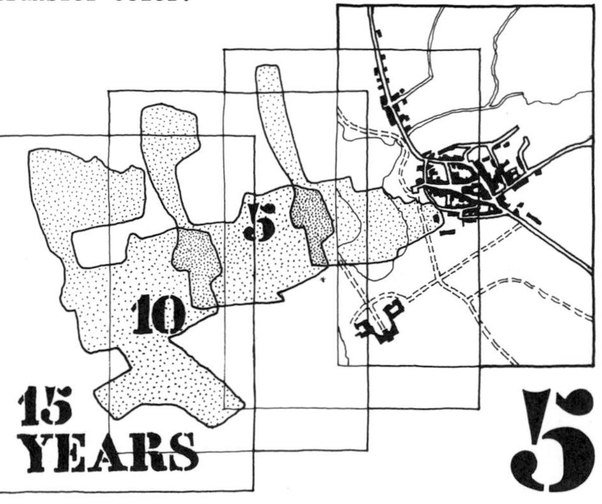

5

How to Bind a Report

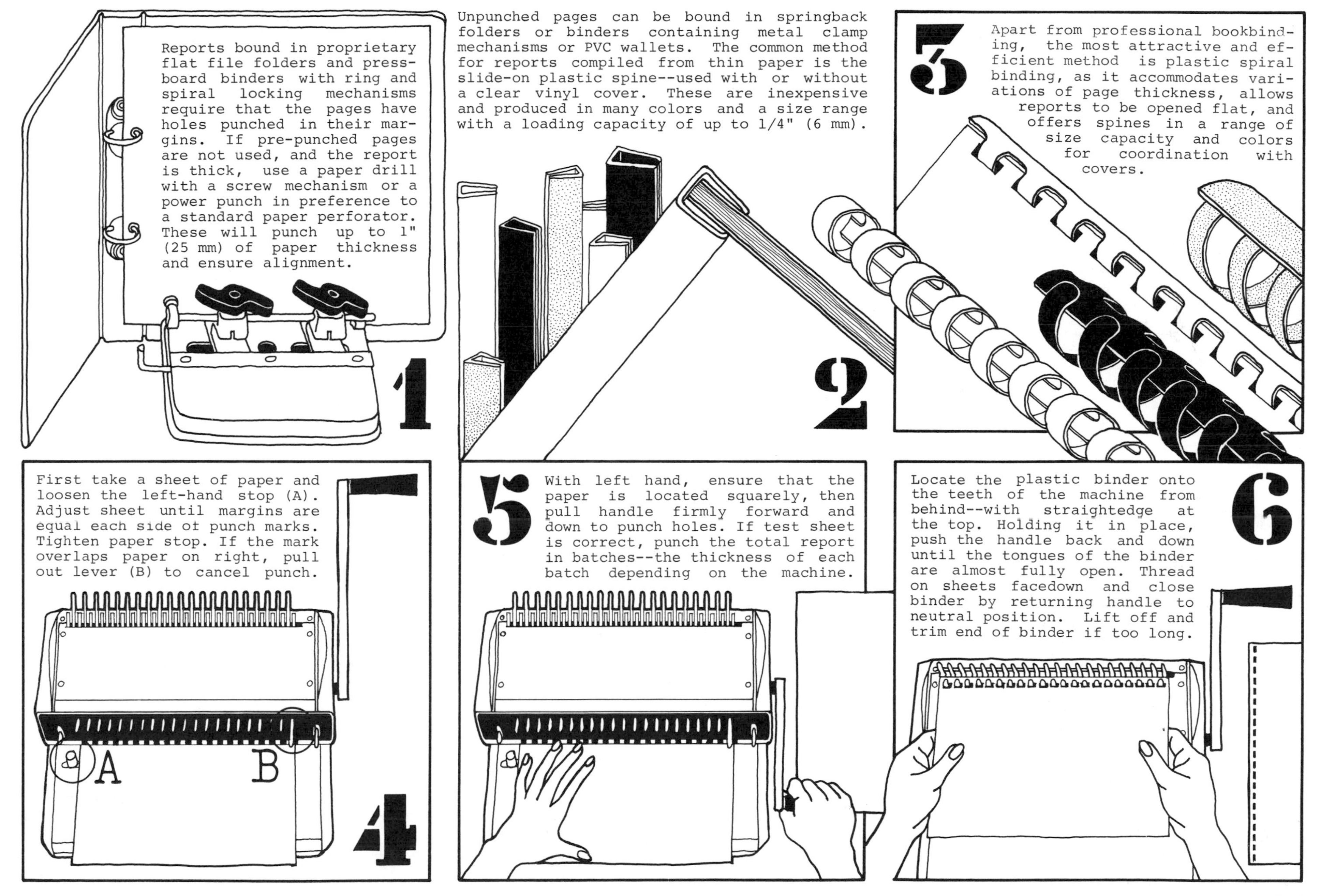

1 Reports bound in proprietary flat file folders and pressboard binders with ring and spiral locking mechanisms require that the pages have holes punched in their margins. If pre-punched pages are not used, and the report is thick, use a paper drill with a screw mechanism or a power punch in preference to a standard paper perforator. These will punch up to 1" (25 mm) of paper thickness and ensure alignment.

2 Unpunched pages can be bound in springback folders or binders containing metal clamp mechanisms or PVC wallets. The common method for reports compiled from thin paper is the slide-on plastic spine--used with or without a clear vinyl cover. These are inexpensive and produced in many colors and a size range with a loading capacity of up to 1/4" (6 mm).

3 Apart from professional bookbinding, the most attractive and efficient method is plastic spiral binding, as it accommodates variations of page thickness, allows reports to be opened flat, and offers spines in a range of size capacity and colors for coordination with covers.

4 First take a sheet of paper and loosen the left-hand stop (A). Adjust sheet until margins are equal each side of punch marks. Tighten paper stop. If the mark overlaps paper on right, pull out lever (B) to cancel punch.

5 With left hand, ensure that the paper is located squarely, then pull handle firmly forward and down to punch holes. If test sheet is correct, punch the total report in batches--the thickness of each batch depending on the machine.

6 Locate the plastic binder onto the teeth of the machine from behind--with straightedge at the top. Holding it in place, push the handle back and down until the tongues of the binder are almost fully open. Thread on sheets facedown and close binder by returning handle to neutral position. Lift off and trim end of binder if too long.

Short- and Long-Term Storage

1

Diazo prints fade if exposed to sunlight. For portability and temporary storage they, together with drawings on tracing paper and film, can be rolled for insertion into airtight cardboard and plastic tubes. More sophisticated vinyl carrying tubes with handles are available. However, drawings should not be left rolled for long periods, as they are difficult to straighten out and those using dry-transfer material can bubble.

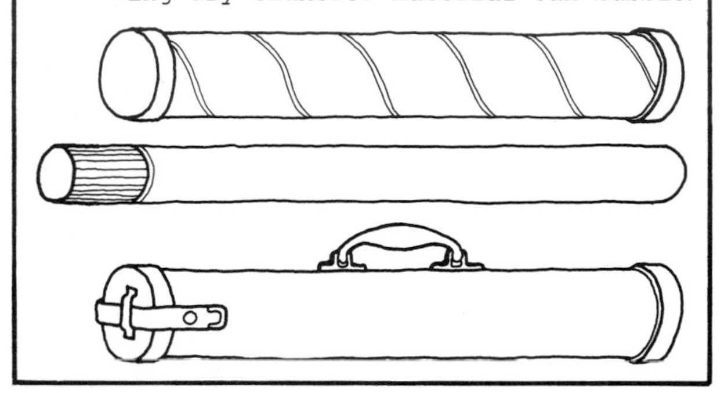

2

A do-it-yourself portfolio can be made from two glue-sized sheets of heavy board and some pieces for flaps, with the spine and flap hinges made from canvas or denim (from an old pair of jeans) and glued in position. Insert tapes through reinforced eyelets, knot, and secure with small patches of glued fabric.

3

All kinds of artwork are best stored flat. For portability plus long-term storage, the portfolio is ideal. These range from the traditional board version to the more expensive zippered carrying cases. It is wise to invest in a large size, as a smaller portfolio tends to restrict its owner to working only on paper sizes which fit within its dimensions.

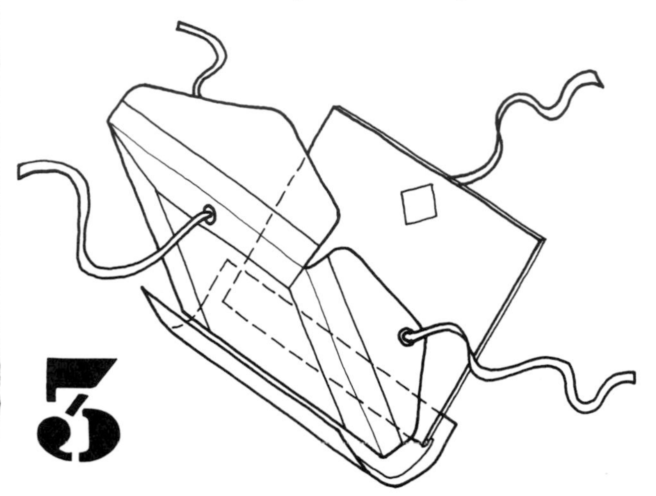

4

For permanent storage, all drawings are best contained in dust-free steel or timber plan chests, in shelved lockers, or hung in vertical filing cabinets. For permanent display, artwork can be framed behind glass or plastic or, using a proprietary process, bonded for posterity within acrylic sheets.

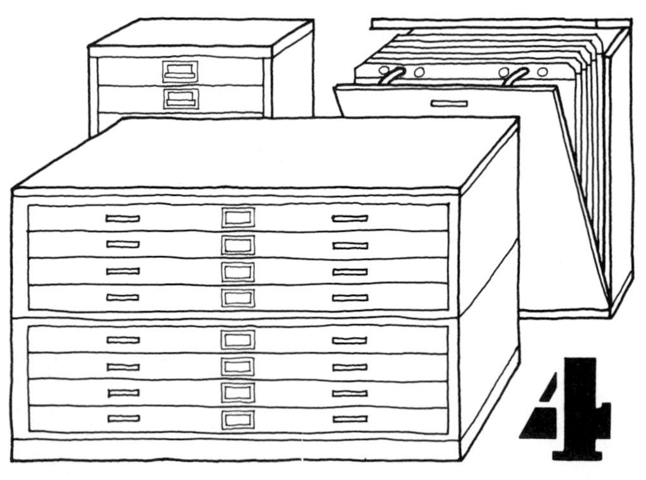

5

It is a good idea to photograph all important drawings and, especially, presentation models. Models should then be stowed in sealed polythene bags and, size permitting, stored in cardboard boxes. For permanent display, models can be exhibited in a showcase made from five cut sheets of acrylic--glued with acrylic cement.

6

Microfilm retrieval systems represent the sophisticated archive. Original drawings are microfilmed and mounted in aperture cards. Copies can be made from microfilm negatives and these or the microfilm originals viewed--enlarged--on microviewers. Enlarged prints can be made using diazo or offset litho reprography. As microfilm reproduction can only be as good as the original, special technical pen nib sizes and stencils are available for drawings destined for microfilm archives.

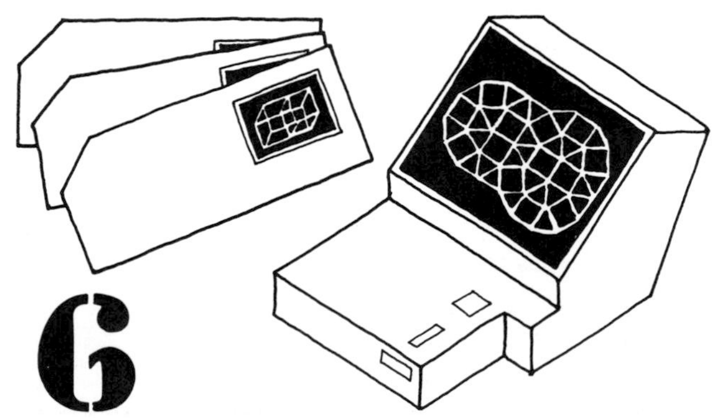

How to Cut Glass and Acrylic Sheets

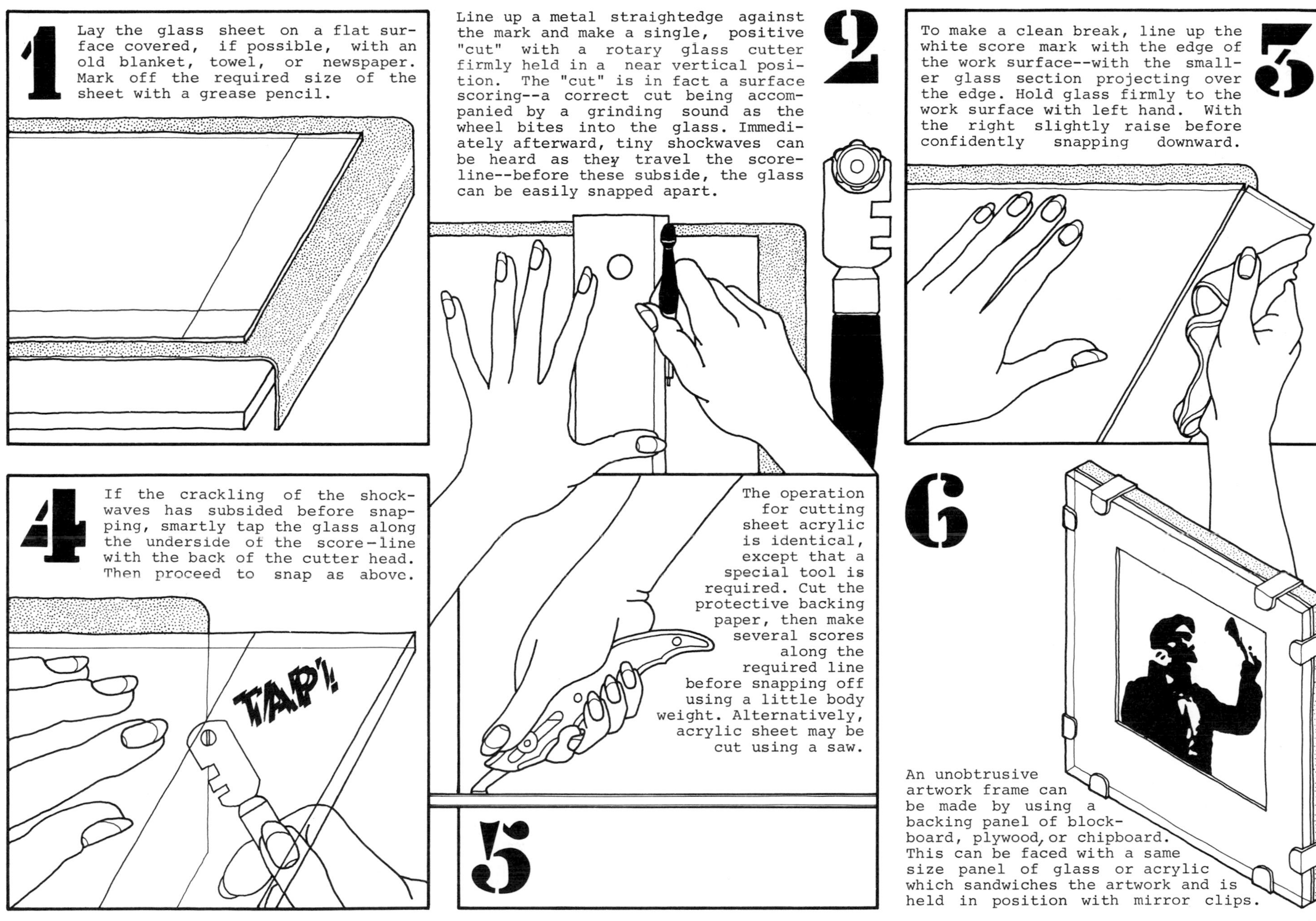

1 Lay the glass sheet on a flat surface covered, if possible, with an old blanket, towel, or newspaper. Mark off the required size of the sheet with a grease pencil.

2 Line up a metal straightedge against the mark and make a single, positive "cut" with a rotary glass cutter firmly held in a near vertical position. The "cut" is in fact a surface scoring--a correct cut being accompanied by a grinding sound as the wheel bites into the glass. Immediately afterward, tiny shockwaves can be heard as they travel the scoreline--before these subside, the glass can be easily snapped apart.

3 To make a clean break, line up the white score mark with the edge of the work surface--with the smaller glass section projecting over the edge. Hold glass firmly to the work surface with left hand. With the right slightly raise before confidently snapping downward.

4 If the crackling of the shockwaves has subsided before snapping, smartly tap the glass along the underside of the score-line with the back of the cutter head. Then proceed to snap as above.

5 The operation for cutting sheet acrylic is identical, except that a special tool is required. Cut the protective backing paper, then make several scores along the required line before snapping off using a little body weight. Alternatively, acrylic sheet may be cut using a saw.

6 An unobtrusive artwork frame can be made by using a backing panel of blockboard, plywood, or chipboard. This can be faced with a same size panel of glass or acrylic which sandwiches the artwork and is held in position with mirror clips.

INDEX